KYLIX
Power Solutions

with Don Taylor, Jim Mischel,
and Tim Gentry

Don Taylor

Jim Mischel

Tim Gentry

Publisher
Steve Sayre

Acquisitions Editor
Charlotte Carpentier

Product Marketing Manager
Tracy Rooney

Project Editor
Greg Balas

Technical Reviewer
Eric Harmon

Production Coordinator
Carla J. Schuder

Cover Designer
Jody Winkler

Layout Designer
April E. Nielsen

The Coriolis Group, LLC
14455 North Hayden Road
Suite 220
Scottsdale, Arizona 85260

(480) 483-0192
FAX (480) 483-0193
www.coriolis.com

Library of Congress Cataloging-in-Publication Data
Taylor, Don
    Kylix power solutions with Don Taylor, Jim Mischel & Tim Gentry / by Don Taylor, Jim Mischel & Tim Gentry.
        p.   cm.
    ISBN 1-57610-960-7
    1. Application software--Development.   2. Kylix.   3. Linux.   I. Title: Kylix power solutions.   II. Mischel, Jim, 1961- .   III. Gentry, Tim.   IV. Title.
QA76.76.A65 T415   2001
005.2'82--dc21   2001028057

Printed in the United States of America
10 9 8 7 6 5 4 3 2 1

The Coriolis Group, LLC • 14455 North Hayden Road, Suite 220 • Scottsdale, Arizona 85260

A Note from Coriolis

Coriolis Technology Press was founded to create a very elite group of books: the ones you keep closest to your machine. In the real world, you have to choose the books you rely on every day very carefully, and we understand that.

To win a place for our books on that coveted shelf beside your PC, we guarantee several important qualities in every book we publish. These qualities are:

- *Technical accuracy*—It's no good if it doesn't work. Every Coriolis Technology Press book is reviewed by technical experts in the topic field, and is sent through several editing and proofreading passes in order to create the piece of work you now hold in your hands.

- *Innovative editorial design*—We've put years of research and refinement into the ways we present information in our books. Our books' editorial approach is uniquely designed to reflect the way people learn new technologies and search for solutions to technology problems.

- *Practical focus*—We put only pertinent information into our books and avoid any fluff. Every fact included between these two covers must serve the mission of the book as a whole.

- *Accessibility*—The information in a book is worthless unless you can find it quickly when you need it. We put a lot of effort into our indexes, and heavily cross-reference our chapters, to make it easy for you to move right to the information you need.

Here at The Coriolis Group we have been publishing and packaging books, technical journals, and training materials since 1989. We have put a lot of thought into our books; please write to us at **ctp@coriolis.com** and let us know what you think. We hope that you're happy with the book in your hands, and that in the future, when you reach for software development and networking information, you'll turn to one of our books first.

Coriolis Technology Press
The Coriolis Group
14455 N. Hayden Road, Suite 220
Scottsdale, Arizona
85260

Email: ctp@coriolis.com
Phone: (480) 483-0192
Toll free: 800)410-0192

*To my benefactor, Jesus of Nazareth: The gift you so freely gave
I could not possibly have earned in a thousand lifetimes.
—Don Taylor*

*For the Faculty and Staff of the Marine Military Academy in Harlingen, TX. Semper Fi.
—Jim Mischel*

*To those who have sacrificed above and beyond the call in my life—to my Lord Jesus
Christ for saving my soul, to my lovely wife for her patience and love,
and to my selfless parents for an education that left me where I am today.
—Tim Gentry*

About the Authors

Don Taylor (Poulsbo, WA) has been a commercial software developer since 1979, and a best-selling computer book author since 1995. He has used Delphi since its first release, and was the founder of the Turbo User Group, the official support group first recognized by Borland International for all its programming products. Don and his wife, Carol, recently celebrated their 20th wedding anniversary. He plays guitar, and loves to play and sing 50's and 60's rock 'n' roll music, and is perhaps best known for creating the fictional character Ace Breakpoint, Non-Traditional Programmer.

Jim Mischel (Round Rock, TX) is a software developer and author, who has been developing commercial software since 1982. He has developed software for banks, service-oriented businesses, embedded systems, and computer games. Jim has written widely on computer-related topics since 1989, and has authored or co-authored seven books on programming topics. When he's not behind the keyboard, you can find Jim putting in the miles on his bicycle, or brewing up another batch of beer in the kitchen.

Tim Gentry (Bremerton, WA) has been a commercial developer since 1985. He has developed software for a variety of industries, including cellular telephony, aerospace, finance, online commerce and negotiation, and computer gaming. He currently works for Sierra Online, doing network programming for the SWAT team. When he's not staring into a monitor, you'll likely find him on his motorcycle, either braving the Seattle commute, or taking one of his kids for a ride.

Acknowledgments

First, thanks to my wonderful coauthors, Jim and Tim. Without your sacrificial efforts, this book would never have come to fruition. It's been great getting to know both of you better in the process. You guys are great!

I feel I've been blessed with the most incredible team at The Coriolis Group. Thanks to Kevin Weeks, my Acquisitions Editor, for catching the vision for this book and pursuing it. Also, thanks to Greg Balas, my Project Editor, who was there through thick and thin (and there was a lot of thin!), inhaling pressure and exhaling patience. Thanks, Greg. In addition, I would like to thank Carla Schuder, the Production Coordinator, Laura Wellander, the cover designer, April Nielsen, for designing the interior of the book, and Tracy Rooney, Tech Press Marketing Specialist at The Coriolis Group.

I would also like to extend a special thanks to Eric Harmon, my tech reviewer, who had to ask the "tough" questions. Thanks, Eric for keeping us all on track, and for bringing me back to technical reality when my brain went numb. Then, there's Bart Reed, the copyeditor. Bart has been given the most precious editorial gift of all, the ability to stick to the rules when absolutely necessary, but to "go with the flow" when it works out better. It's a sense of balance bestowed upon only a few. Thanks for working with us, Bart. In addition, I would like to thank Ann Norcross for proofreading the book, and Richard Evans for indexing.

Many thanks to my long-suffering wife, Carol, who brought meals to my desk on many occasions, and who has forgiven me for not spending time with her on many more of them. Mom, thanks for your patience, too. To my extended family—Skip, Chela, Chris, and Leann, among others—thanks for your prayers, support, and your friendship.

Finally, Ryan, thanks for the ball cap. It really helped.
—*Don Taylor*

Acknowledgments

First of all, to my coauthors Don and Tim, thanks for the help! In addition to writing a third of the book, Don took on the task of coordinating things with the Coriolis team, and without Tim's knowledge of the Linux environment, we couldn't have pulled this off. The Coriolis staff, as always, did a fantastic job on the book. Our tech reviewer, Eric Harmon, asked some very important questions, and the book is much better for it. Eric, I appreciated all of your comments and questions.

My wife Debra kept me at the keyboard when I wanted to be out biking, and put up with my lack of attention during meals and other social occasions. Thank you, dear, for your patience.

Thanks also to my employers, Sam Goodner and Jim Martin at Inquisite, Inc. They and my co-workers on the Inquisite team encouraged me, and were very understanding when I came in late or left early because I was working on the book.

—Jim Mischel

Where to begin? Don and Jim, thanks for taking a rank newbie under your wings. There's no way I would ever have attempted this on my own, and your experience has proved invaluable along the way. You both amazed me with how much you picked up along the way, and how quickly you did it. Thank you, gentlemen.

My wife, Sheri, and my two sons, David and Stephen—you've not seen anywhere near enough of me lately. None of us realized how long this would take, nor how much work it would actually involve. I love you all, and my sincere apologies for how large a chunk of lifetime this has taken. But, for what it's worth, that stranger that's been sitting in front of the computer for entirely too long is gone, and it's your turn to use the computer now.

The staff at Coriolis—I've heard from other authors that you were professionals from the word "Go," and now I've had a chance to verify that with firsthand experience. Kevin, Greg, Eric, and Bart—you guys are awesome. Thanks for a job *very* well done.

And to a certain group of Everquest crazies on The Rathe: Zhendenfaris, Kevralynn, Kalandra, and Thiefum—*Tabalar has returned.*

—Tim Gentry

Contents at a Glance

Table of Contents

Introduction

When Linus Torvalds announced the first "official" release of Linux (dubbed version 0.02) in 1991, he likely had no idea of the extent of the revolution he would start. Originally developed as a hobby project intended to put the Unix operating system in the hands of any hacker who wanted to experiment with it, Linux quickly captured the imagination of its targeted audience. Today, thousands of serious programmers around the world actively contribute to the maintenance of the kernel, that critical portion of code that serves as the foundation for the Linux operating system.

Flashback: It is 1995, and we're in California, halfway around the world from Linus' native Finland. Borland International has just released Version 1 of Delphi, and for the first time, Windows software developers have access to an industrial-strength tool for rapid development of visual applications. Although it appears to be similar in many ways to Microsoft's Visual Basic, Delphi has full access to the underlying Windows API calls, making it a truly powerful development tool (some even call it "VB without the training wheels"). A second revolution has begun, an innovation that has simplified the creation of a program's visual interface, enabling developers to concentrate on the core aspects of their applications.

Fast forward to the present: Until now, Linux has been acknowledged (with reluctance) by many in the mainstream as an efficient and reliable, if not superior, operating system for servers. These same people are quick to point out, however, that Linux has no place on the desktop, and they cite the lack of serious applications to prove their point. But there are only two valid reasons for the lack of desktop applications: (1) The demand for those programs has not been great enough to warrant the time and expense to create them, and (2) The effort (and cost) to develop such applications has been prohibitive with the tools available. However, the release of Kylix—Delphi for Linux—has turned that world upside down. A synergy has been fused between the rapid application development environment of Delphi, and the blazingly fast, highly stable operational platform called Linux.

Now, a third revolution is about to begin—innovation that easily transports existing applications from Windows to Linux, and that realizes new applications destined to become part of the everyday experience of individuals and businesses around the world. *As a Kylix developer, you are an important participant in that revolution.*

Purpose and Focus of This Book

You will likely buy several books that will help you transition to (or simply learn) Kylix programming. This book was written with the specific intent that it should occupy a special place on your bookshelf.

This book has two primary purposes. First and foremost, it is about solutions—*Power Solutions* that will make your applications stand up and shout! In writing this book, all three of the authors have assumed you are an experienced Delphi programmer moving over to Kylix. But even if you're brand new to Kylix, you will likely face many of the programming challenges covered in the pages that follow, and unless you're a masochist at heart (and I'm not going to go there) you will benefit greatly from the hard-won solutions that fill this book.

The secondary purpose is to get you up and running with Kylix in the absolute minimum time possible. Never had any previous experience with Linux? *No problem.* The first four chapters contain concentrated information intended to imbue you with the essence of Linux, and how it compares with Windows, and to provide you with an easily understood overview of the C language conventions used within Linux system API information. Depending on your programming experience, this may be all you need to transition to Kylix.

This book is a work *by* programmers *for* programmers. (This can be evidenced by a short anecdote. While the proposal for this book was being prepared by the authors—before the first word of text was even written—one of the other authors looked at the table of contents and said to me, "Hey—where can *I* buy a copy of this book?")

The authors have taken a lot of their time to ensure that you will spend the minimum of *your* time finding and implementing the programming solutions you need. Each problem is presented with its solution in a way that not only gives you the answer, but also the critical logic for approaching and solving the problem as well. When appropriate, the solution includes a brief discussion of how the problem was approached under Windows, what is materially different in solving that problem under Linux, and the exact programming strategy used to solve the problem. The discussion is followed, in nearly every case, by a short code example or demo program.

How to Use This Book

If you are new to Linux, you will probably want to read all the chapters in Part One. This will give you a quick overview of the salient features of Linux and how it differs from Windows, and it will act as a platform on which to build specific solutions. If you have not yet used Kylix, you might want to stop at that point, until you get a bit of Kylix experience under your belt.

If you are already comfortable with Kylix (or if you just want to get a feel for problem-solving with this powerful development tool), we suggest you continue reading through Part Two. Some of the solutions presented in Part Two contain detailed discussions of Linux concepts, so you can learn more about Linux just by reading through the solutions. When one solution relates to another, it provides a reference to the other solution. Part Two is, in effect, an "encyclopedia" of solutions that you will revisit again and again, whenever you are faced with a programming challenge. (You might call it Write Once, Read Many.) The full, most up-to-date versions of all source code examples in this book are available online at the book's Web site: **www.kylixpowersolutions.com**.

Special Features

A lot of information is packed into this book, and for that reason we have adopted some formatting conventions intended to make that information easier to understand, navigate, and assimilate. Most of the formatting conventions are self-explanatory, but we'll cover a handful of them here, so we'll be certain we're all playing on the same page.

Tips

Tips give you special information about a topic that make it quicker and easier to accomplish your tasks, provide workarounds to limitations, or make you aware of sources of additional information.

Tip

*All of the code examples provided in this book are available in downloadable form from the book's Web site, located at **www.kylixpowersolutions.com**.*

Warnings

As you would assume, warnings are set off to get your attention, so you can avoid potential problems. Someone else has already made it through the minefield—you might as well follow in his or her footsteps and benefit from their mistakes!

WARNING! *This room is equipped with the Edison Electric Light. Do not attempt to light it with a match. Simply turn the key on the wall by the door. (The use of Electricity for lighting is in no way harmful to health, nor does it affect the soundness of sleep.)*

Chapter Quick-Index

The title page for each chapter in the book contains a list of "key topics." Each key topic listed in the chapters in Part Two is a Power Solution. By flipping to the first page of a solutions chapter, you can see a list of the solutions for that subject area. You can then quickly locate a particular solution within the chapter.

Enough introduction! Turn the page and you can start getting familiar with the Linux environment and how it differs from Windows.

Part I

From Delphi to Kylix

Chapter 1
A Comparison of Environments

If you have already picked up a book on Linux, you're aware that the Land of Linux is expansive and dotted with mountainous peaks that are both tall and steep. At this point you may be wondering how something so seemingly similar to MS-DOS (they both have command lines, right?) and MS Windows can be so entirely different.

When you're in unfamiliar territory and trying to get from one place to another, there's nothing like having a map. This chapter is the first of four chapters that constitute just such a map. They will take you from point A (using Delphi under MS Windows) to point B (using Kylix under Linux) by comparing significant differences between what you are familiar with and what you'll be tackling for the first time.

In this chapter, we will compare the two environments from a 10,000-foot view. Although this comparison won't even pretend to be a comprehensive study of all the differences between these environments, it will at least introduce you to some of the learning curves that you as a "Windows native" will face as you move to Linux. If you're a seasoned Unix or Linux developer, you can safely skim through this chapter on your way to the more Kylix-specific information in the chapters that follow.

Differences between the Environments

For all the differences between Linux and Windows, they are surprisingly similar in many respects. Without getting into religious arguments (a practice we'll try to avoid throughout this book),

Windows adopted many Unix features, in some cases extending them in subtle ways. This means you'll find many of the concepts familiar, and the learning curve that you're required to climb will most likely not be as steep as you might at first fear. However, there are some areas in which you'll benefit from a quick "intelligence report," and that's what we'll try to provide here.

System Differences

Perhaps the single biggest difference between Linux and Windows is that Linux is designed from the ground up as a true multiuser system. Now, when we talk about *multiuser*, we're not referring to the number of users who are simultaneously accessing data from a network drive or to the number of users who have accounts on the system. We're talking here about multiple, concurrent, application-running users, each one no different from a user sitting at the system console. For many applications this will have no impact on the algorithms and programming techniques used to create them. For others, however, the possibility of concurrent access to shared resources raises a whole new crop of interesting problems. Programs that access shared resources (configuration files, hardware devices, and so on) need to allow for several users executing them at the same time.

Security and Permissions

As part of its role as a multiuser system, Linux insists on setting up an account for each user of the system, assigning to each account a login identity and a password. Each account is assigned a level, either as an ordinary user or as a system administrator (also known as *root* and sometimes referred to as the *superuser*). Root has complete control over every aspect of the system and is allowed to make changes that can possibly be devastating to the system. For that reason, even the superuser has an ordinary user account and logs on as root only when doing administrative work.

When you're programming, it's important to remember that Linux has user permission levels that Windows doesn't have (with the exception of Windows NT and Windows 2000). On most Linux systems, ordinary users won't have permission to mount a floppy disk or a CD, mount a networked drive, write (or even *read*, in some cases) most of the files outside their own home directories, or even make system configuration changes to the host machine. All these activities can only be performed by root. Developers (especially system utility developers) need to be aware that not all activities they may want their programs to perform will be allowed if a nonroot user is running the application.

Tip

*Although the statement about ordinary users being unable to mount a floppy disk is true for default installations, there is a Linux package called **mtools** that enables ordinary users to access and manipulate data stored on MS-DOS formatted disks. It is installed by default in most Linux installations. Most of the standard DOS commands are supported, but they are prefixed with an **m** (for example, **mcopy** and* *mdel). See the **mtools** man page for more information. Also, by modifying the file/etc/fstab (while logged on as root), you can allow ordinary users to mount any filesystem that you, the administrator, choose to allow. See the man page on **fstab** for details.*

Configuration

If you have grown accustomed to using the Windows Registry, you may be surprised to find it completely missing from Linux. Although some developers would say this is a good thing, many others have grown fond of the Registry (all right, so "fond" might be overstating things a little bit). In any event, the configuration information you're used to storing in the Registry will now be stored in configuration files. In some ways this is eerily similar to the days of Windows 3.x (with all the added complexities brought by INI files scattered all over the face of the earth). However, Linux doesn't have the "single point of failure" problem that Windows has, where all of the system's configuration information is stored in a single, highly complex database. It's all a matter of perspective. Configuration information under Linux is stored in one of several locations, as outlined in Table 1.1.

The last entry in Table 1.1 deserves explanation. In Linux, *dot files* are files and directories beginning with a dot (.) character. They are similar to Windows hidden files in that they aren't visible in normal directory listings. To make them visible in a directory listing, you need to use the **-a** option to the **ls** file list command. This makes dot files unobtrusive without hiding them altogether. As an example, in your own home directory, look for the file .Xdefaults or look into the directory **.kde**. With the clever use of dot files and dot directories, you can mimic the behavior of the **HKEY_CURRENT_USER** branch of the Registry quite nicely. However, as far as a standardized API for accessing configuration files stored in this manner goes—well, you're out of luck on that one. However, Kylix provides support for INI-format files, which is a big step in that direction.

Interprocess Communication and Libraries

Another area that stands out is the wealth of options Linux programmers have for interprocess communication, or *IPC*. Under Linux, applications (or *processes*, as they're better known in Linux) can communicate in several ways, ranging from simple signals to more complex data-sharing techniques. Although some of these exist under Windows, others do not. IPC methods will be covered in substantially more detail in Chapter 2.

Table 1.1   Configuration information locations.

Information Type	Location
System startup scripts	Stored in files under the /etc/rc.d directory tree, and executed each time the system enters a new runlevel
System configuration	Configuration files in /etc (/etc/hosts and /etc/fstab, for example)
Global application configuration	Configuration files in /usr/local/etc or in /etc
User-specific configuration	"Dot files" in the user's home directories

One final area, deserving of an entire chapter in this book, is the area of dynamic link libraries (DLLs) under Windows. DLLs, as such, don't exist under Linux, but a more flexible (and, correspondingly, more complex) alternative is available for Linux developers—the shared library. Linux shared libraries are covered in detail in Chapter 3.

Development Environment Differences

Are you ready for a little brutal honesty? Until fairly recently, development environments under Linux were substantially more primitive than the ones enjoyed by Windows developers. Integrated development environments (IDEs), although common under Windows, were a rarity under Linux. Seasoned C programmers might argue that all you really require to develop programs for Linux are the *vi* editor and a makefile. Essentially, that would be true—but that is precisely the attitude that has constrained Linux programming to the command-line environment for so long.

Although Linux's use of the X-window system enables graphical user interface-based programs to be developed and executed under Linux, its acceptance as a competent, professional development environment for serious, GUI-based applications has been hindered by the lack of a standard, powerful GUI-based development tool. Kylix is poised to become that standard tool for Linux. Even so, quite a few of the command-line tools used for the last decade or more are still quite useful today. Some of these tools and their uses are outlined in Table 1.2.

Until now, Pascal has never really been a powerhouse in the area of Linux development. Although several command-line Pascal compilers are available, including the GNU compiler, the language suffers from a severe shortage of programming libraries and language-specific

Table 1.2   Traditional development tools and their uses.

Tool Name	Use
make	Automated builds based on dependency rules. Extremely useful in group development for daily builds.
cvs	Project-oriented source code revision management.
adb/gdb	Debuggers (primitive by Kylix's standards) useful for post-mortem debugging.
rpm	Package manager, useful as a *de facto* standard package installer and management tool. Others are available, but rpm seems to be supported on a wider variety of Linux installations than the rest.
man	Displays manual pages for commands, files, and system calls. Try "man man" for details.
zip/unzip	The old faithful compression and archiving utilities (but open-sourced this time). The programs **tar** and **gzip** provide similar functionality and are a pseudo-standard for Linux. If your system doesn't provide zip and unzip, use these instead.
grep	Useful for finding files containing a specific string or regular expression.
Shell scripts	These are batch files on major steroids. Useful for automating repetitive tasks, such as building and packaging.

tools. In fact, one of the more popular Pascal tools has been a utility called **ptoc**, which converts Pascal source code to C. This, by itself, is a sad commentary on the state of Pascal under Linux. Kylix will certainly have an impact on this situation, and it will breathe new life into Pascal development for Linux.

Hopefully you are used to working with revision-control or change-management systems, such as SourceSafe, ClearCase, and CMS. If you are part of a group who doesn't use a revision-control system, I strongly suggest that you start. There's nothing like working with a safety net, knowing that no matter how badly you hack the copy of the code you're working on, you can always restore the previous version (or the one before that, or the one before that) unharmed.

Under Linux, a popular version control tool is CVS (concurrent version system). CVS allows teams of developers to work on sections of code simultaneously, and to safely integrate those changes and track them in a code repository (of course, if you're an individual developer you can still use the tool). CVS makes it easy to retrieve an entire source code package at any revision or release level, which is a blessing when trying to find and fix that bug a customer found in code two releases old. It operates at the project level, working with entire directory trees instead of only with files (like more basic version control packages such as SCCS or RCS), and it invalidates almost every excuse you can make for not using version control. Ignore it at your peril.

The Open Source Difference

I would be remiss if I didn't raise the issue of Open Source as a significant difference between Linux and proprietary operating systems (of which Windows is only one). I'll try to avoid sounding like a Linux and Open Source evangelist here, but the fact remains that Linux does have some notable advantages.

On the programming side, there is the obvious: Most Open Source software can be freely copied and used. There are no licenses to track and, therefore, no related costs or legal risks. As an example, the source code for the Linux kernel is, itself, available for downloading. You can change it to suit your whim, but you must always realize that the changes you make will not likely appear at your customer or client sites, unless you have control over those sites. Major software packages (such as the MySQL database package) are adopting the Open Source movement with open arms, almost on a daily basis. True, nearly all the Open Source material available today is written in C and C++ (up until now, at least, the *de facto* standards for Linux programming). Be aware that it's not just the availability of the code that constitutes "Open Source." It's an open *attitude* among its developers and a removal of limitations upon how that code can be used. A common description of Open Source software is "free as in *speech*, not free as in *beer*," meaning that instead of merely being (monetarily) free, Open Source code is available to be used in other projects without restriction.

This brings me to the second benefit of Open Source for program developers: the availability of the authors. In most cases, you can communicate directly with the author of a program or module via the Internet. Frequently, he or she will answer your questions directly or may provide a reference to someone who can give you the answer you need. (Try doing that with the authors of a proprietary operating system!) Even when you have to pay for support of an Open Source product, you will frequently be working directly with the developers or you will have some sort of access to them.

One final benefit, this time on the marketing side: The deployment of Linux to small- to medium-sized businesses is on the knee of a power curve. Savvy business people recognize the competitive advantage of Linux-based computers that operate on a system that is both highly reliable and free (or nearly free). The only thing holding back a large revolt in this sector is the availability of competitively priced application software written for the desktop. Enter Kylix. As was stated in the introduction to this book, you have just become part of the revolution.

Windowing in Linux

If you have studied operating system or networking system software, you know it is typically built up of layers, each layer adding functionality to the layers beneath. It is the same with windowing and Linux: Two layers provide the windowing functionality—one giving the windowing capabilities, and the other providing the graphical, Windows-like environment.

The X Window System

At the root of all things windowing, there is X. No, that's not an algebraic statement. X is the X Window system, a package developed at the Massachusetts Institute of Technology that provides the core, basic GUI services to the system. X has three major components: The X Server, the X Client, and the X Protocol. The organization of these components is conceptually simple, as shown in Figure 1.1.

The X Client is represented by any X-compatible application, such as the text editors that were installed with KDE or Gnome on your system. X Clients are *hardware neutral*, meaning they have no code for specific displays or input devices. The X Clients use the X Protocol to communicate screen information and input device events with the X Server, which can run on a completely separate machine.

The X Server is ultimately responsible for displaying what the user sees as the application's window on the screen and for relaying input events to the appropriate X Client. Although X Clients are hardware neutral, X Servers are very device dependent. X Servers for many of the more "prominent" graphics adapters are normally shipped with the Linux distribution. On the vast majority of Linux systems, the X Server is the XFree86 package. Among other things, the X Server handles mouse and keyboard input, screen resolution and low-level

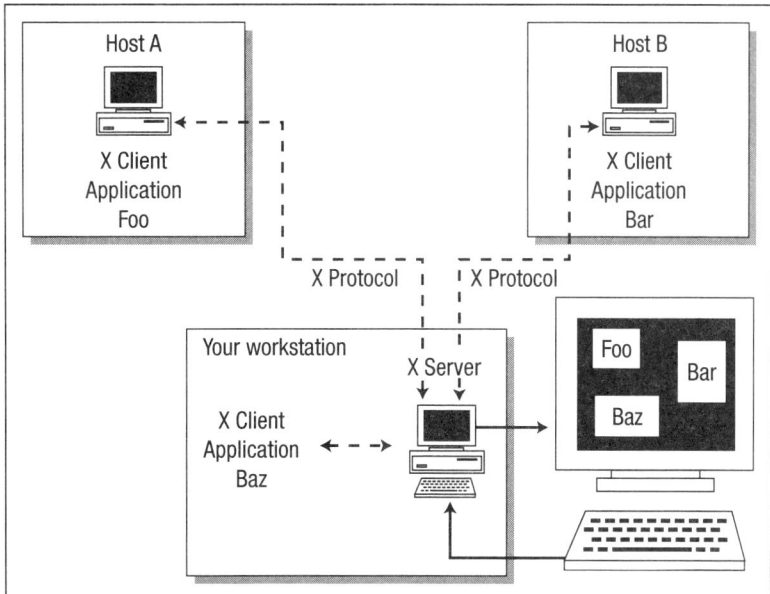

Figure 1.1
Primary components of the X Window system.

device primitives, and core output routines. It also provides a very basic GUI. The XLib libraries are used to develop applications that work at this level. However, applications using XLib are required to draw and create their own onscreen elements (called *widgets*) and handle a great deal of the GUI tasks that you're accustomed to leaving to Windows. XLib applications have no common "look and feel" and are frequently hideously complex to develop and maintain. To draw a parallel to Windows, creating XLib applications is similar to creating Windows applications in Windows 3.0—only worse. A key difference between the X Window system and Windows is that Windows is more monolithic. It is impossible to separate the Windows GUI from the Windows kernel, whereas in Linux the GUI and the kernel are completely separate entities.

The Window Manager

Unless you descend deep into the heart of the windowing system, you'll be spending most of your programming time at the *window manager* level. The window manager is layered on top of X and XLib, and it's the primary interface between the underlying X Window system and the user. It is responsible for drawing and maintaining all the various aspects of the windowing environment, such as window borders, menus, button bars, toolbars, and virtual desktops. It is usually customizable to suit the needs and whims of the user.

Under Windows, you have a single window manager: Windows itself. Under Linux, however, you can fake your choice from a variety of window managers. The primary contenders

Widgets vs. Components

You may be wondering why the "components" you have come to know and love in Delphi have changed their name to "widgets" in Kylix. The reason is that Borland has replaced the Windows-specific Delphi components with Qt, an equivalent set of Linux-compatible objects developed by Trolltech in Norway. These classes implement a set of GUI controls (buttons, scrollbars, and fields, for example) under the X environment, and in that environment GUI controls have always been known as *widgets*. Qt widgets are extremely similar to Delphi VCL (Visual Component Library) components, only with a new name.

The Qt library is an object-oriented GUI software toolkit, written in C++, that's portable to more than a dozen windowed environments. It has been used in a multitude of applications since the release of its first commercial version in 1995, and its use continues to grow.

at this time are KDE and Gnome, but lurking in the wings are other hopefuls such as Window Maker, AfterStep, and Enlightenment. In this book, however, we'll concentrate primarily on the major two (KDE and Gnome). The other environments have dedicated (and vocal) followings, but for the time being they're running a distant third to these two.

Hearing about the wide variety of window managers available may give you the horrifying impression that you'll need to support them all. This actually is nowhere near as difficult as it sounds, thanks partially to Kylix and partially to some magic worked by the authors of the Qt class library.

Borland did its usual job—which is to say, *excellent*—when it created the VCL class library that shipped with Delphi. The abstraction of the notoriously complex Windows SDK was marvelous. It nicely hid complexities and details of displaying screen elements, drawing graphics, handling events, and all the rest of the gory details that go into GUI programming. This abstraction carries over into the new CLX framework in Kylix as well. With Kylix, a **TButton** object is a button in the GUI, regardless of the window manager displaying it. This means that regardless of whether the user of your application is running KDE, Gnome, or Enlightenment, your application will continue to behave as you designed it.

However, an abstraction of GUI programming only goes so far. Simply abstracting a GUI doesn't make the underlying classes work across windowing environments, let alone across operating systems. That's where the Qt library comes in. When porting the VCL library to the CLX framework, Borland wrapped CLX around Qt, further hiding the details of programming under so many different environments. As with Delphi for Windows, if you need to get down and dirty with the underlying window manager (or the OS itself, for that matter), you are free to do so. In several of the solutions presented in this book, we *will* go to those levels. But Kylix, in the true Delphi tradition, makes this surprisingly unnecessary.

Most of you may never need to be familiar with anything deeper then the CLX framework that ships with Kylix. We strongly encourage you to stick with CLX, even if you have a background in X or Qt programming. Sticking with the CLX framework greatly enhances the portability of your source code from Linux to Windows (and whatever other platforms Borland decides to support in the future).

Where to Go for More Information

If you'd like to explore the programming documentation available for KDE, check out **www.developer.kde.org**. For more information on the Qt class library and related products from Trolltech, go to **www.trolltech.com**, and for details on the Gnome window manager, try **www.gnome.org**. Finally, if you would like to know more about the Open Source movement, there is a ton of information at **www.opensource.org**.

Chapter 2
A Linux Boot Camp

Now that you've completed the 10,000-foot overview, it's time to buzz down and take a closer look at some of the differences between the Linux and Windows platforms. In this chapter, you'll examine how files and directories are structured under Linux and then take a rapid tour through several aspects of the Linux operating system from a programmer's perspective. Finally, you'll be introduced to the /proc filesystem.

Be forewarned: Linux (and Unix, upon which it is based), is an industrial-strength product, and there have been many, many books (some containing thousands of pages) written to describe it. The information in this book is intended only to give you a "handle" to grab; in no way can it be a complete introduction to Linux. However, a basic understanding of the material presented in this chapter, and the two chapters that follow, will go a long way in helping you write applications that execute smoothly under Linux. With that caveat firmly in mind, let's get started!

Files and Directories

Like Windows and its predecessor, MS-DOS, Linux maintains programs and data on disk in the form of files, and it lets you organize files within directory structures. We won't attempt to dive into the actual disk-level organization (we'd be rewriting several other books if we did); instead, we will relate the user's view of the Windows file system to the Linux way of life.

13

File and Drive Names

File and directory names under Linux are very similar to UNC naming conventions under Windows. There are, however, some differences, both in the rules and the accepted style. Drive names are quite different—but they're also more descriptive.

Case Matters!

Under Windows, if your directory listing contains a file called OneTrueWay.pas, you can refer to that file as onetrueway.pas or ONETRUEWAY.PAS, and Windows will still recognize and select the appropriate file for you. Under Linux, this is no longer true—file names are *case significant*, and any attempt to refer to a file using a name with mismatched case will fail. If you're stuck "thinking in Windows," that failure could appear very mysterious indeed—and leave you scratching your head.

Legal File Names and Directory Names

Linux file name conventions are very similar to those of Windows, but there are a couple of things that might trip you up for a while. The first of these concerns the little finger of your right hand. Where Windows (for some reason lost in the depths of time) uses the backslash (\) character as a directory separator, Linux (like Unix and many other operating systems) uses the forward slash (/) character. Like Windows, Linux's single separator character is the name of the top-level directory on the system (also called the *root directory*), and all other directories descend from it. Unlike Windows, which has as many root directories as there are drives on the system, Linux has a single root directory, regardless of the number of drives. Other filesystems on other drives and partitions as well as shared drives on other computers are mounted into the local filesystem on *mount points*, which are simply directories added to the filesystem for this purpose.

More about Mounting

The term *mounting* probably originated in the early days of the mainframe computer, when memory was scarce and expensive, and hard disk drives were about the size of an automatic washing machine. It was not unusual during the course of operation to spin down the disk drive and replace a "disk pack" (about the size of a tire on a Yugo) by physically mounting it onto the drive and tightening its handle.

Under Linux, access to data on additional hard drives (whether physically part of the computer or shared over a network), and even individual disk directories, can be "mounted" on the fly to the overall filesystem by using the—you guessed it—**mount** command. In Windows, a new disk drive is always "mounted" at the My Computer level and assigned a unique drive name. Linux, by contrast, connects shared resources (drives or directories) to a mount point that you define (by convention, an empty directory).

Let's say you want the filesystem (directories and files) on the floppy drive (known under Linux by the device designation **/dev/fd0**) to be made part of your Linux filesystem, available in the **/mnt** directory immediately below your **/usr** directory. You could issue the following command:

```
mount /dev/fd0/usr /mnt/floppy
```

Linux uses predefined parameters located in the /etc/fstab file (short for *file system table*) at boot time to configure your filesystem and mount your drives at the designated mount points.

Drives with removable media (such as a floppy disk) must be unmounted and then mounted again whenever new media is inserted—truly a nuisance. The **mtools** package (mentioned in Chapter 1, and automatically installed with many Linux distributions) will do the mounting and unmounting for you automatically.

File and directory names in Linux can be as long as you want them to be, up to 256 characters (anybody who uses that many characters is certifiably masochistic, but that's a little outside the scope of this book). Names can contain any character except the "slash" (/) directory separator character, but you are strongly advised *not* to use a dash (-) as the leading character in a file name.

Tip

*Although the dash (-) character is a perfectly legal character in a file name, it will make life miserable for you if you use it as the first character in a file or directory name. This is because by convention Linux uses the dash character as the command-line "option" character (similar to the slash, as used in Windows). If you try to use any command-line tool (such as **rm**) and specify that name as a command-line parameter, the tool will see the file name as a command-line option, with potentially disastrous results. If you must work with this type of file, try referring to it by its fully qualified name (/home/fflintstone/-xyzzy, for example) or renaming it with the **mv** command (for example, **mv -- -xyzzy xyzzy**) to make your life a bit easier. And, in case you're curious, that "double dash" character (--) in the example tells the **mv** utility there will be no further command-line options, preventing the utility from interpreting **-xyzzy** as a command-line option. Many of the command-line utilities in Linux support this convention, making it a handy thing to remember.*

Drive Names

Another potentially confusing difference between Windows filesystems and Linux filesystems lies in the area of drive names. Under Windows, drives can be named in one of two different ways. Local drives—drives and partitions physically located on your computer—are called "C:," "D:," or "E:" (or any other letter of the alphabet). Networked drives are referred to by "\ \" followed by the name of the networked machine ("\ \foo," for example), followed by the share name on the remote machine. An example of this might be "\ \foo\bar," where "foo" is the remote machine name and "bar" is the share name on that machine. Network drives can also be mapped to an available drive letter using Windows Explorer. The point here is that different physical drives under Windows are always separate from each other. It isn't possible to map a network drive into a directory on your C: drive, for example.

Under Linux, things get a little bit hairier. Until they are mounted, local drives *and the partitions on those drives* are referred to by their name as listed in the /dev (device) directory. The designation /dev/fd0 refers to the first floppy drive on the system, and /dev/fd1 refers to

---

Dancing with Samba

Would you like your Linux machine to share files and printers compatibly with DOS- and Windows-based machines over a network? It can, thanks to a package called *Samba*. Samba was originally developed by Andrew Tridgell, a native Australian who wanted to create a fileserver program for his local network that supported an odd DEC protocol from Digital Pathworks. The project grew over time and eventually became the Samba we know today. Samba uses the Server Message Block (recently renamed *Common Internet File System*) protocol originally taken from IBM's LAN Manager and later extended by Microsoft. Samba uses TCP/IP (not NETBEUI or IPX) to communicate between two network clients. When properly set up, resources shared by a Linux machine running Samba will appear to other users on a network—in fact, unless you tell them otherwise, they will likely assume your Linux box is actually a Windows NT machine. Samba is included with most Linux distributions. It is an Open Source product and is distributed under the GNU General Public License.

---

the second. The first partition on your first IDE hard drive is /dev/hda0, whereas the second partition on the second physical drive is /dev/hdb1. If you have a SCSI hard drive, its first partition is /dev/sda0. Your CD-ROM drive is /dev/cdrom. Confused yet? Don't worry— we'll go into this in a bit more detail shortly.

Networked drives (drives or filesystems exported from other machines on your network) are accessed using a network-based file-sharing protocol, such as Network File System (NFS) or Samba. Similar to the Windows file-sharing techniques, these protocols allow shared disks on other systems to be mounted for use as if they were local drives. Detailed use of these packages is way beyond the scope of this book—entire books have been written on both of these protocols!

Once mounted, the contents of both local drives and network drives appear as ordinary files and directories on your Linux filesystem. Your CD-ROM drive can be made to mount to the /cdrom directory, your Zip disk to the /zip directory, and your Windows partition (for those of you with dual-boot machines) can be mounted to the /dos directory. This makes use of other drives and networked filesystems a snap. Just remember that before these drives can be used, they must be mounted. Unlike Windows, which allows networked drives to be accessed without being mapped to a drive letter, Linux requires that network drives be mounted to the filesystem before they can be accessed.

File Links

Imagine that you have a large file—a dictionary perhaps. This file needs to be accessed by two separate programs, but one program is looking for the file named xyzzy, whereas the other is looking for the same file with the name plugh. You have two choices: Either you can copy the file and eat valuable disk space, or you can create a *file link*.

A file link is a filesystem feature not found in Windows. Links come in two varieties—hard links and symbolic links—and both are created with the **ln** command. Hard links allow the same physical file to be referenced by multiple separate directory entries, each entry pointing to the same file on the system. Deleting a hard link doesn't necessarily delete the associated file; the physical file is not deleted until the last link is deleted. Hard links, however, can't span filesystems.

Symbolic links (also called soft links, or *symlinks*) are similar to hard links, but they have several important differences. Instead of creating a link to the same physical file, a symlink is a separate file that holds a reference to the original file. Because the symlink is a reference to another file, it can span filesystems, overcoming a limitation of hard links.

In our directory example, a hard link would probably be the better choice. It is entirely possible that one of the applications could be deleted (removing its copy of the dictionary file). If a symbolic link was used there would be a 50/50 chance of removing the actual file, rendering the other application useless. With hard links, however, removing one link leaves the file intact until the last link is also removed.

One common use for symlinks (especially symlinks) is in directory management. If you have two versions of a library installed in two separate directories, it is a simple matter to create a symbolic link to one of those directories and then specify the symbolic link instead of the actual directory when compiling. When you need to use the other version of the library, simply change the symlink to point to the other directory. Symbolic links will play an important role in Chapter 3, when we talk about shared libraries.

File and Directory Ownership

Unlike MS-DOS and Win9x/WinMe platforms, Linux is a true multiuser operating system with a full file-permissions scheme. This means it is not only capable of allowing multiuser access to files, but it is also able to limit access to those files to authorized users.

User and Group IDs

Every user on a Linux system has at least two different IDs: a single user ID (or *uid*) and one or more group IDs (or *gid*). Every uid on a system is unique and is assigned to a specific user in the file /etc/passwd. Each user is also assigned to at least one group. Each user's primary gid is assigned in the file /etc/passwd, whereas secondary groups are assigned in the file /etc/group.

Files on the system are owned by an individual user and by a group. Permissions for each of these owners—as well as the world at large—can be specified on every file and directory on the system, giving a great deal of flexibility as to how file access permissions can be set. The easiest example of how this works is to run the following command from within a console on your system and examine the results:

```
ls -l /bin/ls
```

Note that the **ls** program has more command-line options than you can shake two sticks at, but the **-l** option simply lists more information about the file, instead of just listing the file name.

The screen output from this command should look something like the following:

```
-rwxr-xr-x   1 root    root    49844 Sep 24  1999  /bin/ls
```

The first dash gives you some information about the type of file you're examining. The dash indicates this is a normal file. If you were looking at a directory, it would be a "d". If you were examining a link, an "l" would be listed instead. The next set of characters is called the file's *permission mask*, and it's presented in three groups of three characters each. The first set (rwx, in this example) indicates that the *owner* of the file can read, write, and execute the file. The second set (r-x) specifies that the *group* that owns this file can read and execute the file, but not write to it. The last set shows the permissions for all users not covered by the first two sets (these are known as *world permissions*). The owner's name and the group's name are shown, as well as the file size and the last modification time. The command-line utility programs **chmod**, **chown**, and **chgrp** are used to change the file permission mask, file ownership, and file group ownership, respectively.

Note

A permission mask is commonly specified as a three-digit octal number, where each digit represents one of the three sets of permissions on the file. For example, 754 would be equivalent to -rwxr-xr--, and 544 would indicate a permission mask of -r-xr--r--.

The permissions granted on a file are dependent on the permissions of the directory containing the file. Even if the file's permission mask is set to -rwxrwxrwx (777), other users can't access the file if they don't have read and write permissions on the directory where the file is located. This makes it easy to lock down all files in a directory (and in all directories below it) by setting the permissions on that directory to -rwx------ (700).

The Superuser Concept

The concept of user permissions implies that some users are granted more power than others, and this is certainly the case. On all systems there is one "superuser" account, called *root* (not to be confused with the root directory). Root is the system administrator, able to read and write any file or directory on the system.

Root is all powerful (at least on the local system, anyway), but this also means root has tremendous responsibilities. It is entirely too easy for root to delete every file on the system or to change system configuration information in such a way as to render the system a smoldering pile of slag (ask us how we know about this).

The moral of this story is, never, *never* do normal "user-type" work on the system while logged in as root. *Always* create at least one user account for your "normal" work and log in as root only when system maintenance needs to be performed. We guarantee you'll thank us in the long run.

What Are All These Directories, Anyway?

There are so many possible places to put files on a Linux system that it can be difficult to know where to begin looking for files, or even where to put your own. Let's examine a roadmap of some of the major directories on the system and what these directories traditionally contain.

On a typical Linux system, the top level of the file system (the root directory) contains a list of directories similar to the following: bin, dev, etc, home, lib, proc, tmp, usr, and var. Here is a brief look at each of these directories:

♦ */bin*—This is short for *binaries*, which is another name for *executables*. Many system programs reside in this directory tree—some of them quite essential. If you take a look at the list of files in this directory, you might see some that you're already familiar with, such as cp and ls. Normally you would not add files to this directory tree.

♦ */dev*—This is short for *devices*. The entries listed in /dev aren't genuine files but rather special "device files" that enable access to system devices and services. Among many other things, these devices include physical devices such as disk drives and hardware peripherals, but they also include access to software services such as /dev/random (a stream of random data) and /dev/sequencer (access to your MIDI playback capabilities, if you have them). Your programs can even read mouse input, just like reading from a file, simply by accessing /dev/mouse (of course, in a windowed environment this will be counterproductive).

Device-Naming Conventions

Disks in the /dev directory have a consistent naming convention. Devices that begin with "hd" are IDE hard drives, whereas devices beginning with "sd" are SCSI drives. Each drive is assigned a letter: "a" for the first device, "b" for the second, and so on. To provide more detail, each partition on these disks is assigned a number: "1" for the first partition, "2" for the second, and so forth. These designators are then strung together as needed to reference either specific drives or the partitions on them. For example, /dev/hda refers to the first IDE drive on the system (master on the primary IDE controller), and /dev/hda1 indicates the first partition on that drive.

Other devices follow similar schemes: /dev/fd0 is the first floppy drive on the system, /dev/lp0 is the first parallel port (LPT1 on Windows), and /dev/cdrom is—incredibly enough—the first CD-ROM drive.

In addition, /dev/null is a special device that serves as a "black hole"—a write-only filesystem. This is very useful when you need to run a program and completely ignore its output—just redirect it to /dev/null. This device is an output device with infinite space. So, if you ever hear somebody warning you that /dev/null is getting full, ignore him; he's pulling your leg.

♦ */etc*—This directory contains system information and configuration files. Don't put your application's configuration files here—use /usr/local/etc instead.

♦ */home*—This directory is for users' home directories. For example, /home/fflintstone is the home directory for the user with the ID "fflintstone." Development and unit testing should take place in your home directory. When development is complete, applications should then be moved out of your home directory for system and integration testing.

♦ */lib*—This one is short for *libraries*. Shared libraries are similar to Windows DLLs, and they are stored here. This directory is therefore similar to the \Windows\System directory in Windows.

♦ */proc*—This is an interesting "virtual file system." It contains a great deal of information about the current state of the system, all stored in virtual "files" that don't actually take up any physical disk space. We'll go into much more detail on **/proc** and why it's important to you near the end of this chapter.

♦ */tmp*—This is exactly what it sounds like—a temporary storage area for files. By default, all users have write access to this directory. If you need to store a temporary file for any reason, put it here. Many systems have automated scripts that remove older files from this directory as space becomes a problem, but in the interest of "best practices" you should always be sure to have your program remove a file when it is no longer needed.

♦ */usr*—This is an important directory, containing subdirectories that hold some of the system's application programs and their configuration files. Most of these directories are created and populated as part of the process of installing Linux itself onto the system. The directory /usr/X11R6 is a perfect example: It contains the X Window System's executables, configuration files, and support files. The directory that you'll probably access most in /usr, though, is /usr/local and all the directories under it. This set of directories is intended for applications and files specific to your system. For example, optional applications and their configuration files reside in /usr/local/bin and /usr/local/etc.

♦ */var*—This directory holds directories and files that tend to grow in size. Among other things, the system log files, mail and news folders, and print jobs are stored under this directory.

Linux Programming Whirlwind Tour

With the filesystem concepts out of the way, you're about to embark on a whirlwind tour of basic Linux system programming concepts. This is *not* intended to be a complete and thorough tour of Linux system programming—again, many excellent books have been written on that subject. Our intent is merely to bring you up to a level of familiarity that will allow you to start working on the solutions presented in Part Two of this book.

Remember, too, that Kylix's object libraries will insulate you from most of the application programming details. That is why this material is oriented toward basic system programming instead of starting out with application programming concepts. Your first destination is System Call City, home of the kernel's access points.

System Call Concepts

Operating systems have a core component called the *kernel*, which is the protected-mode software layer that, among other things, controls access to the system hardware, synchronizes processes, and implements system security policies. The Linux kernel is loaded during the system boot and then uncompressed into main memory, where it lives until the system is shut down. The kernel runs in protected space; no other application has access to the kernel's memory or methods. This restriction is enforced by the hardware of the CPU (hence the term *protected mode*).

Because applications cannot access the kernel directly, they communicate with the kernel using *system calls*. System calls can be thought of as the access points of the kernel, and as such serve as the mechanism for applications to make use of kernel services.

System calls are fundamentally different from normal system methods, usually called *library functions*. Calling a library function doesn't use the system call mechanism, although library functions can, themselves, make use of system calls. Both library functions and system calls exist to provide services to application programs. However, although it is possible to replace the library functions (by using another programming library, for example), system calls cannot be replaced without installing a new copy of the kernel itself.

In Kylix, many of the standard Linux/Unix system calls and common library functions are available in the **Libc** unit that ships with Kylix. Further documentation of all system calls and library functions can be found in the system **man** page (assuming that the **man** pages package has been installed).

System Call Mechanism

The actual mechanism by which system calls are serviced is unlike a normal method call. Instead of a method call, the application loads the CPU's registers with the parameters that are to be passed to the system call, and then it invokes an interrupt. The kernel's interrupt handler is activated, and it examines the system call's parameters to see which kernel method is to be called. It then calls that method, resets the CPU registers with the appropriate return information, and returns from the interrupt. The application has no knowledge of the addresses of the kernel's internal methods, which helps maintain the security of the kernel and the stability of the system.

By the way, if you want to see which system calls are accessed by an application, use the Linux command **strace**, but be prepared to wade through mountains of information. This is like an X-ray picture of an application, and it can be a very handy low-level debugging technique when the alligators are beginning to circle.

What's the Story, Man?

By tradition, instructional manuals for Unix command-line programs (such as **ls**) have been stored in a special format for display by the manual display program, called *man*. Linux continues that tradition. If you have a question about any standard Linux command, bring up a console from within your window manager and type the following command:

```
man <name of command>
```

If a manual exists for that command, you will be presented with it. To navigate through the manual, use the Enter key to move a line at a time, the spacebar to move forward a page, the backspace key to move back a page, and the Q key to quit the program and return to the command line.

Manuals are sometimes broken into numbered sections. To access a particular section of a manual, use this command:

```
man <section number> <name of command>
```

For more information on the **man** command, type (you guessed it) this:

```
man man
```

Processes and Signals

Under Linux, any program executing on the system is called a *process*. Linux, being a multi-processing operating system, is quite capable of executing concurrent processes for multiple users. Processes include both foreground applications executed by users and background tasks (similar to Windows services, and sometimes called *daemons*) necessary to keep the system running properly.

Every process on the system is guaranteed to have a unique numeric identifier, which will take the form of a nonnegative integer. This identifier is called the *process ID*, or *pid*. Processes can obtain their pid using the **getpid** system call, and users can list processes on the system by using the **ps** command.

Processes are started using a somewhat complicated procedure involving the **fork** system call, and any of several forms of the **exec** system call (for details on the differences between the different versions of **exec**, see the **exec man** page). The **fork** system call creates a second process that is a duplicate of the original process. This duplicate is called the *child process* and is an exact copy of the code and data of the original "parent" process. Execution within the child process begins at the point immediately following the **fork** call that created it. The child process then calls one of the **exec** methods to overwrite itself with a new program that begins executing in its place, while the parent continues executing normally.

Every process has an "environment," similar to the environment variables used in Windows since MS-DOS days (remember the **SET** command?). The environment consists of string pairs. The first string is used as a "lookup key" in the environment list, and the second string contains the value associated with this key. Environment variables are normally used to provide configuration information for the processes, which can read and write their environment settings using the **getvar** and **setvar** library functions.

A process can be terminated in any of several ways: by returning from its top-level method, by calling **exit** or **_exit** (these have been renamed to **__exit** and **_Exit** in Kylix), by aborting execution by calling **abort** (again, renamed to **__abort** in Kylix), or by receiving and acting upon a termination signal.

Signals provide a simple means of communicating with processes. Signals are software interrupts, which constitute one-way communication devices. Signals are sent to the current process using the **raise** system call (renamed to **__raise** in Kylix); signals are transmitted to another process using the **kill** system call and the appropriate pid. (Contrary to its name, **kill** isn't used solely to terminate processes.) Thirty-one different signals are available, of which all but two have specific, reserved meanings. For a list of these signals and their meanings, see the man page for "signal" in Section 7 of the man pages (execute the command **man 7 signal**).

A process can handle signals in one of three ways: It can usually ignore the signal (there are two signals that cannot be ignored, however—**SIGKILL** and **SIGSTOP**, for the curious), it can process the signal itself, or it can let the default action apply. Default handlers are provided for all signals, but specialized signal handlers can be created for every application to allow for customized signal processing. We'll demonstrate this in Part Two of the book.

Threaded Programming

Like Windows, Linux processes can be multithreaded. Indeed, the concepts of threaded programming are similar between the two platforms. Threads have been called *lightweight processes*, and that's pretty accurate, if a bit oversimplified. Threads are cousins to processes, but they are not themselves processes. Like their more complex cousins, threads execute independently of each other, but they execute within a single controlling process and share that process's resources (environment, opened files, global variables, and so forth).

Threads have some significant advantages over the use of multiple processes. Threads are quite small when compared to processes, so they are much cheaper to create. Because they share the resources of the controlling process, they also have a correspondingly smaller impact on memory usage. A multithreaded program has huge advantages over single-threaded programs in situations where the application is required to perform multiple actions that may result in blocking or delay, such as file and socket I/O.

Unfortunately, threads have some disadvantages over multiprocess systems—the biggest being complexity. When multiple threads share common resources, there must be a reliable method employed to control access to those resources; otherwise, resource corruption is almost certain to occur. The methods of controlling concurrent resource access from multiple threads are complex, and special consideration must be given to these methods whenever thread usage is planned. In spite of this, though, the advantages threads provide make them a powerful tool on the Linux programmer's workbench.

Under Linux, the POSIX threading model is used. There is a small horde of library functions used to create and manage threads, and almost all the names of those functions begin with **pthread_**. These functions include **pthread_create** (creates a new thread and starts it running), **pthread_exit** (exits from a completed thread), and **pthread_kill** (aborts execution of a thread from outside of the thread itself). There are many others, all summed up in—you guessed it—your system's man pages.

At this point, if you're already familiar with Kylix, you might be asking why we're talking about the **pthread_** functions when Kylix contains a perfectly useful **TThread** class. It's a good question. The **TThread** class in Kylix wraps around the **pthread_** functions, but in our experience it is always a good idea to know what's going on beneath the hood, especially with something as complex as threading. In this case, having an idea of how threading works under Linux will allow you more flexibility in your **TThread** usage, as well as give you a leg up on the fun debugging that can be required when threads start tying themselves in knots.

Interprocess Communication

As with Windows, there are times when multiple Linux processes must speak with each other. In this section we'll discuss several methods of interprocess communication (IPC). The three methods presented here—pipes, FIFOs, and semaphores—are present in both Windows and Linux, but with vastly different APIs. Linux has several other methods available (such as shared memory and message queues) that are not directly supported under Kylix, so we won't go into them here.

We won't talk about sockets here simply because Borland has thoughtfully provided an excellent set of classes in the Kylix object library that encapsulate socket programming. Sockets make an excellent IPC mechanism in their own right, and you should consider using Borland's implementation, if possible, if for no other reason than the portability of your application code.

Pipes

Pipes are, as the name implies, the communication plumbing of Linux. Pipes are the oldest form of Unix IPC, and they are common to all Unix-based systems. They provide a half-duplex communication channel (that is, data flows only one way) between two processes—most frequently, between a parent and a child process.

Pipes are created using the **pipe** system call. This system call creates the pipe and returns a pair of file descriptors that will be used for writing to and reading from the pipe. At this point the pipe is basically useless, because the same process is holding both ends of the pipe. However, after calling **fork**, the child process also knows the file descriptors (it's an exact duplicate of the parent, remember?), and now the two processes can communicate across the pipe. Most often the child process writes to the pipe and the parent reads it, but there's nothing preventing the reverse from taking place. Both the parent and the child can write to the pipe, but since the pipe is one-way there would be no way for them to distinguish the intended recipient of the data in the pipe. If two-way communication is desired, create two pipes.

The **popen** function simplifies the creation of a pipe to a child process. This function creates a new process (using **fork** and **exec**) that executes a specified program, and it returns a pipe connected to the standard output of the child process. The **pclose** function is used to close a pipe created in this manner.

Although it is possible to set up a pipe with multiple writers, this is rarely done. Pipes are most useful when an IPC channel has a single writer and a single reader. The principle drawback to pipes is that both the reader and the writer must be related—they must share a common ancestor process. When you must have unrelated processes communicate across a pipe, you'll need to turn to FIFOs.

FIFOs

A *FIFO* (sometimes called a *named pipe*) is a special type of file that makes it easy for unrelated processes that share a common file system to exchange data. Once a FIFO has been opened, all the usual file I/O functions (**fopen**, **fread**, and **fwrite**) can be used with it. FIFOs are created with the **mkfifo** function and then opened (by name, hence *named pipes*) by all processes wishing to use the FIFO. It is common for FIFOs to have multiple writers and a single reader, but be aware that multiple writers will have to worry about synchronizing their writes to prevent data from being interleaved as it enters the FIFO. (A common technique for synchronization is to use *semaphores*, which we'll discuss shortly.)

FIFOs are frequently used by server programs, which act as the reader at the downstream end of the FIFO. Because a FIFO looks like a file (including the fact that is has a "well-known" name), it is easy for clients to open the FIFO and write to it. The only complication is that the same technique does not work for sending data back to the clients, because there is no way for multiple readers to distinguish the data coming back down a single FIFO. One solution to this problem is to have the clients send identifying information down the FIFO (the client process's pid works wonderfully for this). The server then creates and opens new FIFOs back to the clients, naming the FIFOs with a variation of the identifying information sent from the client and using the FIFOs to return data to specific clients. As an example, the server process named Fred creates a FIFO named "Fred" so that clients can feed it data. When Fred receives data identified as coming from process id 1234 it creates a new FIFO called Fred_1234 to send data back to the client.

Semaphores

A *semaphore* is an IPC mechanism, but it is fundamentally different from the other types we've discussed in that it's not used to transfer data directly. Semaphores are instead counters used to synchronize access to a shared resource by multiple processes.

A small word of warning is in order: A semaphore is a complex IPC mechanism (of course, this statement holds true whenever you start to discuss shared resources). For that reason, explaining semaphores in detail would require substantially more space than we can provide in this introductory context.

So, let's look at a simple example—a case where a process wants to grab control of a specific resource, locking out other processes that might also want control of that resource from time to time. This example assumes that everyone is "playing fair," and is cooperatively using a common semaphore.

In order to obtain "ownership" of the shared resource, the process must do the following:

1. Test the value of the semaphore that controls access to the resource.

2. If the value of the semaphore is greater than zero, the resource is available. The process decrements the value of the semaphore by one (indicating that it has taken possession of one unit of the resource), and it begins using the resource.

3. If the value of the semaphore is instead zero, the process goes to sleep until the semaphore's value is greater than zero again (because it was set by another process). When the process wakes up, it loops back and resumes at Step 1.

4. When the process is finished with the resource, it increments the value of the semaphore by one, which wakes up any other processes sleeping in Step 3.

What a pain, or at least it would be, if the system didn't automate the process for you. Indeed, it *must* automate the process. Here's why: In a multiprocess (or multithreaded) system, it is highly likely that the executing thread or process could be interrupted between Steps 1 and 2, causing the process to begin using the resource without a guarantee that the resource is actually available. (Hint: What would happen if another process executed *both* Steps 1 and 2, while the first process paused *between* Steps 1 and 2? It's an ugly thought.)

Because of eventualities such as these, the entire process of testing and decrementing a semaphore's value must be atomic and not be interrupted during these steps. For this reason, semaphores are normally implemented inside the kernel. Like a message queue, a semaphore has an ID that can be used by any process on the system (subject to the permissions on the semaphore). A semaphore is created with the **sem_init** library function and it is tested with the **sem_wait** function (which automatically sleeps until the semaphore is available) and the **sem_trywait** function (which returns immediately if the semaphore is not available).

One drawback to semaphores is that individual semaphores are identified by a numeric identifier that isn't published anywhere. Unlike a FIFO, whose name is specified as part of its creation, a semaphore ID is automatically generated by the system when the semaphore is created. At that time, only the creator of the semaphore knows its ID. For other processes to use the semaphore, the creating process must write the ID to a file or some other place accessible to all processes needing to use the semaphore.

Semaphores, once created, remain on the system until destroyed. They are not automatically removed by the system when all processes using them exit; it is the responsibility of processes using semaphores to destroy them as necessary (last process to use the semaphore, turn out the lights). Semaphores can be removed by their owners, with the **sem_destroy** function, or by using the **ipcrm** utility from the command line.

The /proc Filesystem

In Linux there is a mechanism processes can use to obtain information about the system: the **/proc** filesystem. This filesystem was originally designed to provide processes with an easy way to access information about other processes (hence the name). It is now used by almost every part of the kernel that has something interesting to report, including **/proc/ modules**, which contains the list of installable modules currently in use by the kernel, and **/proc/meminfo**, which can provide memory usage statistics.

The **/proc** filesystem contains a series of "pseudo-files" that hold information about the system. Information available from the various files includes data about the CPU, numbers for the major character and block devices, assigned hardware interrupts and I/O port addressing, and the version of the running kernel—just to name a few. Some files are dynamically updated and can give you average system load data, lists of locks held on open files, and operational statistics. A list of the more interesting **/proc** files is shown in Table 2.1.

Table 2.1 Interesting files in the /proc filesystem.

Path Under /proc	Data in the File
cpuinfo	Complete identification information about the current system's CPU
filesystems	Filesystem types supported on this machine
interrupts	IRQ information for the devices installed on the system
ioports	I/O addresses for the devices installed on the system
meminfo	Information about the memory installed on the system, as well as information about current swap file usage
modules	Information about loadable modules currently loaded by the kernel
net/	Current network status and information
pci	Detailed information about PCI devices installed on this system
sys/	Information about current kernel variables and settings

The **/proc** filesystem is something that's unique to Linux (that is, it has no counterpart in Windows). It is *very* cool, and we'll be using it in some of the solutions presented in Part Two of the book. In the meantime, you can read about the files and directories under this filesystem by using the command **man proc** at any shell prompt. Be warned, however, that the **/proc** "files" have had different formats over the years, and it is up to you to make sure your code can handle these formats. *Caveat coder*—let the programmer beware.

Where to Go for More Information

If you would like to learn more about Samba, there is a wealth of information available. Because Samba is typically included with most Linux distributions, the first place to look is on the CD-ROMs that came with your distribution. Beyond that, Samba has its own Web site, located at **www.samba.org**. From that site you can download the source code and lots of documentation. Coriolis publishes *The Samba Black Book*, an excellent source of information, by Dominic Baines, on installing and managing Samba (ISBN 1576104559). An online copy of Eckstein, Collier-Brown, and Kelly's book, *Using Samba*, is available at **sunsite.dk/samba/oreilly/using_samba/**.

The **mtools** package is also included with most Linux distributions. If your distribution did not include it (or if you would like to update your copy), you can download it at **www.tux.org/pub/tux/knaff/mtools/**. If you already have a copy and would like user information, try the **mtools** man page.

For information on the installation and administration of Linux, check out the *Linux Installation and Getting Started Guide* by Matt Welsh, et. al. (available at **www.ibiblio.org/mdw/LDP/gs/gs.html**) and the *Linux System Administration Black Book* by Dee-Ann LeBlanc, published by Coriolis (ISBN 1576104192). For industrial-strength information on Unix system programming, try *Advanced Programming in the Unix Environment* by W. Richard Stevens (Addison Wesley, ISBN 0201563177). Stevens' book is getting a little dated, but for serious system programming geeks it is a must-have book.

Yes, we've said it before, and we'll most likely say it again a time or two. If you haven't installed the man pages package on your system, do it now. Man pages contain a wealth of information—not just about command-line utilities, but also about system calls, library routines, and configuration file formats. A development system without a set of man pages is like a sports car without a driver's seat—it may be functional, but it is difficult—and possibly painful—to realize its full performance and functionality.

Chapter 3
Using Libraries

In this chapter and the next we'll delve into a greater level of detail on some of the critical aspects of developing industrial-strength programs with Kylix. In this chapter we cover the creation of static and dynamic libraries. Linux's support of libraries is very similar to that of Windows. There are two types of libraries: static and dynamic. *Static libraries* contain object code that is statically bound to the executable program at link time. In Linux, static libraries typically have the .a extension. Windows libraries typically have the .lib extension. A static library is nothing more than a collection of individual object files (.obj on Windows, .o on Linux). Linkers for other programming language can search these libraries and include in the executable image just the object files that it needs. Although Kylix can link individual object files, it cannot search a library.

Linking with a static library or an individual object file is similar to linking with a unit (.dcu) file: The library code is included in the final program's executable image. Linking statically has one huge advantage in that your program is contained in a single executable file. But it has some distinct disadvantages, too. If you have a suite of programs that share many of the same modules, each program includes all of that object code, which increases the storage and memory requirements of your application. Static linking also makes it difficult to update your programs. If a common module changes, you have to recompile the entire program suite to provide an update.

Shared libraries solve these problems and add more flexibility. But that flexibility comes at a price: complexity. The end of this chapter contains some information about the complexity and how to manage it. Under Windows, shared libraries are called *dynamic link libraries*, or *DLLs*, and usually have the .dll file extension. The Linux equivalent is the *shared object*, or *SO file*. By convention, shared objects have the .so file extension. Using shared objects under Linux is very similar to using DLLs under Windows.

Creating and Using a Shared Object

Like a Windows DLL, a shared object is a separate file that contains code (procedures and functions) and data that other programs can access. Unlike a unit, whose code is statically bound to your program, references to code in shared objects are resolved dynamically at runtime. Although a shared object contains executable code, you can't "run" the shared object like a program. You need a separate program to call the functions in the shared object. In this section, we're going to create a shared object, and a program that calls the functions in that shared object.

Create a Project Group

Because we'll be making changes to two projects (the shared object and the calling program), the first thing we'll do is create a Kylix project group to contain both projects. Using a project group is much more convenient than continually opening and closing the individual projects to make and test changes.

From Kylix's main menu, select File | New from the menu and then select Project Group from the New Items dialog box. Save the project with the name **HelloGroup.bpg**. In the Project Manager, right-click the top-level node (it will be called *HelloGroup*) and select Add New Project from the pop-up menu. From the New Items dialog box, select Shared Object, and save the project as **hello.dpr**.

Naming Libraries

If you look at the Project Manager window, you'll notice that the library target is named **libhello.so**, rather than just hello. If you compile the project, the output file will be called **libhello.so**. What's going on?

The Linux convention is to prepend "lib" to the name of all library files. Kylix, always the helpful servant, does this for you. Therefore, the **hello.dpr** project file automatically creates the output file libhello.so. The use of library files under Linux is subject to a lot of conventions, which I'll discuss in detail after you see how to call library functions.

The Hello Library

Listing 3.1 shows a very simple shared object that exports just one procedure, **SayHello**, which writes a message to the console. Enter this code into your hello.dpr file and save the file.

Listing 3.1   A simple shared object.

```
{ hello.dpr - a simple shared object }
library hello;

uses
  SysUtils,
  Classes;

{$R *.res}

procedure SayHello; cdecl;
begin
  WriteLn ('Hello from library');
end;

exports
  SayHello index 1 name 'SayHello';

begin
  WriteLn ('library startup code');
end.
```

Libraries start with the reserved word **library** rather than **program** or **unit**. They also have a **uses** statement. You'll notice that, like programs, libraries don't have separate interface and implementation sections. You write your procedures and functions in the library just as you would in a unit or a program and then you specifically *export* those functions that you want to be available to other programs.

The **cdecl** modifier at the end of the procedure definition specifies that the function should use the C calling convention. Although it's not required, it's a good idea to have your exported functions use the C calling convention. If you use some other calling convention, programs written in other languages (C, for example) won't be able to access your library functions.

Whatever calling convention you use (see the Kylix documentation for details about different calling conventions), the function declaration in the library's interface unit (discussed below in "Calling Library Functions") *must* match the calling convention of your exported library function. If the calling conventions don't match, your program will fail when it calls or returns from the exported function. This is a very difficult bug to track down. The other reason to use **cdecl** is simplicity. If you always use the C calling convention for your exported functions, you'll have less chance of creating an interface unit whose function declarations don't match the library's function definitions.

The **exports** statement is what tells the compiler to make specific functions available to other programs, and what to call them. In this example, I've exported the **SayHello** procedure by name and by ordinal number. We'll talk more about the **name** and **index** modifiers later in this chapter. If you have more than one exported function, separate their declarations with commas, like this:

```
Exports
  SayHello index 1 name 'SayHello',
  SayGoodbye index 2 name 'SayGoodbye';
```

This library also has a line of code in the main **begin...end** block. I've included this code to illustrate the order in which things happen. Its use will become apparent later in the chapter.

Calling Library Functions

A library isn't much good without a program to access its functions. In this section you'll create a quick test program to call the **SayHello** procedure in **libhello.so**. In the Project Manager window, right-click the HelloGroup node and select Add New Project from the pop-up menu. Select Console Application from the New Items dialog box, enter the code shown in Listing 3.2, and then save the project as **HelloTest.dpr**.

Listing 3.2   A program to test libhello.so.

```
{ HelloTest.dpr - Libraries example test program }
program HelloTest;

{$APPTYPE CONSOLE}

uses
  SysUtils, HelloIntf;

begin
  WriteLn ('Start library test');
  WriteLn ('Press Enter to call the SayHello function');
  ReadLn;
  try
    SayHello;
  except
    on E:Exception do
      WriteLn ('Error: '+E.Message);
  end;
  WriteLn ('Press Enter to exit the program');
  ReadLn;
end.
```

This program uses the HelloIntf unit, shown in Listing 3.3, which contains the declaration of the **SayHello** procedure.

Listing 3.3   The library interface unit.

```
{ HelloIntf.pas - interface unit for hello library }
unit HelloIntf;

interface

procedure SayHello; cdecl;

implementation

procedure SayHello; external 'libhello.so' name 'SayHello';

end.
```

Create a new module called **HelloIntf.pas** and enter the code shown in Listing 3.3.

HelloIntf.pas is an interface unit that tells Kylix where to find the **SayHello** procedure. The **SayHello** procedure definition in the implementation section specifies that the function is located in an external module called **libhello.so**.

Once you've created the interface unit, save your work and select Build All Projects from the Project menu. Kylix will compile the library and the test program. After the compile is complete, press F9 to run the program. If you did everything correctly, you should see this output on your screen:

```
library startup code
Start library test
Press Enter to call the SayHello function

Hello from library
Press Enter to continue
```

It's possible that you'll get an error message saying that the system can't find the **libHello.so** library. The most likely cause for this error is that the Linux loader is not searching the current directory for libraries.

Making Your Library Accessible

An environment variable called **LD_LIBRARY_PATH** tells Linux where to search for libraries. Linux looks in other places, too (see "Where Linux Looks for Libraries" later on in this chapter), but **LD_LIBRARY_PATH** is a convenient way to change things for testing purposes. You can use this **LD_LIBRARY_PATH** trick for testing on your development machine, but your program's installation script should never change **LD_LIBRARY_PATH** on the user's machine. The section on library conventions describes more acceptable ways to make your libraries accessible.

LD_LIBRARY_PATH is a colon-separated list of directory names. It functions in much the same way as the Windows **PATH** environment variable. To view the current value of **LD_LIBRARY_PATH**, enter this command at the Linux command prompt:

```
echo $LD_LIBRARY_PATH
```

You'll either see a blank line, indicating that **LD_LIBRARY_PATH** has not yet been defined, or you'll see a line that contains a colon-separated list of path names. If you see the string "**:.:**" in the path, or if "**:.**" is at the end, then the current directory ("**.**") is already in the path. Otherwise, you'll need to add the current directory to the path.

The easiest way to add the current directory to **LD_LIBRARY_PATH** is to enter this command:

```
export LD_LIBRARY_PATH=.:$LD_LIBRARY_PATH
```

Of course, you'll have to shut down Kylix and then restart it in order for the IDE to recognize that the environment variable has changed.

If you want to make the change to **LD_LIBRARY_PATH** permanent, shut down Kylix and add the **export** command above to the end of your login script (.bashrc in your home directory). Then log out and log back in. When you start Kylix again, it'll get the new value of the **LD_LIBRARY_PATH** environment variable. **LD_LIBRARY_PATH** is a good solution for development and testing, but it has some problems, which are discussed later in the section titled "Where Linux Looks for Libraries."

Shared Library Conventions

Linux loads shared libraries at program start time. If the system can't find a library that the program needs, the program will abort with an error message. Properly installed, shared libraries allow you to update libraries and still support programs that use older, incompatible libraries, override specific libraries or library functions for a particular program, and make library changes while other programs are running using existing libraries. As you can imagine, supporting all these features requires that you follow a number of conventions when naming and placing your libraries.

Library Naming Conventions

Shared libraries are typically referred to by three different names. These names are called the *real name*, the *soname*, and the *linker name*. All three of these names are files. The real name is the name of the file that contains the actual code of the library. The soname and linker name are symbolic links. The soname symbolic link points to the real name, and the linker name symbolic link points to the soname.

A library's real name starts with the prefix "lib" and is followed by the library's name, the phrase ".so", followed by a period, the major version number, a period, the minor version number, and another period and the release number. For example, our library might be called **libhello.so.1.1.1**, meaning version 1.1, release 1. The final period and release number are considered optional. The minor release number is changed whenever you make significant changes to the library's operation. You should only change the major release number when the library's interface changes. The soname is simply the real name without the minor version and release numbers. The soname for the library named previously would be **libhello.so.1**.

Finally, the linker name is the name that the compiler uses when requesting a library. This is just the soname without the version number. In the example, the linker name would be libhello.so. Typically, the soname points to the latest library version that has the soname's major version number, and the linker name points to the soname with the highest major version number.

Why Three Names?

The simple answer is flexibility. The library can be updated with a minimum of hassle. To update a library that has the same major version number, simply copy the new library to your system and update the soname symbolic link. For example, if you were to deploy the sample library to a system, you would copy it to the **/usr/lib** directory (or one of the other standard places—see "Where Do Libraries Go," later on in this chapter). You would also create symbolic links for the soname and the linker name, by issuing these two commands from the Linux command line:

```
ln -s /usr/lib/libhello.so.1.1 /usr/lib/libhello.so.1
ln -s /usr/lib/libhello.so.1 /usr/lib/libhello.so
```

Note that you will probably need to be logged in as root in order to create or modify files in the **/usr/lib** directory. The **/usr/lib** directory would then contain the three files shown in Table 3.1 (in addition to whatever else is there).

Later, if you wanted to update the library to version 1.2.1, you would copy **libhello.so.1.2.1** to the **/usr/lib** directory and update the **libhello.so.1** symbolic link so that it points to the new library. You could then delete **libhello.so.1.1.1**.

Table 3.1   Files and links created when deploying the sample library to /usr/lib.

File Name	Description
libhello.so.1.1.1	The real name. This file contains the actual library object code.
libhello.so.1	The soname. This file is a symbolic link to **libhello.so.1.1.1**.
libhello.so	The linker name. This file is a symbolic link to the soname **libhello.so.1**.

To update to a new major library version, you would copy the new library to **/usr/lib**, create a new soname symbolic link, and update the linker name to point to the new soname. For example, if you release version 2 of the library, called **libhello.so.2.1.1**, you would copy it to **/usr/lib**, create a new soname called **libhello.so.2**, and update **libhello.so** to point to the new soname. The commands to update the links are as follows:

```
ln -s /usr/lib/libhello.so.2.1.1 /usr/lib/libhello.so.2
rm /usr/lib/libhello.so
ln -s /usr/lib/libhello.so.2 /usr/lib/libhello.so
```

Your **/usr/lib** directory would then contain five files, as shown in Table 3.2.

Where Do Libraries Go?

Earlier, I mentioned **/usr/lib** as the directory into which you should place libraries. That's one place. Other possibilities are **/lib** and **/usr/local/lib**. In general, libraries that are required to boot the system should be placed in the **/lib** directory. You would normally put other libraries in **/usr/lib** or **/usr/local/lib**. The Filesystem Hierarchy Standard, available at **www.pathname.com/fhs**, describes the current conventions. I strongly recommend that you read this document and follow the conventions when deploying your libraries.

Where Linux Looks for Libraries

The list of directories that the Linux loader searches for shared libraries is stored in the file **/etc/ld.so.conf**. See Table 3.2 for a list of files and links in the sample library in **/usr/lib**. Searching in all these places would be inefficient, however, so Linux uses a caching arrangement. The file that the loader *actually* searches is **/etc/ld.so.cache**. This file is created by the **ldconfig** program, which you must run after you add or remove a shared library or change the list of directories in **/etc/ld.so.conf**. To run **ldconfig**, make sure you're logged in as root, and then enter this command:

```
ldconfig
```

ldconfig will scan your system and update the cache file where necessary. If you want to see the directories and files that **ldconfig** is scanning, specify the verbose option, like this:

```
ldconfig -v
```

Table 3.2   Files and links after updating the sample library in /usr/lib.

File Name	Description
libhello.so.1.1.1	The real name for version 1 of the library.
libhello.so.1	The version 1 soname. This is a symbolic link to **libhello.so.1.1.1**.
libhello.so.2.1.1	The real name for version 2 of the library.
libhello.so.2	The version 2 soname. This is a symbolic link to **libhello.so.2.1.1**.
libhello.so	The linker name. This is a symbolic link to **libhello.so.2**.

In addition to the directories specified in **/etc/ld.so.conf**, the **LD_LIBRARY_PATH** environment variable specifies a list of directories that should be searched before the standard set of directories. **LD_LIBRARY_PATH** is handy for development and testing, but you shouldn't rely on it for normal use. For an explanation of why, see the document, "Why **LD_LIBRARY_PATH** Is Bad" at **www.visi.com/~barr/ldpath.html**.

Here, then, is the loader's library search order:

1. The paths specified in the **LD_LIBRARY_PATH** environment variable.

2. The list of paths specified in **/etc/ld.so.cache**.

3. The **/usr/lib** directory.

4. The **/lib** directory.

These are the most common methods of controlling the library search algorithm. For more detailed information, see the "Program Library HOWTO" document referenced at the end of this chapter.

Kylix Support for Library Conventions

Kylix supports the Linux library conventions by allowing compiler directives to change the compiler's default behavior. The four library-specific compiler directives are shown in Table 3.3.

To follow convention, then, the sample shared object should define a version and a soname, and the application that references it should be updated to use the version-specific soname.

Table 3.3   The four library-specific compiler directives.

Directive	Purpose
{$SOPREFIX 'string'}	Overrides the default "lib" prefix in the output file name. For example, if you want to create a design-time package called *dclhello*, you would specify **{$SOPREFIX 'dcl'}**. If you want no prefix, you would specify **{$SOPREFIX ''}**.
{$SOSUFFIX 'string'}	Adds the specified suffix to the output file name before the .so extension. For example, **{$SOSUFFIX '-2'}** would create **libhello-2.so**.
{$SOVERSION 'string'}	Adds a version string to the file name after the .so suffix. To create version 1.2.4, for example, you would specify **{$SOVERSION '1.2.4'}** to create **libhello.so.1.2.4**.
{$SONAME 'string'}	Specifies the library's soname. This is the internally coded library name in the shared object file's dynamic string table. This doesn't change the name of the output file but instead causes the compiler to create a symbolic link to the actual file. For example, if you specify **{$SOVERSION '1.2.4'}** and **{$SONAME 'libhello.so.1'}**, the compiler will create **libhello.so.1.2.4**, which contains the actual library code, and **libhello.so.1**, which is a symbolic link that points to **libhello.so.1.2.4**.

In the **hello.dpr** file, add the following two lines directly below the line that contains the **library** keyword, as shown here:

```
library Sample;
{$SOVERSION '1.1.1'}
{$SONAME 'libhello.so.1'}
```

In the interface unit, HelloIntf.pas, change the library name in the **SayHello** procedure declaration to **'libhello.so.1'**, like this:

```
procedure SayHello; external 'libhello.so.1' name 'SayHello';
```

Build both projects and run the program. You should get the same results as before. However, you'll notice that the compiler creates **libhello.so.1.1.1** and **libhello.so.1**. The **libhello.so** file that is still in your directory is the old version. You should delete it. Note that the compiler did not create a linker name file (**libhello.so**) that points to the soname. If you want that link, you'll have to create it yourself using the **ln** command.

Fun with Function Names

When I created the sample library, I used the **name** and **index** modifiers in the **exports** statement to name the library function. That statement reads as follows:

```
exports
  procedure SayHello; index 1 name 'SayHello';
```

The **index** modifier is supported in Kylix for Linux for cross-platform compatibility. A Windows DLL can export functions by index, as well as by name, but the ELF format used by Linux can only export by name. The Kylix for Linux compiler will issue this warning message

```
        Warning: Symbol 'INDEX' is specific to a platform
```

if it encounters an **index** modifier in an **export** statement, but the code will compile correctly.

In this particular case, the **name** modifier isn't really required, because you're not really renaming the function. If you were to write the following, you would get the same result:

```
exports
  SayHello;
```

The exported function name would still be **SayHello**. In some cases, though, you might want a function's external name to be different from the internal function name. The **name** modifier allows you to do this. For example, if you want the exported name to be **WriteHello**, you would change the name with the **name** modifier, like this:

```
exports
  SayHello name 'WriteHello';
```

If you make this change, you'll have to change the interface unit, too. The original interface unit declaration looks like this:

```
procedure SayHello : string; external 'libhello.so.1';
```

In order to reference the newly renamed function, you would need to change it to read as follows:

```
procedure SayHello : string; external 'libhello.so.1' name 'WriteHello';
```

Alternatively, you could create a new declaration in the interface unit for the **WriteHello** procedure, like this:

```
interface

procedure SayHello; cdecl;
procedure WriteHello; cdecl;

implementation

procedure SayHello; external 'libhello.so' name 'WriteHello';
procedure WriteHello; external 'libhello.so' name 'WriteHello';
```

Calling either **SayHello** or **WriteHello** will result to a call to the **WriteHello** procedure in the library **libhello.so.1**.

The reason for the **name** modifier in function declarations is that some libraries export function names that are not valid Pascal identifiers. For example, an exported library function called **xy$format** would require a function declaration with a **name** modifier, because **xy$format** is not a valid Pascal identifier.

Loading Libraries Dynamically

If you look back at the output from your program test, you'll notice that the library's startup code (the code in the main **begin…end** block of **hello.dpr**) was executed before your program got control. This happens because the Linux loader resolves references to shared libraries when the program is started, which causes the library startup code to be executed.

If the loader can't find one of the referenced libraries, it will fail to load the program. This behavior is fine in cases where the majority of the program depends on the existence of the shared libraries in order to function. But if only small or infrequently used parts of the program require functions in shared libraries, requiring the libraries to be present all the time is unreasonable. In this case, you want the ability to load library functions dynamically as they're required.

Dynamically loading library functions is more involved than having Linux do it at program startup, but it's a lot more flexible. The changes you have to make are all in the application program. The library file remains the same. Listing 3.4 contains a modified library interface unit called **HelloDynm.pas** that supports dynamic linking.

Listing 3.4   Loading libraries dynamically.

```
{ HelloDynm.pas -- Dynamic interface to libhello }
unit HelloDynm;

interface

procedure SayHello;

implementation

uses SysUtils, Libc;

const
  STR_LIB_NAME = 'libhello.so.1';
  STR_HELLO_NAME = 'SayHello';

type
  HelloProc = procedure; cdecl;

const
  libHandle : Pointer = nil;

function GetLibraryHandle : Pointer;
begin
  if libHandle = nil then
  begin
    libHandle := dlOpen (STR_LIB_NAME, RTLD_LAZY);
    if libHandle = nil then
      raise Exception.CreateFmt
        ('Unable to open library "%s"', [STR_LIB_NAME]);
  end;
  Result := libHandle;
end;
```

```
function GetLibrarySymbol (const fName: String): Pointer;
begin
  Result := dlSym (GetLibraryHandle, PChar(fName));
  if Result = nil then
    raise Exception.CreateFmt
      ('Unable to locate function "%s" in library "%s".',
        [STR_LIB_NAME, fName]);
end;

procedure SayHello;
const
  HelloPtr : HelloProc = nil;
begin
  if not Assigned (HelloPtr) then
    HelloPtr := GetLibrarySymbol (STR_HELLO_NAME);
  HelloPtr;
end;

initialization

finalization
  if Assigned (libHandle) then
    dlClose (libHandle);

end.
```

Hey, I *said* it was more involved. You end up writing code to do what the Linux loader does automatically. But there is a serious benefit to all of this code—you have much better error recovery, and *you* control when libraries are loaded.

Most of the work is done in the **GetLibraryHandle** and **GetLibrarySymbol** functions. **GetLibraryHandle** simply checks to see if the **libHandle** global variable has been assigned. If it hasn't, the function makes a call to the Linux runtime library function **dlopen**, which locates and loads the library.

GetLibrarySymbol passes the library handle returned from **GetLibraryHandle** and the name of the symbol to be created to the **dlsym** function, which will locate an exported library function. When a program calls the **SayHello** function, the function obtains a pointer to the exported library function, calls that function through the pointer, and returns the result. The finalization section of the module checks to see if the library has been loaded and, if so, releases it by calling **dlclose**.

The **GetLibraryHandle** and **GetLibrarySymbol** functions will throw exceptions if their calls to **dlopen** or **dlsym** fail. The calling program can handle these exceptions by informing the user of the problem and requesting that the proper library be installed—all without having to exit the program or lose the user's data. This is in sharp contrast to functions in shared libraries, which must be located at program startup in order for the program to work at all.

To test this new unit, create a new file called **HelloDynm.pas** and enter the code shown in Listing 3.4. Then, replace the reference to the **HelloIntf unit** in **HelloTest.dpr** with a reference to the new **HelloDynm** unit. Finally, compile and run the program. The output to your screen should be as follows:

```
Start library test
Press Enter to call the SayHello function

library startup code
Hello from library
Press Enter to continue
```

Note that now, the library startup code is not executed until your program loads the library, which happens during the call to **SayHello** rather than at program startup.

Library Initialization and Finalization

The ELF standard specifies that if a library exports a function called **_init**, that function will be called when a program loads the library. Similarly, if a library exports a function called **_fini**, it will be called when a program releases the library. Kylix doesn't support the **_init** and **_fini** functions directly. If you export these functions in your library, they will not be called when the library is opened or closed. Instead, Kylix provides the initialization and finalization sections in units, which are automatically executed when the library is opened and closed, respectively.

Where **dlopen** Looks for Libraries

If the file name passed to the **dlopen** function contains an absolute path, the Linux loader will look only in that location for the library. Similarly, if the file name contains a relative path, the loader will append the relative path to the current directory and look only in that location for the library. If the file name doesn't contain path information, **dlopen** uses the same search order the Linux loader uses:

1. The paths specified in the **LD_LIBRARY_PATH** environment variable.

2. The list of paths specified in **/etc/ld.so.cache**.

3. The **/usr/lib** directory.

4. The **/lib** directory.

If you expect many programs to share your library, your best option is to follow the Linux convention for library naming and placement. On the other hand, if your library is specific to your application, placement and naming is entirely up to you. It's probably best if you maintain the .so file extension, but versioning is optional, and you may want to place the library in the same directory as your executable program in order to make updates easier. This also prevents cluttering up the **/usr/lib** or **/usr/local/lib** directory with application-specific libraries that aren't generally useful to other programs. See the Filesystem Hierarchy Standards document at **www.pathname.com/fhs** for other recommendations.

Cross-Platform Issues

If you isolate the operating system library function calls to just a few parts of your code, you don't have to make major changes to your library source code in order for it to work with both Kylix and Delphi. There are some issues that you have to keep in mind when writing a cross-platform library.

Calling Convention

The "normal" calling convention for Linux libraries is **cdecl**. Under Windows, the recommended calling convention for DLLs is **stdcall**. Because of this, your library's code needs to conditionally define the function-calling conventions, and so does the interface unit. For example, you would write something similar to the following to declare your library functions:

```
function GetHelloMessage : string;
  {$IFDEF MSWINDOWS} stdcall; {$ENDIF} {$IFDEF LINUX} cdecl; {$ENDIF}
```

You have to do something similar in your interface units, but there you have the added complication of the library name.

Library Name

Your library name will probably be different under Linux from what it is under Windows. For example, the sample library in this chapter is libhello.so.1, but under Windows I'd probably just call it **hello.dll**. How, then, does one write an interface unit that will compile under both platforms?

There are actually two answers: The first is to write two sets of declarations in your interface unit—one set for Windows and one set for Linux, resulting in code like this:

```
{$IFDEF LINUX}
  procedure SayHello; cdecl; external 'libhello.so.1';
```

```
  {$ELSE}
    procedure SayHello; stdcall; external 'hello';
  {$ENDIF}
```

This might be reasonable if you have only a handful of functions in your library, but it can become unwieldy very quickly. A better way to do this is to create a constant that contains the library name, like this:

```
const
{$IFDEF LINUX}
  libname = 'libhello.so.1';
{$ELSE}
  libname = 'hello';
{$ENDIF}

procedure SayHello;
  {$IFDEF MSWINDOWS} stdcall; {$ENDIF} {$IFDEF LINUX} cdecl; {$ENDIF}
  external libname;
```

The individual function declarations are longer, but at least you only have to maintain one set of them.

Library Handle Type

The **dlopen** function returns a Pointer value to identify the library after it has been opened. The corresponding Windows function, **LoadLibrary**, returns an **HModule**, which is just an integer. Again, you have two choices. You can rewrite the **GetLibraryHandle** and **GetLibrarySymbol** functions (and any other pieces that use the value returned from **dlopen** or **LoadLibrary**) for each system, or you can conditionally define a **TLibHandle** type definition, like this:

```
type
// define library handle type
{$IFDEF LINUX}
  TLibHandle = Pointer;
{$ELSE}
  TLibHandle = HModule;
{$ENDIF}
const
// define null value for library handle
{$IFDEF LINUX}
  LibHandleNull = nil;
{$ELSE}
  LibHandleNull = 0;
{$ENDIF}
```

ShareMem

Under Windows, Kylix requires you to include a unit called **ShareMem** as the first unit in your program's and your library's **uses** clause if the program will be sharing dynamically allocated memory with the library. The Linux version of Kylix does not have this requirement. You will have to conditionally include the **ShareMem** unit in your cross-platform projects.

Library Startup Code

Library startup code is the one place where you may run into trouble writing cross-platform library code. Windows DLLs can contain a function called **DLLProc** that is notified when a process or thread attaches to or detaches from the DLL. There is no corresponding mechanism in the Linux world. In a Linux library, all initialization and shutdown processing must take place in the initialization and finalization sections of the library's units or in the library's main **begin...end** block (in the .dpr file).

The initialization and finalization sections work for Windows DLLs, too, so your best bet is to avoid the **DLLProc** function in your Windows DLLs if you can. If you must use a **DLLProc** function in your Windows DLL, then you'll need to use an **$IFDEF** directive to prevent it from being included in the Linux version of your library.

The Cross-Platform Interface Unit

Making the changes described previously and adding the Windows-specific code to load the DLL results in the cross-platform dynamic interface unit shown in Listing 3.5. This unit compiles with both Kylix and Delphi.

Listing 3.5   The cross-platform library interface unit.

```
{ HelloDynmX - Cross-platform dynamic library interface unit }
unit HelloDynmX;

interface

procedure SayHello;

implementation

uses SysUtils,
{$IFDEF LINUX}
  Libc
{$ELSE}
  Windows
{$ENDIF}
  ;
```

```
const
  {$IFDEF LINUX}
    STR_LIB_NAME = 'libhello.so.1';
    LibHandleNull = nil;
  {$ELSE}
    STR_LIB_NAME = 'sample';
    LibHandleNull = 0;
  {$ENDIF}

  // function names in library
  STR_HELLO_NAME = 'SayHello';

type
  {$IFDEF LINUX}
    TLibHandle = Pointer;
  {$ELSE}
    TLibHandle = HModule;
  {$ENDIF}

  HelloProc = procedure;
    {$IFDEF LINUX} cdecl; {$ELSE} stdcall; {$ENDIF}

const
  LibHandle : TLibHandle = LibHandleNull;

function GetLibraryHandle : TLibHandle;
begin
  if libHandle = libHandleNull then
  begin
    {$IFDEF LINUX}
      libHandle := dlopen (STR_LIB_NAME, RTLD_LAZY);
    {$ELSE}
      libHandle := LoadLibrary (STR_LIB_NAME);
    {$ENDIF}

    if libHandle = libHandleNull then
      raise Exception.CreateFmt
        ('Unable to open library "%s"', [STR_LIB_NAME]);
  end;
  Result := libHandle;
end;

function GetLibrarySymbol (const fName: String): Pointer;
var
  bErr : boolean;
```

```
begin
  {$IFDEF LINUX}
    dlerror; // call to clear error code
    Result := dlsym (GetLibraryHandle, PChar(fName));
    bErr := (dlerror <> nil);
  {$ELSE}
    Result := GetProcAddress (GetLibraryHandle, PChar(fName));
    bErr := (Result = nil);
  {$ENDIF}
  if bErr then
    raise Exception.CreateFmt
      ('Unable to locate symbol "%s" in library "%s".',
        [STR_LIB_NAME, fName]);
end;

procedure SayHello;
const
  HelloPtr : HelloProc = nil;
begin
  if not Assigned (HelloPtr) then
    HelloPtr := GetLibrarySymbol (STR_HELLO_NAME);
  HelloPtr;
  dlClose (LibHandle);
  LibHandle := LibHandleNull;
end;

initialization
  // no initialization--needed for finalization

finalization
  if libHandle <> LibHandleNull then
  begin
    {$IFDEF LINUX}
      if dlclose (libHandle) = -1 then
    {$ELSE}
      if not FreeLibrary (libHandle) then
    {$ENDIF}
        raise Exception.CreateFmt
          ('Error closing library "%s".', [STR_LIB_NAME]);
  end;
end.
```

Conversion of the library itself (Sample.dpr) is much easier, requiring only that you include the **ShareMem** unit for the Windows DLL version and that you add code to change the function-calling convention for each platform, like this:

```
procedure SayHello;
 {$IFDEF LINUX} cdecl; {$ELSE} stdcall; {$ENDIF}
```

Similar changes would be required to the SampleIntf.pas module if you wanted to make it cross platform.

Where to Go for More Information

The Program Library HOWTO, available at **www.linuxdoc.org/HOWTO/Program-Library-HOWTO/index.html**, gives a very detailed explanation of how libraries are used in Linux, and it documents the **dlopen**, **dlclose**, and **dlsym** functions. As with many Linux HOWTO documents, the code examples are very "C centric," but the rest of the document is very thorough and applies to libraries written in any language. If you're interested in how all this stuff works under the hood, see the "Other Information Sources" page of this document for links to documentation of the Executable and Linkable Format (ELF).

Chapter 4

Essential C for Kylix Programmers

As we mentioned in Chapter 2, Pascal has never been a primary development language under Linux. The huge majority of third-party libraries are written in C or C++ and have interfaces and sample code built for those languages. Very few Pascal libraries exist for Linux, and those that do exist are so compiler specific they probably will not be usable by Kylix. This means that you, as a Kylix programmer, have a choice to make. If you don't want to wait for someone else to write the units you need, you can either rewrite the functionality of the libraries themselves or create modules that wrap around these libraries and provide yourself with an API. If you chose the former, then just walk away slowly, and we'll see you in several years when you've completed the project. If you chose the latter, however, you'll be glad to know that Kylix makes it reasonably straightforward to create interface units that enable your applications to access C libraries.

Note that we said "reasonably straightforward," not necessarily "easy." In some cases, it won't even be possible, especially where the libraries in question have been written in C++ specifically for that language's use. We firmly believe, however, that the number of Kylix-compatible libraries will grow with time, and our fond hope is that this chapter will soon become unnecessary.

In the meantime, you may all too frequently find yourself needing to read source code examples written in C—a heady challenge for a dedicated Pascal programmer. The C language can be substantially more terse than Pascal, and because of this it can seem cryptic at times. A high-level understanding of some of the constructs of the C programming language will help you understand C API documentation and code examples.

In this chapter, we present the core of information you'll need to understand C interfaces and programming examples, and we even demonstrate how you can create Pascal interface units for C libraries. Don't worry—we're not trying to make a C programmer out of you. In fact, if you already have a working knowledge of C programming, you can probably jump down to the section titled, "Using C Libraries from Kylix."

Pascal Programmer's C Tutorial

We'll approach C programming from the ground up, making notes of programming constructs and language features that are unique to C, as well as features that are similar, but with important differences. We'll start with the data types.

C and Pascal Data Types

Primitive data types in C can be divided into three categories—integer types, real types, and "other" types—as shown in Table 4.1. The C **long long** data type is not supported on all compilers, and it occasionally goes by other names (**__int64** in Microsoft and Borland C++ compilers, for example). Although its usage is quite rare, it is included here for the sake of completeness.

As with all C data types, pointers can be created to any of these integer types. These pointers will be discussed a little further on. In the past, there was a real problem with real (or *floating-point*) data types because their implementation could vary from compiler to compiler. This meant the **float** and **double** data types were not portable, especially between languages. Now, however, most compilers follow the IEEE standard for single- and double-precision representations, thus greatly enhancing the portability of these types. Even so, if your applications make use of these types when accessing C libraries, make certain to test the results thoroughly (see Table 4.2).

Enumerated types, or **enums**, are used in C to create an integer-type variable that can take on one of a specific set of symbolic values (see Table 4.3).

The Story of *int*

Those with a C background might notice the absence of the 16-bit version of **int** in Table 4.1. Historically, the size of the **int** data type has depended on the C compiler in use and was originally intended to be the same size as the word size of the machine for which the application was being compiled. These days, it is almost always a 32-bit value, but even that fact is not guaranteed. As newer compilers and machine architectures are introduced, this will almost certainly become a 64-bit type. This ambiguity makes the use of the **int** data type unpopular for API usage, so you're not likely to see it often. If you do, you'll need to determine from other sources what size is intended.

You'll likely find **int** most troublesome when you're making use of older libraries, possibly porting software from 16-bit Windows code. In that case, you'll need to pay attention to the requirements of that software's API and make sure you're using an appropriately sized integer type in your code.

Table 4.1   Comparable integer data types.

C Type	Pascal Type	Description	Range
char	ShortInt	8-bit signed integer	-128 .. 127
short	SmallInt	16-bit signed integer	-32,768 .. 32,767
int	Integer or LongInt	32-bit signed integer	-2,147,483,648 .. 483,647
long	LongInt	32-bit signed integer	-2,147,483,648 ..2,147, 483,647
long long	Int64	64-bit signed integer	-9,223,372,036,854,775,808 .. 9,223,372,036,854,775,807
unsigned char	Byte	8-bit unsigned integer	0 .. 255
unsigned short	Word	16-bit unsigned integer	0 .. 65,535
unsigned int	Cardinal or LongWord	32-bit unsigned integer	0 .. 4,294,967,295
unsigned long	LongWord	32-bit unsigned integer	0 .. 4,294,967,295
unsigned long long	None	64-bit unsigned integer	0 .. 18,446,744,073,709, 551,615

Table 4.2   Comparable real data types.

C Type	Pascal Type	Description	Range
float	Single	Single-precision floating point	Approximately 3.4E-38 .. 3.4E+38
double	Double	Double-precision floating point	Approximately 1.7E-308 .. 1.7E+308
long double	Extended	"Triple-precision" floating point	Varies

Table 4.3   Comparable "other" data types.

C Type	Pascal Type	Description
enum	Enumerated type	An enumerated list of specific integer values, expressed as a type
(Any integer type)	Boolean	Boolean value (true or false)
char *	Pchar or ^Char	Pointer to a quantity of type **Char**
void *	Pointer	Untyped pointer

These values are listed, or *enumerated*, in the declaration of the **enum** itself, as shown in the following code:

```
enum TestStatus { pending = -1, passed, failed };
```

This example creates a new type called **TestStatus**. Variables of this type can be assigned any of the three values contained in the enumeration list, as shown here:

```
enum TestStatus ts = pending;
```

This creates a **TestStatus** variable and sets its value to the symbolic constant "pending." This is very similar to, but not interchangeable with, Pascal's enumerated type; a close Pascal equivalent to the declaration above would be the following:

```
type
 TestStatus = (pending, passed, failed);
```

The C version differs slightly, in that the integral value of an **enum** can be specified in the list or, if left unspecified, starts at zero and increments through each element in the enumeration list. From a Pascal perspective, the preceding C declaration creates an **int**-sized variable and sets it to the value -1.

In C, there is no explicit Boolean type. Instead, a Boolean value is represented by any integer type or any expression that evaluates to an integer type. Boolean false equates to a zero value, whereas any nonzero value corresponds to a Boolean true. Should you need to pass a Boolean value to a C API, simply pass it as an appropriately sized integer type with the value set either to 0 (for false) or 1 (for true).

Strings as they exist in Pascal are not duplicated in C. Instead, C uses arrays of characters, terminated by a single null character (a character with the value of zero). This format is called a *null-terminated* or *zero-terminated string*, also sometimes referred to as an *ASCIIZ string*. C "strings" are passed around as character pointers ("**char *str**" in C), which is duplicated in Pascal with the **PChar** type.

Tip

*As a convenience, Kylix automatically stores a zero byte at the end of long and wide strings. This makes it easy to reference long and wide strings as null-terminated strings simply by casting those strings to a **PChar** type.*

Unlike Pascal, C has no string manipulation operators. Instead, strings in C are managed by a small horde of string-manipulation functions, such as **strcat**, **strlen**, and **strdup**. Should you wish to make use of these functions yourself, they are also available in Kylix when you use the **SysUtils** unit.

Variables, Structures, Unions, and Types

C has two ways to store structured data: via **struct** and via **union**. A C **struct** is very similar to Pascal's **record**, and they can be used almost interchangeably. The following examples show a C **struct** and its equivalent Pascal **record** type:

```
struct Item
    {
    long    item_number;
    long    price;
```

```
        short   in_stock;
        };

    type Item = record
        ItemNumber: LongInt;
        Price: LongInt;
        InStock: ShortInt;
    end;
```

It must be noted that these aren't exactly equivalent. The Pascal example produces a new type called Item, whereas the C example does not. In order for the C example to do this, the **typedef** keyword must also be incorporated, which would be applied as follows:

```
typedef struct
    {
    long    item_number;
    long    price;
    short   in_stock;
    } Item;
```

The **typedef** keyword is used in C to create a new type (in this case, a type called Item), which can be used just like any other "official" type in the language. Without the use of the **typedef** keyword, variables would have to be defined with the accompanying **struct** keyword, like the following:

```
struct Item item_info;
```

The **struct** keyword could be omitted, if the **typedef** keyword is used to create a new type.

A **union** in C is similar to a variant record in Pascal. Both are a group of variables, each occupying the same memory space within the record. Here is an example of a C **union** and its corresponding variant record in Pascal:

```
typedef union
    {
    long            register_val;
    unsigned short word_0, word_1;
    unsigned char  byte_0, byte_1, byte_2, byte_3;
    } Register_32;

type Register_32 = record
    case Byte of
        val32:  (RegisterVal: LongInt);
        val16:  (Word0, Word1: ShortInt);
        val8:   (Byte0, Byte1, Byte2, Byte3: Byte);
end;
```

In each example, the byte-sized fields occupy the same memory space as the 4-byte field. In fact, this is a fairly common usage in C, especially where there is a need for low-level access to the individual bytes of a variable.

If you're called upon to create a record that mimics a specific C **struct** or **union**, pay close attention to the sizes of the individual fields that make up the record and use the appropriate Pascal types that duplicate the C types. They must match, and they must be specified in the same order; otherwise, mysterious data errors will result.

C Operators

C has more operators than you can shake *two* sticks at, and some Pascal programmers might sorely be tempted to use those sticks to beat on the C language designers' heads. You'll see these operators in code examples, and although most of them have direct equivalents in Pascal, some are purely unique to C (but for most of these exceptions there are workarounds).

Table 4.4 outlines operators with similar functions in C and Pascal. The basic mathematic operators are overloaded in Pascal, so they can also serve as set and string operators. This is

Table 4.4   Equivalent operators in C and Pascal.

C Operator(s)	C Description	Pascal Operator(s)
+	Numeric and pointer addition	+
-	Numeric and pointer subtraction	-
*	Numeric multiplication	*
/	Integer and real division (dependent on operands' types)	**Div and /**
%	Modulus division	**Mod**
-	Numeric negation (unary operator; applied to integer types)	-
=	Assignment	:=
==	Equality test	=
&&	Logical **AND** (used in conditional expressions)	**And**
||	Logical **OR** (used in conditional expressions)	**Or**
!	Logical **NOT** (used in conditional and logical expressions)	**Not**
<< and >>	Bitwise left and right shifts	**Shl and Shr**
&	Bitwise **AND**	**And**
|	Bitwise **OR**	**Or**
^	Bitwise **XOR**	**Xor**
&	Address of (unary operator; applied to variable or function)	@
*	Pointer dereference (unary; applied to a pointer type)	^
->	Structure selection; applied to a pointer to a structure	. or ^.
.	Structure selection; applied to a structure instance	.
sizeof()	Returns the size of a variable or type	**SizeOf()**
(<type>)	Type cast (for example, **"(int)x"**)	**<type>() (e.g. Integer(x)**

not the case in C, which has no "set" types and uses functions for string manipulation. The numeric comparison operators ("<", ">", ">=", and "<=", for example) are all identical to the corresponding Pascal operators, however.

As you can see, many of the operators are similar, but they have different representations. Several of the operators are applied in different ways—for example, the unary pointer dereference operator in C is applied on the left of the operand, whereas in Pascal it is applied on the right—and some operators have different semantics, but many of the same operations are supported. Several operators in C are unique to that language, however. These are the conditional operator, the autoincrement and autodecrement operators, the arithmetic assignment operators, the 1's complement operator, and the comma operator.

The Conditional Operator

The *conditional operator* is a ternary operator (an operator taking three operands) that takes the form "?:". In use, it looks like the expression within the parentheses in the following code:

```
x = (y == 0 ? "false" : "true");
```

The first operand in the conditional operator is any expression that evaluates to a Boolean value (remember that *Boolean* in C is simply an integer value evaluated with an eye toward whether it is a zero or nonzero value). In this case, "**y == 0**" is the expression. The second operand is the value the entire operation will return if the first operand evaluates to true, and the last operand is what the operation will return if the first operand is false. In Pascal, this example would be rewritten like so:

```
if y = 0 then
    x := 'false'
else
    x := 'true';
```

Use of the conditional operator isn't common because it can make program source more difficult to read.

Autoincrement and Autodecrement Operators

As their names suggest, the autoincrement (**++**) and autodecrement (**--**) operators increment and decrement integer and pointer variables. They are similar to the Pascal **Inc** and **Dec** procedures, but with two subtle differences. First, unlike a Pascal procedure, these operators (like all other C operators) are actually *functions* that result in a value being returned for the operation. Second, the operator can be placed in front of or behind the operand. Although the operand is incremented or decremented regardless, this placement affects the value taken by the operation. Because the semantics of the two operators are identical, the following code will serve as an example for both:

```
short foo = 10;
short bar = ++foo;
short baz = foo++;
```

At the end of this example, the variable *foo* will contain the value 12, as you would expect. You would probably guess that the variable *bar* will contain the value 11, because ++*foo* is evaluated as the value of the operand *after* the increment takes place—the operator is placed in front of the operand. It may come as a bit of a surprise, however, to learn that the value of *baz* is also 11. Because the operator is placed *behind* the operand, the operation will evaluate to the content of the operand *before* the increment takes place.

You'll frequently see the autoincrement and autodecrement operators used in situations where their evaluation is ignored. In this case, the placement of the operator in front of or behind the operand makes absolutely no difference, and the effect of the operator is identical to the Pascal **Inc** and **Dec** procedures. For example, the C statement

```
x++;
```

is identical to the Pascal statement

```
Inc(x);
```

Arithmetic Assignment Operators

Non-C programmers sometimes regard the arithmetic assignment operators as unnecessary shorthand, but their use is extremely common, so they are dealt with here. These operators combine any of the arithmetic and bit-manipulation operators with the assignment operator, as illustrated in the following example:

```
xyzzy += 7;
plugh |= 1;
```

These two lines can be rewritten in Pascal as follows:

```
xyzzy := xyzzy + 7;
plugh := plugh Or 1;
```

As you can see, the observation that these operators are a kind of shorthand is directly on target, but as virtually any C programmer will tell you, shorthand is brevity, and brevity is frequently regarded in C as a good thing.

The 1's Complement Operator

The *1's complement operator* (**~**) is used to convert any integer type to its 1's complement value. This conversion involves inverting all the bits used to represent the operand. For example, the integer value 17 (binary 00010001) would be converted to the value -18 (binary 11101110). This operator is most often used to create logical masks for bit manipulation, where a single bit in a variable needs to be set to zero.

The 1's complement operator in Pascal is an alternate form of the **not** keyword. If **not** is applied to a Boolean value it simply negates the value. If, however, it is applied to an integer type it performs a 1's complement operation. To demonstrate, here are two equivalent examples. First, in C:

```
const unsigned char BIT_FOUR_MASK = 0x10;
...
unsigned char val;
...
val &= ~BIT_FOUR_MASK;      /* turn off bit FOUR */
```

Here it is in Pascal:

```
const
    BitFourMask: Byte = $10;
var
    Value: Byte;
...
Value := Value And ( Not( BitFourMask ) );
```

The Comma Operator

That brevity we mentioned earlier can sometimes come back in strange forms. In C, there are occasions where programmers want multiple statements to execute serially but to syntactically be a single expression (this is frequently seen in **for** loops, which will be discussed shortly). The comma operator is simply a comma placed between statements for exactly this purpose. The result is a multistatement expression that takes on the value of the statement following the final comma. Pascal has no similar functionality. This doesn't present a problem, because Pascal really has no need of it. It can, however, be confusing for Pascal programmers used to seeing C statements separated by semicolons to suddenly see what appear to be statements separated by commas. We'll show an example of the comma operator in the section on the C **for** loop, later.

Control Statements and Looping

Like Pascal, C has several looping constructs. Two are similar to Pascal looping mechanisms (**while** and **do/while** loops). A third (the **for** loop) shares the same name as a Pascal looping mechanism but operates somewhat differently.

while and *do/while* Loops

C's **while** loops are almost identical to Pascal's **while** loops, with one notable exception: Where Pascal's loop condition must evaluate to a Boolean value, C's loop condition can be an expression that evaluates to any integer type. The loop will continue until the expression evaluates to zero, or until the loop is forced to exit prematurely. This means that all the following are legal loop conditions in C:

```
while ( i++ )
while ( j = j - 2 )
while ( some_function_that_returns_an_integer() )
```

Other forms are possible, and common. This arrangement affords a great deal of flexibility in loop conditionals, occasionally at the cost of added complexity or lowered readability.

C's **do/while** loops take the following form:

```
do
    statement;
while ( expression );
```

C's **do/while** loops are very similar to Pascal's **repeat/until** loops, with the notable difference that C repeats *while* the expression is true, and Pascal repeats *until* the expression is true.

for Loops

The **for** loop can be considered another kind of shorthand statement in C. A **for** loop (or, more correctly, a **for** *statement*) is extremely flexible and expressive, but can become quite complex. It is similar in concept to Pascal's **for** loop in that a loop counter is initialized and updated through the lifetime of the loop, taking on a new value for each loop iteration. The basic form of a C **for** statement is as follows:

```
for ( expression1; expression2; expression3 )
    statement;
```

The statement forms the body of the loop and will be executed zero or more times, depending on the three expressions inside of the parentheses. The first expression is the *initialization expression*. It is evaluated once as the **for** statement begins and is usually used to initialize one or more loop counter variables. The second expression is similar to the conditional expression in a **while** loop. Like a **while** loop, this expression is evaluated each time the loop begins. The loop will terminate when this expression evaluates to zero (or if the loop is explicitly terminated). The final expression is the *modifier expression*. It is evaluated at the end of each iteration of the loop and is most often used to increment the loop index variable.

Here's a simple example of a **for** loop:

```
for ( idx = 0; idx < 10; idx++ )
    printf( "%d ", idx );
```

This example simply prints the numbers 0 through 9. The initialization expression initial-izes the variable **idx** to 0. The conditional expression keeps the loop iterating while the value of **idx** is less than 10. The modifier expression increments the value of **idx** each time a loop iteration is finished. The Pascal equivalent of this loop is as follows:

```
For idx := 0 to 9 do
    Write( idx, ' ' );
```

Several twists are legal with the **for** statement, however. Each of the expressions within the parentheses is optional. In other words, each can be replaced with the "empty statement," which consists of nothing more than a semicolon. The following statement is perfectly legal (but not very useful because it will simply loop forever, doing nothing):

```
for ( ; ; );
```

In C, it is perfectly legal for the program to modify the value of the loop index inside the body of the **for** loop. In Pascal, this results in a compile-time error.

Finally, each expression can also be a comma-separated list of statements (as outlined with the comma operator, earlier). Here's an example:

```
for ( i = 0, j = 0;
    str[i] != 0;
    j += ( str[j] == ' ' ? 1 : 0 ), str[i++] = str[j++] );
```

Although it won't win any prizes in the readability department, this statement is a perfectly legal C **for** statement. (In case you're curious, it removes all single spaces from a text string contained in the array of **char** called **str**.) Unfortunately, some C programmers—some, not all—seem to regard statements such as this as acceptable code, which can make your job of reading sample code very difficult. (I once heard a C critic remark, "There's got to be some-thing wrong with a language that makes it easy to point to a statement and say, 'I'll bet you can't guess what *that* line of code does.'")

Loop Termination: *break* and *continue*
Like Pascal, C provides two structured mechanisms for forcing the early termination of a loop. These two mechanisms are the **break** and **continue** statements, and they behave iden-tically to Pascal's **Break** and **Continue** procedures. The **break** statement causes execution

of the loop to be terminated immediately, with execution continuing at the first statement outside the current loop. The **continue** statement, however, causes the remainder of the current iteration of the loop to be skipped, with execution resuming at the evaluation of the loop's termination expression.

Pointers

Although Pascal supports *pointers*, Pascal programmers make nowhere near as much use of them as C programmers. In C, pointers are the lifeblood of the program, used everywhere, and understood by everyone. (Well, *most* everyone, anyway—even diehard C programmers occasionally get lost.)

A *pointer* is simply an address of a specific location in memory. Among other things, pointers enable programmers to pass parameters by reference (discussed shortly), to work with dynamically allocated memory, and to efficiently and effectively represent complex data structures. Pointers are closely interlinked with arrays as well.

Consider this example in C:

```
short idx = 20;
short *ptr;
```

Here, we've declared an integer variable, **idx**, as well as **ptr**, a pointer to an instance of the **short** type. So far, the pointer is uninitialized, meaning that it is pointing to a random location in memory. Attempting to dereference the pointer at this point would very likely result in a program crash. To cause **ptr** to point to the variable **idx**, the following statement would be used:

```
ptr = &idx;
```

Using this pointer by dereferencing it now will indirectly use the **idx** variable. For example,

```
*ptr = 30;
```

will cause the value stored in the **ptr** variable to be set to 30.

A common use of pointers is to step through arrays and other data structures. The following example steps through the contents of an array called **values**, printing its contents to the screen:

```
int values[6] = { 5, 10, 15, 20, 25, 0 };
int *ptr = values;
while ( *ptr != 0 )
    printf( "%d ", *ptr++ );
```

Two lines deserve special attention. The first is when **ptr** is declared. Notice that **values**, a reference to an **int** array, is assigned to **ptr**, an **int** pointer. All arrays in C can be referenced as pointers simply by omitting the indexing operation. In this case, **values** (by itself, without indexing) is equivalent to an **int** pointer, allowing the assignment to succeed. You'll see this most often with C's use of character arrays to represent strings. These arrays will be passed around frequently using the base name of the array as a "**char ***" type.

The second line of note is the last line of the example, specifically "***ptr++**". The effect of this expression is to obtain the *dereferenced* value of the pointer for printing and then to increment the pointer itself. Incrementing a pointer in this manner causes the pointer to advance by the same number of bytes as the size of the type of the pointer, as determined by the compiler. (Pascal's **Inc** and **Dec** procedures work in this same manner when incrementing pointers.) No memory is changed by this action, despite the appearance of the expression. Should you wish instead to increment the contents of the memory location referenced by the pointer, the following expression must be used:

```
(*ptr)++;
```

Note the use of parentheses to explicitly control the order of evaluation of the individual operators.

Another common use for pointers is in the representation of linked records, such as those found in linked lists. Most often, these records (or *nodes*) are dynamically allocated. First, the declaration of a node structure is created:

```
typedef struct Node
    {
    char *item_name;
    struct Node *next;
    } Node;
```

This will create a new type called **Node**. The two uses of the type name in the first and last lines are necessary to support the definition in the fourth line. C does not support forward references, so the **Node** type can't be referenced before it is created in the last line.

Next, we create the first node in the linked list, dynamically allocating the memory using the **malloc()** function:

```
Node *first = (Node *)malloc( sizeof( Node ) );
first->item_name = "hammer";
first->next = NULL;
```

Note the use of the cast to convert the untyped (**void**) pointer normally returned by **malloc()** to a **Node** pointer, as well as the use of the **sizeof()** operator to specify the number of bytes to allocate. Also note the use of the structure selection operator ("**->**", also called the *arrow operator*) to refer to fields in the newly allocated **Node**, as well as the use of the value **NULL** to initialize the pointer to the nonexistent next node in the list. **NULL** in C is equivalent to **nil** in Pascal.

Finally, we create the next element of the list and set the first element to point to it:

```
Node *ptr = (Node *)malloc( sizeof( Node ) );
ptr->item_name = "pliers";
ptr->next = NULL;
first->next = ptr;
```

Now, traversing the list is as simple as using the following **for** loop:

```
for ( ptr = first; ptr != null; ptr = ptr->next )
    {
    printf( "%s\n", ptr->item_name );
    }
```

In Pascal, this entire example would be coded in the following way:

```
type
    PNode = ^Node;
    Node = record
        ItemName: PChar;
        Next: PNode;
    end;

var
    First: PNode;
    Ptr: PNode;

New ( First );
First^.ItemName := 'hammer';
First^.Next := nil;

New ( Ptr );
Ptr^.ItemName := 'pliers';
Ptr^.Next := nil;
First^.Next := Ptr;

Ptr := First;
while ( Ptr <> nil ) do
begin
    WriteLn ( Ptr^.ItemName );
    Ptr := Ptr^.Next;
end;
```

Like Pascal, C also supports pointers to functions. Although the Pascal form of declaring a function is fairly simple, the C form can be notoriously difficult to decipher. Here's a simple Pascal example that creates a new type called **FunctionPtr**, a pointer to a function that returns an integer and takes a single integer as an argument:

```
Type
    FunctionPtr = Function ( j: Integer ): Integer;
```

Here's the identical C statement:

```
typedef int ( *FunctionPtr )( int j );
```

As long as the function signatures remain simple, this isn't too difficult to read. When the signatures become more complex, however, function pointers are some of the most difficult C code to read. Even experienced C programmers sometimes have to stop, take a deep breath, and proceed with caution when confronted with a complex function pointer declaration.

Functions and "Procedures"

Many of the conventions for declaring and calling functions and procedures are similar in C and in Pascal. Syntactically in C, there is no difference between a function and a procedure. A "procedure" in C is simply a function defined as returning **void**.

All C functions defined as returning anything except **void** must use the **return** statement to return a value to the caller. Here's an example:

```
return value;
```

In Pascal, the equivalent is to assign the return value to a special nondeclared variable called **Result**. The Pascal equivalent to the C **return** example is the following:

```
Result := Value;
Exit;
```

Like in Pascal, arguments to C functions can be passed by reference or by value. Unlike Pascal, however, there are no special language keywords (such as **var** in Pascal) to identify an argument that is passed by reference. Instead, C uses pointers when passing by reference, as in the following example:

```
void someFunction( int valueParam, int *varParam)
    {
    valueParam++;
    *varParam += 10;
    }
```

The function in this example accepts two parameters, changing the value of both of them before returning. The first argument, *valueParm*, is passed by value, so the change in the variable's value back in the calling function is unchanged. The second argument, *varParam*, is passed by reference. In the calling method, this variable will be modified before the *someFunction* method returns.

Miscellaneous Odds and Ends

This section is a catchall for several differences between C and Pascal that don't really belong anywhere else. These items include array indexing, dynamic memory allocation, and the C preprocessor.

Array Indexes

In Pascal, programmers are free to declare their arrays with indexes spanning any ordinal values. In C, however, array indexes always range from 0 to the size of the array (minus 1, because the array index starts at 0). For example, given the array definition

```
int values[10];
```

valid array index values for the *values* array are 0 through 9. It is important to remember that array indexes *always* begin at 0 in C.

Another major difference in array usage has to do with multidimensional arrays. In Pascal, multidimensional arrays are referenced as follows:

```
value := Arr[i, j];
```

If this syntax is used in C, it means the programmer is trying to do something crazy with the comma operator. In C, the equivalent statement would be the following:

```
value = Arr[i][j];
```

Dynamic Memory Allocation

In Pascal, dynamic allocation of things that are of a known size is quite similar to C. In C, the functions **malloc()** and **free()** are used to allocate and deallocate dynamic memory, just like the procedures **GetMem** and **FreeMem** in Kylix. Given the Pascal example

```
GetMem( Ptr, SizeOf( SomeRecord ) );
```

the equivalent C statement would be as follows:

```
ptr = malloc( sizeof( SomeRecord) );
```

Both allocate a chunk of memory that has been sized appropriately to contain a record of type **SomeRecord**.

Pascal also uses the **New** and **Dispose** procedures to allocate memory. C doesn't have this mechanism, but C++ uses a similar one in the form of the **new** and **delete** operators.

The C Preprocessor

This topic could easily open an entire new can of worms, but it needs to be discussed. The C preprocessor is a powerful and extremely useful part of the C language, but it is also single-handedly responsible for some of the most wanton and despicable acts of code obfuscation ever performed.

Okay, enough theatrics. At its heart, the C preprocessor is a textual substitution mechanism that is activated in the first pass of the C compiler. It is used for purposes such as constant replacement, string internationalization, and running code macros (although better ways of doing each of these tasks exist). The substitution mechanism takes a simple form, as this example shows:

```
#define DAYS_IN_YEAR 365
#define EMPLOYEE_NAME "Joe Smith"
#define WEEKS_IN_YEAR DAYS_IN_YEAR / 7
```

Each of these defines a preprocessor macro, consisting of a token, such as **DAYS_IN_YEAR**, and a substitution, such as the constant 365. Another way of thinking of this is creating a compile-time variable that contains the substitution text. After this directive is processed, all occurrences of the token in the source code will be replaced with the substitution text. For example, the preceding directives could be used as shown in the following code fragment:

```
printf( "%s is paid weekly, %d times per year.",
        EMPLOYEE_NAME, WEEKS_IN_YEAR );
```

The preprocessor will produce the following code, which will then be compiled normally:

```
printf( "%s is paid weekly, %d times per year.",
        "Joe Smith", 365 / 7 );
```

In this capacity, the preprocessor macro is similar to Pascal's **Const** declarations, but with one very significant difference: *type checking*. Preprocessor macros create untyped constants (they're just textual substitutions, remember?) and, as such, have the capacity to create errors in the code that can be very difficult to track down.

Another popular use for the preprocessor is for conditional compilation. In addition to its textual substitution mechanism, the preprocessor has limited logical constructs. The **#ifdef** directive and its associated **#else** and **#endif** directives allow code to be conditionally compiled, based on the content of any preprocessor macros. For example, consider the following code:

```
#ifdef DEBUG
    logMessage( "Entering initialization code" );
#endif
```

Here, the code intended to generate the debug message will only be compiled if a preprocessor macro called "**DEBUG**" has been defined using the **#define** directive. It's important to note that this logic is performed at compile time, not execution time; if the **DEBUG** macro has not been defined, the statement isn't even compiled into the program. Kylix supports identical functionality using the **{$IFDEF}** and **{$ENDIF}** directives.

You will see this simple example extended to provide conditional compilation of platform-specific code. Different macros will be defined based on the current platform in use, and blocks of conditionally compiled code will be compiled based on these macro definitions. It looks ugly (even C purists usually won't argue that fact), but it gets the job done efficiently and is much easier than maintaining separate source files for each platform supported.

A final common use for the preprocessor is in source file inclusion. This is so common, in fact, that it is performed in almost every C source file ever created. Blocks of C code, usually macro definitions, type declarations, and function definitions are saved in *header files*. The names of these files usually have the extension ".h." Header files correspond to the interface sections of Pascal source files and can be shared by multiple C source files with the use of the **#include** preprocessor directive. This directive is similar to the Pascal **uses** statement in that executing the directive informs the compiler of the types, methods, and constants contained in the included header file. A common directive in C is

```
#include <stdio.h>
```

which textually inserts the contents of the file **stdio.h** in place of the **#include** directive. The stdio.h file contains a horde of function and constant declarations that pertain to C's standard I/O library, and including this file gives the compiler all the information it needs to generate code that relies on that library.

Header files will often be your primary source of information when creating the interface units necessary to use third-party C libraries from within your Kylix code. Learning to read the declarations contained in a library's header files is an absolute necessity if you wish to use these libraries and avoid reinventing the wheel.

The Perils of C++

Although C++ uses much of the same syntax as C, it has a few more features that can throw some real challenges in your direction. Some of these features make it extremely difficult (and sometimes impossible) to use third-party libraries written specifically for C++ programs. We could easily write an entire book on feature differences between the two languages, but that is far, far beyond this book's scope. Instead, we'll focus on the three differences you will encounter most often as you peruse third-party libraries: overloaded functions, member functions, and exceptions.

Overloaded Functions

In C, all functions must have unique names. In C++, however, it is perfectly legal for two functions to have identical names, as long as they have different parameter lists. For example, the two functions

```
int set_value( int value );
int set_value( char *value );
```

will cause a compiler error in C but are valid functions in C++. To accommodate this new functionality and still be able to use existing tools, the designers of the C++ language incorporated the signature of the function (the number and types of its parameters) into the function name stored in the compiled object code. In this way, existing linkers, debuggers, and other software tools could still be used with overloaded functions. This process of incorporating the function signature into the compiled object code is appropriately called *name mangling*. For example, the function

```
int TestFunction( int x, char *y, float z );
```

is mangled to

```
TestFunction__FiPcf
```

by the C++ compiler.

Although this is a reasonably elegant solution to the problem of how to represent overloaded functions in compiled object files, it certainly causes a problem for anyone attempting to translate it for use with Kylix. The mangled function name isn't obvious from the code, and without it there's no way for you to tell Kylix which function in a C++ shared library you want to use.

There is a solution, but it isn't pretty. Once you've determined the shared library you wish to use, you can examine the list of functions it exports using the *nm* utility. This utility lists the functions exported from an object file or a shared library. In the case of a C++ library, these names will be mangled. The program **c++filt** can unmangle the names, however, allowing you to see them and perform a cross-reference that will enable you to specify the appropriate function name in your interface library. Here's how to do it.

First, run the **nm** application from the command line, passing the name of the shared library on the command line and piping the output of the command through the **c++filt** utility. The output on your screen will look something like the following:

```
holly% nm test.so.1 | c++filt
00000000 T TestFunction(int, char *, float)
00000000 t gcc2_compiled.
```

The first column (the sequence of digits) contains the address of the function within the shared library, whereas the third column contains the names of the functions exported by this library. Notice the readable function definition output by the **c++filt** utility. You can use these "unmangled" function names to locate the function you want to call from your code. Now run the same command again, this time omitting the **c++filt** utility. This time the screen output will look like this:

```
holly% nm test.so.1
00000000 T TestFunction__FiPcf
00000000 t gcc2_compiled.
```

Find the function with the same address, and you've found the mangled name that you'll need to specify in the external definition in your interface library.

We told you it wasn't pretty. In fact, it's not infallible, either. It falls apart miserably when member functions are used (you'll see why in moment). But it is at least a start. This method, although painful, will work for C++ functions that are not member functions or function templates and that do not throw exceptions.

Member Functions

In C++, member functions (functions associated with a class) must pass the address of the object on which they're being invoked as the first parameter to the function. Normally the C++ compiler does this automatically and transparently. You're not using a C++ compiler, however, and you don't know (and can't even get) the address of the C++ object, anyway. Until Borland releases a combination package of Kylix and Borland C++, similar to its Windows offering, C++ member functions will be unavailable to Kylix programmers.

Exceptions

Exceptions in C++ are similar to exceptions in Kylix: They provide a method for notifying the caller of the current function of errors that occurred during processing. The mechanisms used by C++ and by Kylix, however, will almost certainly be incompatible. Again, until Borland releases a combination C++/Kylix package, any C++ function that is declared to throw an exception will be unavailable to Kylix programmers.

Using C Libraries from Kylix

We started on this adventure with the promise that you can use existing C libraries in your Kylix programs by developing a Pascal interface for them. To do that, you needed the ability to read source code written in C. It's now time to roll up your sleeves and see how this process can be accomplished. We're going to incorporate a third-party library into a Kylix project.

The library used is a small encryption library that implements the Blowfish encryption algorithm, originally designed by Bruce Schneier. This is a publicly usable encryption library, unencumbered by patent and free for all forms of use. Its API is small enough that we'll have no problem covering it completely in this book yet "real world" enough that it will serve as a good introduction to interfacing Kylix with third-party libraries. A link to the package is provided at the end of this chapter.

It should be noted before going any further that there are already implementations of Blowfish available for Delphi, and they may well be portable to Kylix. Performing that port would likely be a better use of your time than writing this particular interface. However, writing the interface will serve as an example of putting the principles learned in this chapter to use.

Quite a few third-party libraries are distributed as static libraries, which Kylix is unable to access. For those libraries, the first thing required is to recompile the library's source as a shared library, as referenced in Chapter 3. To do this, you'll need to visit the command line for a short time, where you'll learn some of the basics about makefiles. If the third-party library you want to use is distributed as a shared library already, feel free to skip this step (you may very well be glad you did).

Making Programs with **Make**

Makefiles are used as parameter scripts to the make program, which automates a build process, compiling only source files that have changed since the last build. Numerous books and articles have been written about using the make program, so we won't go into extensive detail here. You can consult those books, but a good source of information on makefiles can be found in the man pages installed on your system. (If you're an old hand with MS-DOS and command-line versions of Turbo and Borland Pascal, you may already be familiar with a variant of makefiles and the make utility.)

In its simplest form, a makefile might look like this:

```
hello: hello.c
        gcc -c -o hello hello.c
```

This minimal makefile establishes several rules that will be used by the make program to build an executable program called "hello". The first line establishes a dependency, namely that the file hello (called the *target*) is dependent on the file hello.c (the *dependency*). When

make is run, it will check to see if hello.c has been changed more recently then the file hello. If it hasn't changed, make will exit without doing anything. If it has changed, however, the command on the next line will be executed to bring the target up to date with the dependencies. There can be multiple dependencies for a single rule, and the list of commands can be as long as required. Commands that are too long can be split across multiple lines, if needed, by leaving a backslash character (\) as the final character of the split lines.

One other aspect of makefiles that you'll need to understand involves makefile variables. Variables are used in most makefiles to simplify maintenance and to make complex rules easier to understand. For our purposes, they can make it substantially easier to update a makefile that will produce a shared library.

Variables are defined using a standard-looking assignment, such as the following:

```
CFLAGS=-c
```

This variable can now be used anywhere in the makefile by using the notation **$(CFLAGS)**, which will be replaced with the content of the variable when make is run. You can extend this minimal makefile using variables, as follows.

```
CFLAGS=-c
APPNAME=hello
SRCFILES=hello.c
$(APPNAME): $(SRCFILES)
        gcc $(CFLAGS) -o $(APPNAME) $(SRCFILES)
```

When make is run against this makefile, the effect is exactly the same as the previous two-line minimal makefile. (Although nothing was gained in this example, the principles will come into play when the makefile is modified to produce the shared library.)

To keep things manageable for this example, we've "skeletonized" the makefile that comes with the Blowfish library source. Listing 4.1 contains the makefile that will be modified to produce the shared library.

Listing 4.1   The skeletonized makefile.
```
CC=gcc
CFLAGS=-g
AR=ar r
RANLIB=ranlib

LIB=libcrypto.a
LIBOBJ=bf_skey.o bf_ecb.o bf_enc.o bf_cfb64.o bf_ofb64.o

lib:    $(LIBOBJ)
        $(AR) $(LIB) $(LIBOBJ)
        $(RANLIB) $(LIB)
```

Modifying this makefile to produce a shared library is actually fairly easy. If you've not visited the URL mentioned at the end of Chapter 3, you might want to do so now and look at the sections of the document titled "Creating a shared library" and "Installing and using a shared library." This will make things a little easier to understand.

To produce a shared library, the C compiler must be run with the **–fPIC** flag (in addition to any flags already in use) to create position-independent code. Adding this flag to the **CFLAGS** variable definition line will take care of this, making the **–fPIC** flag be used anywhere the compiler is run:

```
CFLAGS=-g -fPIC
```

One other task must be done to create a shared library—gathering the compiled object files into a ".so" file. This makefile uses the ar and ranlib applications to create a static library, but those commands will be replaced with the command required to create the *shared* library:

```
lib:    $(LIBOBJ)
        $(CC) -shared -Wl,-soname,libblowfish.so.1 \
            -o libblowfish.so.1.0.1 $(LIBOBJ) -lc
```

Again, looking at the URL from the end of Chapter 3 will help to make these commands slightly clearer. That document also covers the installation of the newly created shared library, which won't be covered here. The final form of the makefile is shown in Listing 4.2.

Listing 4.2   The makefile used to produce the Blowfish shared library.
```
CC=gcc
CFLAGS=-g -fPIC
AR=ar r
RANLIB=ranlib

LIB=libcrypto.a
LIBOBJ=bf_skey.o bf_ecb.o bf_enc.o bf_cfb64.o bf_ofb64.o

lib:    $(LIBOBJ)
        $(CC) -shared -Wl,-soname,libblowfish.so.1 \
            -o libblowfish.so.1.0.1 $(LIBOBJ) -lc
```

Whew. Enough of the command-line stuff already! In the next section, you'll return to Kylix and create the interface unit required to actually use the new shared library.

Writing the Interface Unit

Now that you have a shared library, you can write the interface unit for it. To do that, we'll use two files as source material. The first file will be the header file for the library—in this case, **blowfish.h**. Remember, this file contains the declarations of the types, constants, and functions that make up the API for the library. The second source of information will be the documentation of the libraries API contained in the file *blowfish.doc*. Examining the header file for the library, you'll find the C source shown in Listing 4.3.

Listing 4.3   Blowfish.h, the C header file for the Blowfish library.

```
/* Copyright (C) 1995-1998 Eric Young (eay@cryptsoft.com)
 * All rights reserved.
 *
 * Redistribution and use in source and binary forms, with or without
 * modification, are permitted provided that the following conditions
 * are met:
 * 1. Redistributions of source code must retain the copyright
 *    notice, this list of conditions and the following disclaimer.
 * 2. Redistributions in binary form must reproduce the above copyright
 *    notice, this list of conditions and the following disclaimer in the
 *    documentation and/or other materials provided with the distribution.
 * 3. All advertising materials mentioning features or use of this software
 *    must display the following acknowledgment:
 *    "This product includes cryptographic software written by
 *     Eric Young (eay@cryptsoft.com)"
 *    The word 'cryptographic' can be left out if the routines from the
 *    library being used are not cryptographic related :-).
 * 4. If you include any Windows specific code (or a derivative thereof)
 *    from the apps directory (application code) you must include an
 *    acknowledgment:
 *        "This product includes software written by Tim Hudson
 *        (tjh@cryptsoft.com)" *
 * THIS SOFTWARE IS PROVIDED BY ERIC YOUNG "AS IS" AND
 * ANY EXPRESS OR IMPLIED WARRANTIES, INCLUDING, BUT NOT LIMITED TO, THE
 * IMPLIED WARRANTIES OF MERCHANTABILITY AND FITNESS FOR A PARTICULAR PURPOSE
 * ARE DISCLAIMED. IN NO EVENT SHALL THE AUTHOR OR CONTRIBUTORS BE LIABLE
 * FOR ANY DIRECT, INDIRECT, INCIDENTAL, SPECIAL, EXEMPLARY, OR CONSEQUENTIAL
 * DAMAGES (INCLUDING, BUT NOT LIMITED TO, PROCUREMENT OF SUBSTITUTE GOODS
 * OR SERVICES; LOSS OF USE, DATA, OR PROFITS; OR BUSINESS INTERRUPTION)
 * HOWEVER CAUSED AND ON ANY THEORY OF LIABILITY, WHETHER IN CONTRACT, STRICT
 * LIABILITY, OR TORT (INCLUDING NEGLIGENCE OR OTHERWISE) ARISING IN ANY WAY
 * OUT OF THE USE OF THIS SOFTWARE, EVEN IF ADVISED OF THE POSSIBILITY OF
 * SUCH DAMAGE.
 */

#ifndef HEADER_BLOWFISH_H
#define HEADER_BLOWFISH_H

#ifdef  __cplusplus
extern "C" {
#endif
```

```
#define BF_ENCRYPT   1
#define BF_DECRYPT   0

/* If you make this 'unsigned int' the pointer variants will work on
 * the Alpha, otherwise they will not. Strangely using the '8 byte'
 * BF_LONG and the default 'non-pointer' inner loop is the best
 * configurationfor the Alpha */
#define BF_LONG unsigned long

#define BF_ROUNDS   16
#define BF_BLOCK    8

typedef struct bf_key_st
    {
    BF_LONG P[BF_ROUNDS+2];
    BF_LONG S[4*256];
    } BF_KEY;

#ifndef NOPROTO

void BF_set_key(BF_KEY *key, int len, unsigned char *data);
void BF_ecb_encrypt(unsigned char *in,unsigned char *out,BF_KEY *key,
    int enc);
void BF_encrypt(BF_LONG *data,BF_KEY *key);
void BF_decrypt(BF_LONG *data,BF_KEY *key);
void BF_cbc_encrypt(unsigned char *in, unsigned char *out, long length,
    BF_KEY *ks, unsigned char *iv, int enc);
void BF_cfb64_encrypt(unsigned char *in, unsigned char *out, long length,
    BF_KEY *schedule, unsigned char *ivec, int *num, int enc);
void BF_ofb64_encrypt(unsigned char *in, unsigned char *out, long length,
    BF_KEY *schedule, unsigned char *ivec, int *num);
char *BF_options(void);

#else

void BF_set_key();
void BF_ecb_encrypt();
void BF_encrypt();
void BF_decrypt();
void BF_cbc_encrypt();
void BF_cfb64_encrypt();
void BF_ofb64_encrypt();
char *BF_options();

#endif
```

```
#ifdef   __cplusplus
}
#endif

#endif
```

Let's take a look at the preprocessor directives first. Immediately following the copyright comment, you'll see a common feature of C header files. The construct

```
#ifndef HEADER_BLOWFISH_H
#define HEADER_BLOWFISH_H
    (the rest of the header file here…)
#endif
```

prevents the header file from being included multiple times, which would cause the compiler to complain bitterly about types being redefined and various other maladies. You can safely ignore it here.

The next lines contain another construct that will be fairly common in header files you will view. The preprocessor macro "**__cplusplus**" is defined in C++ compilers only, and the use here is to inform a C++ compiler that everything defined in this file uses C naming conventions, not C++. This prevents the C++ compiler from generating references to external functions that contain name mangling. This, too, you can safely ignore, other than to take note of the fact that you're dealing with a library that exports standard C names (as opposed to mangled C++ names).

The next lines simply declare two constants: **BF_ENCRYPT** and **BF_DECRYPT**. These symbols are for the use of the caller, so you'll create a couple of constants of your own to match. These constants will be used when passing in the parameters named "enc" in the procedure declarations that follow:

```
Type
Const
    BF_ENCRYPT = 1;
    BF_DECRYPT = 0;
```

The next lines define another preprocessor macro, named **BF_LONG**, which will be replaced with **unsigned long** wherever it occurs in the source. The **unsigned long** data type corresponds with the Kylix **LongWord** data type. You have two choices here: You can simply remember the fact that **BF_LONG** and **LongWord** are synonymous, and do the replacement yourself, or you can declare a new type and use it in the interface unit. Both approaches work, but defining your own type makes it much easier to port the code later. We'll declare a new type here, calling it **BF_LONG**:

```
Type
    BF_LONG = LongWord;
```

The next two lines declare constants that will be used in the library itself and that you need in order to size some data fields correctly. You can just add them to the **Const** section already started, like so:

```
Const
    BF_ROUNDS = 16;
    BF_BLOCK = 8;
```

Now you'll need to translate the **struct** the library needs into something you can provide. You've already got the type defined (**BF_LONG**), which makes this particular structure easy to create. Because the 4×256 constant will never change, you can evaluate it as 1,024 before it's put into code. While you're at it, you can create a new pointer type that will make using this in function declarations a bit easier:

```
Type
    BF_KEY = Record
        P: Array[1 .. BF_ROUNDS + 2] of BF_LONG;
        S: Array[1 .. 1024] of BF_LONG;
    end;
    PBF_KEY = ^BF_KEY;
```

That completes the structures and constants that you'll need to use the library. What remains to be translated are the function declarations that make up the actual library API. Note that there are two blocks of declarations, each with identical function names. The first block contains complete declarations of the functions' parameter lists, whereas the second block contains only function names. In older C code (so-called "K&R" C, named for the inventors of the language), function declarations didn't contain the parameter lists. As time went on, however, the value of fully declared function declarations (also called *function prototypes*) became widely known. For older compilers, however, quite a few libraries include function declarations without parameter lists.

In this header file, the programmer is using conditional compilation based on the **NOPROTO** macro. If this macro is *not* defined, the compiler will use the fully formed function prototypes in the first block. If it *is* defined, the compiler will use the empty prototypes in the second block. Because Kylix supports fully prototyped functions, you can ignore the second block completely.

To translate the method declarations, you need to translate both the return type of the method and the parameter list. For this library, translating the return types is easy, because all but one of the functions are declared with void return types. These functions translate to procedures in Pascal. To translate the parameter lists, use Tables 4.1, 4.2, and 4.3 to find the Pascal type that exactly matches the corresponding C parameter's type and use it to create the parameter declaration. Let's look at the first function more closely.

The first function, **BF_set_key**, takes three parameters. The first is a pointer to a **BF_KEY** structure. When you pass a pointer to a function, it's a safe bet the function will be modifying the structure that it points to, and that's the case here. This parameter will be declared as a pointer to a **BF_KEY** structure, just as it is in the C declaration. You can use the pointer type that you so thoughtfully declared with the record type:

```
Procedure BF_set_key( key: PBF_KEY; . . .
```

The second parameter is an **int**. Remember that the size of this type is dependent on the C compiler used to compile the library. On most platforms (including Linux), this will be a 32-bit quantity, but you'll want to make sure. You can use a **LongInt** in this declaration:

```
Procedure BF_set_key( key: PBF_KEY; len: LongInt; . . .
```

The final parameter is a pointer to an unsigned **char** variable. This type of declaration is frequently used as a pointer to an untyped arbitrary region of memory, especially when paired with a length parameter, as it is here. To make it easier for you to use this parameter in this way, you can use a generic pointer type to represent this parameter:

```
Procedure BF_set_key( key: PBF_KEY; len: LongInt; data: Pointer );
```

Under most circumstances, the declaration would be complete here. However, because you're calling a C function instead of a Pascal procedure, you need to inform the compiler of that fact. The **cdecl** keyword is used to force the Kylix compiler to follow the C calling conventions when generating code for this method. Here, then, is the final form of the procedure declaration:

```
Procedure BF_set_key( key: PBF_KEY; len: LongInt; data: Pointer ); cdecl;
```

Note

C and C++ use different conventions for passing parameters to functions than Pascal. In Pascal, the default method involves the caller pushing parameters on the stack from left to right, while the called subroutine removes them from the stack. In C, however, parameters are pushed onto the stack from right to left, and the caller is responsible for both pushing parameters onto the stack AND removing them after the subroutine returns. Because of these differences it is vitally important that the correct calling conventions be used when calling external C functions.

The procedure behind translating the remaining functions and completing the interface section is similar. When the procedure completes, you have the following declarations:

```
Procedure BF_ecb_encrypt( in: Pointer; out: Pointer;
                          key: PBF_KEY; enc: LongInt); cdecl;
Procedure BF_cbc_encrypt( in: Pointer; out: Pointer; length: LongInt;
                          ks: PBF_KEY; iv: Pointer; enc: LongInt ); cdecl;
```

```
Procedure BF_cfb64_encrypt( in: Pointer; out: Pointer; length: LongInt;
                            schedule: PBF_KEY; ivec: Pointer;
                            num: PlongInt; enc: LongInt ); cdecl;
Procedure BF_ofb64_encrypt( in: Pointer; out: Pointer; length: LongInt;
                            schedule: PBF_KEY; ivec: Pointer;
                            num: PlongInt ); cdecl;
Function BF_options(): PChar; cdecl;
```

You're getting closer. Now all that's left is to provide definitions in the implementation section of the function and procedures declared in the interface section. To do this, you can use external definitions, pointing the compiler to the shared library that contains the actual implementations of these methods. To do this in a maintainable manner, go back to the constants section and add a new constant to represent the name of the .so file. Then use that constant in the external definitions:

```
Const
    BFmodule = 'libbf.so.1';
```

The first procedure, **BF_set_key**, will be "implemented" in the interface unit, as follows.

```
procedure BF_set_key;          external BFmodule name 'BF_set_key';
```

The effect of this line is to tell the compiler to generate code that looks at runtime for the file libbf.so.1 and to use the implementation of the function **BF_set_key** in that file to resolve all references to that function in the source.

The complete final form of the interface unit is shown in Listing 4.4. When compiled, this unit is used in exactly the same way as any other Kylix unit. Simply include the unit name (blowfish) in your **uses** clause, and you're ready to roll.

Listing 4.4 Blowfish.pas, the complete interface unit for the third-party blowfish library.

```
unit Blowfish;

interface

Const
      BF_ENCRYPT = 1;
      BF_DECRYPT = 0;
      BF_ROUNDS = 16;
      BF_BLOCK = 8;
      BFmodule = 'libbf.so.1';

Type
      BF_LONG = LongWord;
```

```
          BF_KEY = Record
                  P: Array[1 .. BF_ROUNDS + 2] of BF_LONG;
                  S: Array[1 .. 1024] of BF_LONG;
          end;
          PBF_KEY = ^BF_KEY;


Procedure BF_set_key( key: PBF_KEY; len: LongInt; data: Pointer ); cdecl;
Procedure BF_ecb_encrypt( input: Pointer; out: Pointer;
                          key: PBF_KEY; enc: LongInt); cdecl;
Procedure BF_cbc_encrypt( input: Pointer; out: Pointer; length: LongInt;
                          ks: PBF_KEY; iv: Pointer; enc: LongInt ); cdecl;
Procedure BF_cfb64_encrypt( input: Pointer; out: Pointer; length: LongInt;
                            schedule: PBF_KEY; ivec: Pointer;
                            num: PlongInt; enc: LongInt ); cdecl;
Procedure BF_ofb64_encrypt( input: Pointer; out: Pointer; length: LongInt;
                            schedule: PBF_KEY; ivec: Pointer;
                            num: PlongInt ); cdecl;
Function BF_options: PChar; cdecl;


implementation

procedure BF_set_key;        external BFmodule name 'BF_set_key';
procedure BF_ecb_encrypt;    external BFmodule name 'BF_ecb_encrypt';
procedure BF_cbc_encrypt;    external BFmodule name 'BF_cbc_encrypt';
procedure BF_cfb64_encrypt;  external BFmodule name 'BF_cfb64_encrypt';
procedure BF_ofb64_encrypt;  external BFmodule name 'BF_ofb64_encrypt';
function  BF_options;        external BFmodule name 'BF_options';

end.
```

Where to Go for More Information

The Blowfish library used as an example in this chapter comes as part of the SSLeay library by Eric Young. Although that library is no longer being actively maintained, the source can still be found in many locations. The example here came from **www2.psy.uq.edu.au/~ftp/Crypto/blowfish/libbf.tar.gz**. The example itself, including the code from this chapter, is available on this book's Web site.

The HOWTO document referenced at the end of Chapter 3 is a vital resource for creating shared libraries. Again, it is available at **www.linuxdoc.org/HOWTO/Program-Library-HOWTO/index.html**. The net is full of C programming references and tutorials. Owing to the transient nature of the Web, we'll not provide specific links to any of them here, but a quick search at **www.google.com** for "C programming tutorial" or "C programming reference" will yield all the links you can eat.

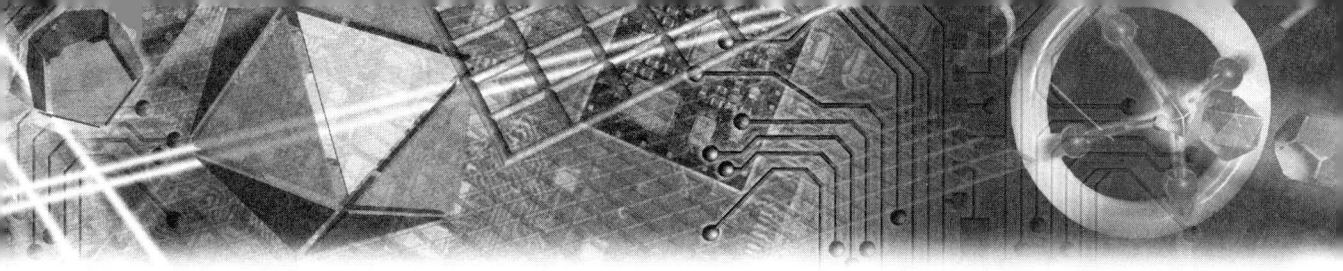

Part II

Essential Kylix
Programming Solutions

Chapter 5
Process Control

Welcome to Part II. So far we have taken you on a journey from Windows programming with Delphi to an understanding of the more important aspects of Linux and the C programming language. For the remainder of this book, we'll be "rolling up our sleeves" and presenting detailed solutions to a wide range of programming challenges you will face, from launching programs from programs to connecting help files to Kylix and creating your own custom help viewer.

Each solution consists of a description of the task to be accomplished, a statement of the strategy to be employed, and a detailed program example. In many cases we have reduced the code printed here to relevant snippets to make reading easier. Complete source code listings are available on this book's Web site at **www.kylixpowersolutions.com**. Please be aware that the code presented in the following chapters is far from "production quality." The intent of the solution examples is simply to demonstrate the strategy presented and give you a platform on which to build.

Although you can treat this book as a "problem solver"—an encyclopedia of sorts to consult for a specific situation—we highly recommend you read through every one of the solutions. Solutions often rely on techniques presented in other solutions, and we frequently use this method to present alternative ways to approach a problem. To gain the most from this book, it's best you read it through—at least once.

This chapter and the next discuss process management and interprocess communications. In this chapter we will describe the Linux process model, show how to create, destroy, and modify processes, and demonstrate how to obtain information about processes from within your Kylix programs. The next chapter is strictly about interprocess communications—that is, how to share information among processes.

Solution 5.1: Replacing the Current Process with a New Program

Often you'll want a program to finish its processing and then launch another program to perform some other task. The first program will exit immediately after launching the second program. Under Windows, you would typically call **CreateProcess** to launch the new program and then exit. The problem with this approach is that it incurs the overhead of creating a new process. It may be possible under Windows to replace a process with a new program, but it's not directly supported in the API.

The Linux runtime library has seven different functions that will replace the current process with a different executable image, without incurring the overhead of creating a new process. The seven functions shown in Table 5.1 are very similar, differing only in how they pass command-line arguments and environment strings to the called program.

Table 5.1 Functions that replace an existing process with a new executable.

Function	Description
execv	function **execv (PathName: PChar; const argv: PPChar): Integer; cdecl;** Executes the file named by **PathName**, passing it the arguments in the array pointed to by **argv**. The called program inherits the calling program's environment strings.
execve	function **execve (PathName: PChar; const argv: PPChar; const envp: PPChar): Integer; cdecl;** Executes the file named by **PathName**, passing it the arguments in the array pointed to by **argv** and the environment strings in the array pointed to by **envp**.
execvp	function **execvp (const Filename: PChar; const argv: PPChar): Integer; cdecl;** Executes the file named by **Filename**, passing it the arguments in the array pointed to by **argv**. The called program inherits the calling program's environment strings. If **Filename** contains slashes (that is, it is an absolute or relative path), this function performs exactly as **execv** does. If **Filename** contains no slashes, **execvp** searches for the program in the directories specified in the calling program's **PATH** environment variable. Because this function searches **PATH**, there's no guarantee which version of the program it will locate. As a result, you should avoid this function in programs that run with root permissions.
execl	function **execl (__path: PChar; __arg: PChar): Integer; cdecl; vararg;** Executes the file named by **__path**, passing it the arguments that follow the file name. The arguments list is terminated with a nil pointer. The called program inherits the calling program's environment strings.

(continued)

Table 5.1	**Functions that replace an existing process with a new executable** *(continued).*

Function	Description
execle	function **execle (__path: PChar; __arg: PChar): Integer; cdecl; varargs;** Executes the file named by **__path**, passing it the arguments that follow the file name and the environment strings pointed to by the last parameter. The arguments list is terminated with a nil pointer.
execlp	function **execlp (__file: PChar; __arg: PChar): Integer; cdecl; varargs;** Executes the file named by **__file**, passing it the arguments that follow the file name. The arguments list is terminated with a nil pointer. The called program inherits the calling program's environment strings. If **__file** contains slashes (that is, it is an absolute or relative path), this function performs exactly as **execl** does. If **__file** contains no slashes, **execlp** searches for the program in the directories specified in the calling program's **PATH** environment variable. Because this function searches **PATH**, there's no guarantee which version of the program it will locate. As a result, you should avoid this function in programs that run with root permissions.
fexecve	function **fexecve (FileDesc: Integer; const argv: PPChar; const envp: PPChar): Integer; cdecl;** Executes the file referenced by the file descriptor **__fd**, passing it the arguments in the array pointed to by **argv** and the environment strings pointed to by **envp**. This function is implemented only in the GNU library.

The **PPChar** type used by some of these functions is a pointer to an array of **PChar** strings. For example, the program arguments are defined like this:

```
const
  PROGRAM_ARGS : array [0..3] of PChar = ('called', 'by', 'execTest', nil);
```

You pass this array by taking its address with the @ operator, like this:

```
rslt := execv (PROGRAM_NAME, @PROGRAM_ARGS);
```

All of these functions return –1 if they fail to launch the program. The global variable **errno** indicates the reason for failure. If the function is successful, it doesn't return. See the **exec** man page (man exec) for more information.

Which function you use depends on how you want to specify the command-line arguments, whether or not you want to specify an environment, and whether or not you want to search the **PATH** environment variable for the executable program. Use the summary descriptions in this list to select the function that best meets your needs.

♦ The **"v"** functions (**execv**, **execve**, **execvp**, and **fexecve**) let you specify the command-line arguments in an array.

- The **"l"** functions (**execl**, **execle**, and **execlp**) let you specify the command-line arguments as parameters in the function call.

- The **"e"** functions (**execve**, **execle**, and **fexecve**) let you specify the called program's environment strings.

- The **"p"** functions (**execvp** and **execlp**) will search the **PATH** environment variable for the executable file.

A couple of scenarios aren't covered by these functions. If you want to use one of the **"p"** functions, but you want to pass specific environment strings, you'll have to do some extra work. You can locate the program in the **PATH** environment variable by using some other method and then call **execve** or **execle** to pass the environment strings. Alternatively, you can modify the calling program's environment so that it's in the state you want before you call **execvp** or **execlp**.

If you want to pass the calling program's environment explicitly, you can pass the global variable **envp**. This technique is especially useful if you want a program launched by **fexecve** to inherit the caller's environment. If you want to launch a new program in a separate process, you'll need to use the **fork** function, which is covered in the next solution.

Warning

*The **exec** family of functions brings with it some rather serious security vulnerabilities, due to the functions' ability to pass the current environment to another process. For this reason, you should never use an **exec** routine with a setuid program (see Solution 5.12, "Running a Program As the Superuser," for more information on **setuid**). The functions **execv**, **execvp**, **execl**, and **execlp** are always vulnerable to this threat, leaving only **execle**, **execve** and **fexecve** as "safe." Even so, these functions must be called with a safe path to the executable file.*

Solution Example: The **execTest** Program

The **execTest** program shown in Figure 5.1 illustrates how to use the **exec** family of functions in a Kylix program. The program allows you to select which of the functions you want to call and also lets you set the command-line parameters and environment strings that will be passed to the called program.

The **execTest** program will not let you edit the command line for the "l" functions, because those functions require that the command-line arguments be passed as function parameters. Similarly, you cannot edit the environment strings unless you've selected one of the "e" functions.

The **execTest** program's main form consists of about 400 lines of Pascal code, most of which are concerned with bookkeeping and are of little real interest in this discussion. The code that actually calls the **execXXX** functions is encapsulated in the Go button's **OnClick** event handler, shown in Listing 5.1.

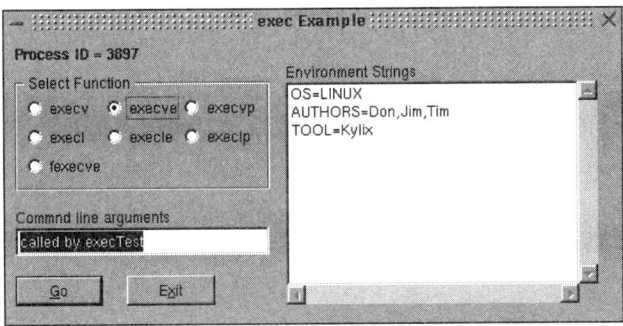

Figure 5.1
The **execTest** program.

Listing 5.1   The Go button's **OnClick** event handler.

```
procedure TfrmExecMain.btnGoClick(Sender: TObject);
const
  // program args used by the 'l' functions
  Args : array [0..3] of PChar =
    ('called', 'by', 'execTest', nil);
var
  pargs : PPChar;
  penv : PPChar;
  fd : integer;
begin
  pargs := nil;
  penv := nil;
  try
    if bEnableFlags[rgFunction.ItemIndex].bArgs then
      pargs := CreateArgsArray (edCmdLine.Text);
    if bEnableFlags[rgFunction.ItemIndex].bEnv then
      penv := CreateEnvArray;

    case rgFunction.ItemIndex of
      0 : execv  ('launched', pargs);
      1 : execve ('launched', pargs, penv);
      2 : execvp ('launched', pargs);
      // execl functions require command line args as params
      3 : execl  ('launched', Args[0], Args[1], Args[2], nil);
      4 : execle ('launched', Args[0], Args[1], Args[2], nil, penv);
      5 : execlp ('launched',  Args[0], Args[1], Args[2], nil);
      6 :
      begin
        // open the file and then call fexecve
        fd := Libc.open('launched', O_RDONLY);
```

```
        try
          if fd = -1 then
          begin
            ShowMessage ('Error opening file');
            exit;
          end;
          fexecve (fd, pargs, penv);
        finally
          Libc.__close (fd)
        end;
      end;
    end;
  finally
    FreePCharArray (pargs);
    FreePCharArray (penv);
  end;
  // values for errno are in Libc.pas
  // For example: ENOSYS = 38
  ShowMessage (Format ('Error %d launching program', [errno]));
end;
```

The code at the beginning of this function creates argument and environment string arrays to be passed to the selected function. Creation of these arrays is controlled by an array of constants (called **bEnableFlags**) that defines for each of the functions whether it accepts command-line arguments or environment strings as array pointers. The code that builds the environment strings array ensures that the environment strings array passed to the **execXXX** function contains the full default environment in addition to the environment strings that the user enters in the edit window. This isn't necessary if you're calling an application that doesn't use environment strings, but X applications (of which the launched program is one) depend on many environment strings in order to locate and communicate with the X Server. Without these environment strings, the X application will fail on initialization. Rather than trying to identify and include each of those variables (which may change between releases or depend on which windowing environment is running), I've included all the default environment strings. If the user enters a string that's already in the environment (**PATH**, for instance), the value that the user enters will overwrite the value from the default environment.

In all cases, **execTest** attempts to start a new program called "launched." This program, shown in Figure 5.2, displays the process ID (which you can compare with the process ID displayed by **execTest**), the command-line arguments, and the environment strings passed to the program. The code for the launched program's main form is shown in Listing 5.2.

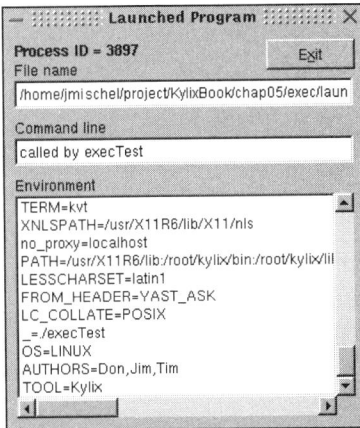

Figure 5.2
The launched program.

Listing 5.2   The launched program's main form.

```
{
  frmLaunched - Simple program to display command line and environment
}
unit frmLaunched;

interface

uses
  SysUtils, Libc, Types, Classes, QGraphics, QControls, QForms, QDialogs,
  QStdCtrls;

type
  TfrmLaunchedMain = class(TForm)
    Label1: TLabel;
    edCmdLine: TEdit;
    lblProcID: TLabel;
    Label2: TLabel;
    mmEnvironment: TMemo;
    btnExit: TButton;
    lblFilename: TLabel;
    edFilename: TEdit;
    procedure btnExitClick(Sender: TObject);
    procedure FormCreate(Sender: TObject);
  end;

var
  frmLaunchedMain: TfrmLaunchedMain;

implementation

{$R *.xfm}
```

```
procedure TfrmLaunchedMain.btnExitClick(Sender: TObject);
begin
  Close;
end;

procedure TfrmLaunchedMain.FormCreate(Sender: TObject);
var
  i : Integer;
  p : PPChar;
  s : string;
begin
  // display process ID
  lblProcID.Caption := Format ('Process ID = %d', [getpid]);

  // and program name. 0 means current module
  edFilename.Text := GetModuleName (0);

  // Display command line arguments
  s := ParamStr(0);
  for i := 1 to ParamCount do
    s := s + ' ' + ParamStr(i);
  edCmdLine.Text := s;

  // Display environment
  mmEnvironment.Clear;
  p := envp;
  while p^ <> nil do
  begin
    mmEnvironment.Lines.Add (p^);
    inc (p);
  end;
end;

end.
```

Note

*Many Linux programming references will tell you that **ParamStr(0)** (or **argv[0]** in C programs) contains the name of the program. This is not necessarily true, as you can see from Figure 5.2. The name of the program is "launched," yet the first parameter is "called." Placing the name of the executing program in the first position is simply a convention that is neither universally accepted nor universally followed. If you want to follow the convention when calling programs with the **execXXX** functions, you must place the called program's name as the first command-line argument in the function call. If you need to obtain the name of the running program, you can call the **GetModuleName** function, which is located in the **SysUtils** unit. The code in Listing 5.2 contains an example of using **GetModuleName**.*

Solution 5.2: Launching a Child Process

You may want to launch a new process but keep the existing process running. This is the standard behavior of the Windows **CreateProcess** API function, although the mechanism is much different from the one under Linux. Under Linux, you use the **fork** function or one of its variants. The **fork** function creates a child process that is a clone of the existing process, which includes copying the parent's entire address space into the child process's address space. If an error occurs, **fork** returns –1 to the parent process (the process that called **fork**), and no child is created.

If **fork** is successful, things get a little more interesting. In the parent process, **fork** returns the process ID of the newly created child process, and execution continues with the statement following the call to **fork**. In the child process, execution *begins* with the statement following the call to **fork**, and the return value is 0. It's as if **fork** returned twice—once in the parent and once in the child. This code snippet shows how you use the return value from **fork** to determine if it's the child or the parent that is executing:

```
var
  forkResult : __pid_d;
begin
  forkResult := fork;
  {
    In the parent process, execution continues here.  If fork was
    successful, forkResult will contain the process ID of the new child
    process. If fork failed, then forkResult will be -1.

    In the child process, execution begins here, with forkResult
    containing 0 to indicate that this is the child process.
  }
  case forkResult of
    -1 : WriteLn ('Error creating child process');
     0 : WriteLn ('Child process is executing');
     else
       WriteLn ('Parent process is executing. Child is ', forkResult);
  end;
```

Solution Example: Creating a Child from a Command-Line Program

The **forkTest** program shown in Listing 5.3 illustrates the procedure of forking to create a child process from a command-line program.

Listing 5.3   Using the **fork** function to create a child process.

```
{ forkTest.dpr - Illustrate using fork to create a child process }
program forkTest;

{$APPTYPE CONSOLE}
```

```
uses Libc, SysUtils;

var
  forkResult : __pid_t;

procedure DoChildProcess;
begin
  WriteLn ('Child: ProcessID = ', getpid);
  sleep (10);
  WriteLn ('Child: Exiting');
end;

procedure DoParentProcess;
begin
  WriteLn ('Parent: Child ProcessID = ', forkResult);
  sleep (5);
  WriteLn ('Parent: Exiting');
end;

begin
  WriteLn ('Parent: ProcessID = ', getpid);
  forkResult := fork;
  case forkResult of
    -1 : WriteLn ('Error creating child process');
     0 : DoChildProcess;
     else
        DoParentProcess;
  end;
end.
```

When you run this program, it immediately creates a child process. The parent then sleeps for 5 seconds before exiting, and the child sleeps for 10 seconds before exiting. (For more detailed information on "sleeping" processes, see Solution 5.7, "Reducing System Load.") You can use the **ps** program in a separate console window to see that two processes are running. You'll notice that when the parent exits, you regain control of the console window, but the child process outputs its "exiting" message to the console five seconds later. Typically, you would have the child process write its information to a log file, either by specifying a log file or by having the child redirect standard output and standard error.

The **fork** function creates a clone of the parent. How, then, do you start a new process with a new program? By combining **fork** and **execv**. The parent calls **fork** to create a new process. The child then calls **execv** to replace the cloned parent program with a new program. The modified **DoChildProcess** procedure, shown in Listing 5.4, illustrates this technique.

Listing 5.4   Launching a new program from a forked child.

```
procedure DoChildProcess;
const
  ProgramArgs : array [0..2] of PChar = ('ps', '-ef', nil);
```

```
begin
  WriteLn ('Child: ProcessID = ', getpid);
  WriteLn ('Child: Parent = ', getppid);
  sleep (7);
  WriteLn ('Child: launching ps');
  execvp ('ps', @ProgramArgs);
  perror ('Child: Error launching program');
end;
```

Solution Example: Creating a Child from a GUI Application

Creating a child from a Kylix GUI application requires somewhat more work than creating a child process from a command-line application. The most important difference is that your GUI programs can't simply fork and continue. If you try it in a GUI program, the child will start to initialize and then cause an endless stream of X Window errors. The errors occur because the child process is trying to share the parent's connection to the X Server—something the X Server doesn't support.

To create a child process from a GUI application, you have to fork and then call one of the **execXXX** functions to replace the process with a new program, even if you want to create a new instance of the same program. It's also a good idea to close any open file handles in the child before calling the **execXXX** function. Listing 5.5 shows how it's done.

Listing 5.5   Creating a child from a GUI application.
```
procedure TForm1.Button1Click(Sender: TObject);
var
  pid : pid_t;
  i : integer;
  open_max : integer;
  fname : String;
begin
  pid := fork;
  case pid of
    -1 : ShowMessage ('Error in fork');
     0 :
     begin
       { Child closes all file descriptors but stdin, stdout, and stderr }
       open_max := sysconf (_SC_OPEN_MAX);
       for i := stderr+1 to open_max-1 do
         fnctl (I, F_SETFD, FD_CLOEXEC);
       fname := GetModuleName (0);
       execlp (PChar (fname), PChar (fname), nil);
     end;
     else
       Memo1.Lines.Add (Format ('Forked to child pid %d', [pid]));
  end;
end;
```

Solution 5.3: Launching a Program and Waiting for Its Completion

There will be times when you want to run another application from your program and wait for its completion for some necessary operation, such as the creation of a log file. Note that the goal here is to run another specific application; if you merely wish to accomplish a task and wait for it in your application, you would likely choose to create a separate program thread for that purpose.

To launch another (child) process, you will once again use the **fork** library routine. The **wait** is accomplished through one of the—you guessed it—**wait** routines. In this case, the **waitpid** function is used, which waits for a specified process ID to change state, and, if no error is detected, returns a value equal to the process ID it was waiting for.

Solution Example: The **forkWait** Program

Listing 5.6 is a short console application that forks a child process and then uses the **waitpid** library function. The process ID returned from the call to **fork** is used in the call to **waitpid**, and the value returned by **waitpid** is also compared to that value, to guarantee it was the child process that exited.

Listing 5.6   Waiting for completion of a forked child.

```
{
  forkWait - Illustrate forking to a child
  process and waiting for it to complete before
  continuing.
}

program ForkWait;

{$APPTYPE CONSOLE}

uses
  Libc,
  SysUtils;

var
 forkResult : __pid_t;
 waitResult : __pid_t;

procedure DoChildProcess;
var
 s : String;
begin
 writeln;
 writeln('Child: ProcessID = ', getpid);
```

```
   write('Child: Press the [ENTER] key...');
   readln(s);
   writeln('Child: Exiting');
end;

begin
 writeln;
 writeln('Parent: ProcessID = ', getpid);
 forkResult := fork;
 case forkResult of
  -1 : writeln('Error creating child process');
   0 : DoChildProcess;
 else begin
       waitResult := waitpid(forkResult, nil, 0);
       if waitResult <> forkResult
         then writeln('Parent: Error terminating child process')
         else writeln('Parent: Exiting');
      end;
 end; { case }
 writeln;
end.
```

The following output is from a session running the **forkWait** console application. As you can see, the **Parent** process starts and then waits for the **Child** to complete its operation (reading a text line from the console). Once that operation is complete, the **Child** exits and the **Parent** is free to continue—in this case to exit.

```
User@machine:~ > ForkWait

Parent: ProcessID = 765

Child: ProcessID = 766
Child: Press the [ENTER] key…
Child: Exiting

Parent: Exiting

User@machine:~ >
```

Solution 5.4: Creating a Background Process

If you view your own process list (**ps** command), all you see are processes that you have started. But if you view the entire list (**ps –e**), you'll see that there are many processes running all the time. Some of these processes—such as the Internet services (inetd), sendmail, and cron—are running in the background, but you never see them. They provide essential services and write their information to log files.

It doesn't make much sense to put a GUI program in the background, so the discussions in this section are concerned only with command-line applications. If you want to put a program in the background programmatically, all you need do is call the **daemon** library function, which has the following declaration:

```
function daemon (NoChDir: Integer; NoClose: Integer): Integer; cdecl;
```

If **NoChDir** is 0, the program's current directory is set to the filesystem root (/); otherwise, the current directory is not changed. If **NoClose** is 0, then **stdin**, **stdout**, and **stderr** are redirected to **/dev/null**. If **NoClose** is not 0, the standard files are not redirected. The **daemon** function returns 0 if it's successful and –1 if an error occurs.

You should almost always set **NoChDir** to 0 so that the program's current directory gets set to the root. This ensures that the process doesn't leave a directory in use, which might prevent the administrator from unmounting a filesystem or performing other maintenance. The only time you should set **NoChDir** to 1 is if your background program requires some files during its operation. In that case, you should call **chdir** to set the program's working directory to the directory that contains the files it needs.

Solution Example: The **bgTest** Program

Listing 5.7 shows a program called **bgTest**, which outputs a message and then goes to the background. The program then goes into a sleep loop until it's terminated by some outside source (usually by the **kill** command).

Listing 5.7   The bgTest program.

```
{ bgTest.dpr - Illustrates background processes }
program bgTest;

{$APPTYPE CONSOLE}

uses SysUtils, Libc;

begin
  WriteLn ('bgTest: Process ID = ', getpid);
  WriteLn ('Program going to background');

  if daemon (0, 0) = -1 then
    WriteLn (Format ('Error %d calling daemon', [errno]))
  else
    repeat
      sleep (60);
    until false;
end.
```

The following output shows a typical session, where I started the program, verified its existence with **ps**, and then stopped the program from the console with the **kill** command (I've edited the output of the **ps** command to eliminate most of the other processes):

```
user@machine:~ > bgTest
bgTest: Process ID = 5479
Program going to background
user@machine:~ > ps -e
5479 ?        00:00:00 bgTest
5480 pts/0    00:00:00 ps
user@machine:~ > kill 5479
user@machine:~ >
```

You could also use the **killall** command to terminate all instances of **bgTest** by name. For example, if you had three instances of the program running, the command **killall bgTest** would terminate all three instances.

Solution 5.5: Destroying a Process

Normally you'll want a program to run to normal completion. For a noninteractive application, completion is defined as "when it's finished." Interactive applications, on the other hand, terminate when the user tells them to. However, if your main program spawns other processes, you need a way to tell those programs to exit when the user closes your program.

Under Linux, destroying a process requires that you send a signal to the process by calling the **kill** function. A *signal* is an interprocess communication mechanism that we will discuss in full detail in Chapter 6. For the moment, just accept the fact there is a signal called **SIGTERM** that, when received by a process, is a request for that process to terminate its operation in a proper manner.

Solution Example: The **CrashTestDummy** Program

I'll be killing an executing process in this example, so I'll need a process to kill—and because we're ultimately talking about GUI programming, it should use a GUI process. That function will be served by **CrashTestDummy**, a simple program that displays its own process ID and offers an exit button. **CrashTestDummy** can be seen in operation in Figure 5.3; its program listing appears in Listing 5.8.

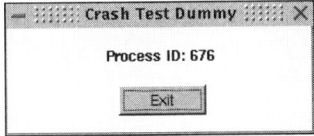

Figure 5.3
The **CrashTestDummy** program.

Listing 5.8 Code for the **CrashTestDummy** program.

```
{
  frmDummy - A simple program used by other demo programs for
    display and destruction...
}
unit frmDummy;

interface

uses
  SysUtils, Types, Classes, QGraphics, QControls, QForms, QDialogs, Libc,
  QStdCtrls, QExtCtrls;

type
  TDummyForm = class(TForm)
    Panel1: TPanel;
    ExitBtn: TButton;
    DummyLabel: TLabel;
    procedure ExitBtnClick(Sender: TObject);
    procedure FormActivate(Sender: TObject);
  private
    { Private declarations }
  public
    { Public declarations }
  end;

var
  DummyForm: TDummyForm;

implementation

{$R *.xfm}

procedure TDummyForm.ExitBtnClick(Sender: TObject);
begin
 Close;
end;

procedure TDummyForm.FormActivate(Sender: TObject);
begin
 DummyLabel.Caption := 'Process ID: ' + IntToStr(getpid);
end;

end.
```

A 'Nix Programming Tradition

Throughout the years, the Unix (and now Linux) communities have developed an arsenal of console utilities that accomplish a wide array of tasks. Although it might be your first thought to write every line of your Kylix application from scratch, we suggest you consider calling standard utilities to accomplish complex, system-related tasks. In the 'nix community, it's Standard Operating Procedure to call these programs, frequently from shell scripts and sometimes even from compiled applications. The reason is simple: *They work.* There are slight variations between versions of Unix (and even distributions of Linux) that can result in side effects you can't imagine.

These standard command-line utilities have proven themselves over time. You will see us using them—by themselves and in combination—in the solutions in this book, and we suggest that you do the same. Just a word to the wise.

Solution Example: The **ProcStuff** Unit

The sample program I'm going to build will have the capability to selectively kill instances of a program. To accomplish that feat, I need to build a list of all instances of a process, given the name of that process. The **ProcStuff** unit, which appears in Listing 5.9, will help us do that—and more.

Listing 5.9   Code for the **ProcStuff unit.**

```
unit ProcStuff;

interface

uses SysUtils, Classes, Libc;

const
  NO_ERR    =  0;
  NOT_FOUND = -1;
  PIPE_ERR  = -2;
  MISC_ERR  = -3;

type
  PProcInfoRec = ^TProcInfoRec;
  TProcInfoRec =
   record
     PID : Integer; { process id }
     Status : String; { process status }
     uName : String; { name of process initiator }
     CmdName : String; { name of process (no path) }
   end; { record }

{
  - For a given process ID, return the process
    status, the login of the user who invoked the
```

```
          process, and the command line used to invoke it.
          Return value indicates success.
    }
    function GetProcessStatus(    PID : Integer;
                              var Status : String;
                              var UName  : String;
                              var Cmd    : String) : Integer;

    {
      - For a given process name, return a pointer
        to a list of records that contain the process
        ID, its status and the name of the user who
        initiated the process. If no matches were
        found, return nil.
    }
    function GetProcessListByName(Cmd : String)
      : TList;


implementation

function ParseToSpace(var InStr : String) : String;
var
 OutStr : String;
begin
 OutStr := '';
 while (Length(Instr) > 0) and (InStr[1] = ' ') do
  Delete(Instr, 1, 1);
 while (Length(Instr) > 0) and (InStr[1] <> ' ') do
  begin
    OutStr := OutStr + InStr[1];
    Delete(InStr, 1, 1);
   end; { while }
 Result := OutStr;
end; { ParseToSpace }


function GetProcessStatus(    PID : Integer;
                          var Status : String;
                          var UName  : String;
                          var Cmd    : String) : Integer;
const
 PIPE_CMD : PChar = 'ps -eo pid,stat,user,args | grep ';
 PIPE_TYPE : PChar = 'r'; { read from the pipe }
var
 CmdArr : array[0..512] of char;
 StrArr : array[0..1024] of char;
 F : PIOFile;
 s : String;
 ErrResult : Integer;
 PtrResult : Pointer;
```

```
 Found : Boolean;
 PSLine : String;
begin
 ErrResult := NO_ERR;
 StrPCopy(CmdArr, PIPE_CMD);
 StrPCopy(StrArr, IntToStr(PID));
 StrCat(CmdArr, StrArr);

 F := popen(CmdArr, PIPE_TYPE);
 if F = nil
  then ErrResult := PIPE_ERR
  else begin
        Found := False;
        repeat
         PtrResult := fgets(StrArr, 1024, F);
         if PtrResult <> nil
          then begin
                PSLine := StrPas(StrArr);
                PSLine := Copy(PSLine, 1, Length(PSLine) - 1);
                s := ParseToSpace(PSLine);
                Found := StrToInt(s) = PID;
                if Found
                 then begin
                       { Parse out the values }
                       Status := ParseToSpace(PSLine);
                       UName  := ParseToSpace(PSLine);
                       Cmd    := ParseToSpace(PSLine);
                      end;
               end;
        until Found or (PtrResult = nil);

        if (PtrResult = nil) and (ErrResult = NO_ERR)
         then ErrResult := NOT_FOUND;
        if (pclose(F) = -1) and (ErrResult = NO_ERR)
         then ErrResult := PIPE_ERR;
       end;

 Result := ErrResult;
end;

function GetProcessListByName(Cmd : String)
   : TList;
const
 PIPE_CMD : PChar = 'ps -eo pid,stat,user,args | grep ';
 PIPE_TYPE : PChar = 'r'; { read from the pipe }
var
 CmdArr : array[0..512] of char;
 StrArr : array[0..1024] of char;
 F : PIOFile;
```

```
        PtrResult : Pointer;
        AList : TList;
        Found : Boolean;
        PSLine : String;
        ProcRec : PProcInfoRec;
        PID : Integer;
        Status : String;
        UName : String;
        CmdName : String;
      begin
       AList := TList.Create;
       StrPCopy(CmdArr, PIPE_CMD);
       StrPCopy(StrArr, Cmd);
       StrCat(CmdArr, StrArr);

       F := popen(CmdArr, PIPE_TYPE);
       if F = nil
        then begin
              Result := nil;
              AList.Free;
              Exit;
             end;

       repeat
        PtrResult := fgets(StrArr, 1024, F);
        if PtrResult <> nil
         then begin
               PSLine := StrPas(StrArr);
               PSLine := Copy(PSLine, 1, Length(PSLine) - 1);
               PID := StrToInt(ParseToSpace(PSLine));
               Status := ParseToSpace(PSLine);
               UName := ParseToSpace(PSLine);
               CmdName := ParseToSpace(PSLine);
               CmdName := ExtractFileName(CmdName);
               Found := CmdName = Cmd;
               if Found
                then begin
                      ProcRec := New(PProcInfoRec);
                      ProcRec.PID := PID;
                      ProcRec.Status := Status;
                      ProcRec.UName := UName;
                      ProcRec.CmdName := CmdName;
                      AList.Add(ProcRec);
                     end;
              end;
         until PtrResult = nil;
```

```
  pclose(F);

  Result := AList;
end;

end.
```

The **ProcStuff** unit contains two functions. **GetProcessStatus** takes a process ID as an argument and returns several pieces of information—the process status, the name of the user who initiated the command, and the command line entered to initiate the program. **GetProcessListByName** takes the name of a process and returns a list of **TProcInfoRec** records containing the process ID, username, and command-line information, where the command line matches the process name supplied.

Note

*You cannot trust the command line to contain a fully qualified path. The command line obtained from the **/proc** filesystem (either directly or through a utility such as **ps**) will consist of the command exactly as submitted to Linux by the initiator. For example, the command lines*

```
dothisthing
```

and

```
/home/username/dothisthing
```

***may** (or **may not**) be executing the same file. Finding a match, then, does involve some ambiguity, and in some cases (as you'll see in a moment), you may find it prudent to ask the user which is the correct process to kill.*

Both **GetProcessStatus** and **GetProcessListByName** use an interprocess communication technique called *piping*. For the moment, I'm going to gloss over the mechanics of that technique (it will be covered in Chapter 6) and just zero in on the net result: running the **ps** utility and collecting its output. As a matter of fact, I'll do something just a bit more clever: running two console applications in end-to-end fashion.

The **GetProcessListByName** function's goal is to return a list of matching processes by name. To accomplish that goal, it effectively executes the command line

```
ps -eo pid,stat,user,args | grep <command name>
```

where **<command name>** is the matching string we pass into **GetProcessListByName**. If you've done a bit of work at the MS-DOS command line, you probably recognize the pipe symbol (|) in the middle of this line. I'm making a very specific call to **ps** and then I'm passing its output to the **grep** utility. If I was to state the intent of this command line in

English, it would be "Give me a report of every process executing on the system, including only the information fields pertaining to the process ID, status, username, and command line, in that order. From that list, extract only those entries that contain the specified case-sensitive command name in one or more of those fields."

Pretty specific, but not perfect: It's possible that a user on the system can have a name identical to the specified command name (not likely, but we know if something *can* happen…). To eliminate the ambiguity, **GetProcessListByName** parses each entry returned, making sure the match occurred in the command line field.

Why not just use the **/proc** filesystem? That's a good question. First, it is very possible that the permissions of the user running a program will not match those required to access the information of some of the processes listed in **/proc**. Second, finding processes by command name in the **/proc** system requires examining every process. Unless you're doing that a lot and are trying to absolutely minimize the impact on the system, it's just more expedient to call the two console utilities. Finally, I wanted to demonstrate an alternative way to accomplish a task under Linux. ("Solution 5.9, Getting Detailed Process Information," will delve deeply into extracting detailed information from the **/proc** filesystem.)

Solution Example: The **KillerApp** Program

With all this as background, we're finally ready to put together a simple demo of selectively killing executing processes. Figure 5.4 shows the **KillerApp** program, poised to delete one of the instances of the command specified in the constant **PROCESSNAME**—in this case, **CrashTestDummy**.

The code for **KillerApp** is shown in Listing 5.10. For each instance on its list, **KillerApp** will query the user as to whether to kill the process. If the user answers in the affirmative,

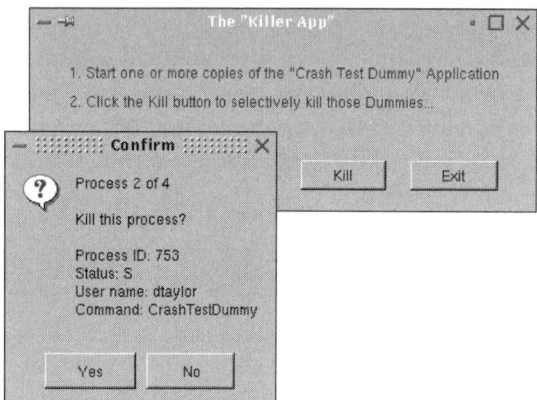

Figure 5.4
The **KillerApp** program.

the process is terminated (by request) by calling the **kill** library function with the process ID as its only parameter.

Listing 5.10   Code listing for the KillerApp program.

```
{
  frmKiller - Demonstrate selective killing of instances of
  a process by name
}
unit frmKiller;

interface

uses
  SysUtils, Types, Classes, QGraphics, QControls, QForms, QDialogs,
  QStdCtrls, Libc, ProcStuff;

type
  TfrmKillerMain = class(TForm)
    KillBtn: TButton;
    ExitBtn: TButton;
    Label1: TLabel;
    Label2: TLabel;
    procedure ExitBtnClick(Sender: TObject);
    procedure KillBtnClick(Sender: TObject);
  private
    { Private declarations }
  public
    { Public declarations }
  end;

const
 LF = ^J; { ASCII linefeed/newline }
 PROCESSNAME = 'CrashTestDummy';

var
  frmKillerMain: TfrmKillerMain;

implementation

{$R *.xfm}

procedure TfrmKillerMain.ExitBtnClick(Sender: TObject);
begin
 Close;
end;
```

```
procedure TfrmKillerMain.KillBtnClick(Sender: TObject);
var
 i : Integer;
 L : TList;
 PRec : PProcInfoRec;
begin
 L := GetProcessListByName(PROCESSNAME);
 if L.Count > 0
  then for i := 0 to L.Count - 1 do
   begin
    PRec := L.Items[i];
    with PRec^ do
     if MessageDlg('Kill Process ',
        'Process ' + IntToStr(i + 1) + ' of ' + IntToStr(L.Count)
         + LF + LF
        + 'Kill this process?' + LF + LF
        + 'Process ID: ' + IntToStr(PID) + LF
        + 'Status: ' + Status + LF
        + 'User name: ' + UName + LF
        + 'Command: ' + CmdName + LF,
        mtConfirmation, [mbYes, mbNo], 0) = mrYes
      then kill(PID, SIGTERM);
   end { for }
   else ShowMessage('No matches found for ' + PROCESSNAME);

 L.Free;
end;

end.
```

Solution 5.6: Prioritizing Processes

Every process has an associated *priority* that defines how often it gets a time slice from the scheduler. In Linux, the minimum priority value is −20 and the maximum is 19. A lower priority value means that the process gets more attention. When talking about process priorities, less is more.

A process with a priority value of 19 will only run when nothing else in the system wants to run. With a priority of 0, the process will share the CPU with other normal-priority processes (the most common), and anything negative will give the program a bigger share of the available CPU time, causing the program to run very fast in comparison to other active processes.

In general, user commands are started with a base priority of 0. Users can change their processes' priorities in the range 0 to 19 by using the **nice** and **renice** commands. Only the superuser may assign a negative priority value to a process. In addition, only the superuser may reduce a process's priority value. That is, if a user's process has a priority value of 10, the user is free to increase the value, but not decrease it. Therefore, if you start a process with priority 0 (normal) and then use **renice** to set its priority to 10, you cannot go back later and use **renice** to set its priority to 5.

In your programs, you can obtain a process's priority by calling the **getpriority** function, and you can set a process's priority by calling **setpriority**. The functions have these declarations:

```
function getpriority (__which: __priority_which_t; __who: id_t): integer;
function setpriority (__which: __priority_which_t; __who: id_t;
  __prio: integer): integer;
```

Table 5.2 shows the valid values for the **__which** parameter.

The **getpriority** function returns the priority of the process. Because –1 is a valid priority value, a –1 return value from **getpriority** is ambiguous: you don't know whether it's an error or the real value. The way to get around this problem is to clear the value of **errno** before calling **getpriority** and then check **errno** if the return value is –1. Here's an example:

```
var
  prio: integer;
begin
  errno := 0;
  prio := getpriority (PRIO_PROCESS, 1234);
  if (prio = -1) and (errno <> 0) then
    perror ('Error getting priority')
  else
    WriteLn ('Priority = ', prio);
end.
```

The **setpriority** function returns 0 on success and –1 on failure. If **setpriority** returns –1, **errno** contains the error code.

You can change the priority of all processes in a process group by specifying **PRIO_PGRP** and passing the process group ID. To set the priority for all of a user's processes, specify **PRIO_USER** and supply the user's ID.

Table 5.2   __which parameter values for the getpriority and setpriority functions.

Name	Value	Meaning
PRIO_PROCESS	0	**__who** is a process ID.
PRIO_PGRP	1	**__who** is a process group ID.
PRIO_USER	2	**__who** is a user ID.

Solution Example: The **priTest** Program

The **priTest** program, shown in Listing 5.11, calls **fork** to create a child process and sets that process's priority value to 10, which will make the child process execute much more slowly than the parent process. Both processes then go into an infinite loop in which they output the value of a loop counter, execute a counting delay loop, and repeat. When you run the program, both processes will output information to the console. You'll see that the parent runs much faster than the child. This program executes an infinite loop—you'll need to use the **kill** command to terminate the parent and child processes.

Listing 5.11   The priTest program.

```
{
  priTest - illustrate process priorities
}
program priTest;

{$APPTYPE CONSOLE}

uses SysUtils, Libc;

var
  forkRslt : __pid_t;
  i,
  LoopCount : integer;
  s : String;
begin
  forkRslt := fork;
  if forkRslt = 0 then
  begin
    s := 'Child';
  end
  else if forkRslt > 0 then
  begin
    s := 'Parent';
    // set child's priority
    if setpriority (PRIO_PROCESS, forkRslt, 10) = -1 then
      perror ('Error setting priority');
  end
  else
  begin
    perror ('Error in fork');
    exit;
  end;

  LoopCount := 0;
  repeat
    WriteLn (Format ('%s=%d', [s, LoopCount]));
```

```
    inc (LoopCount);
    // little delay loop
    for i := 1 to 10000000 do
      ;
  until false;
end.
```

Solution 5.7: Reducing System Load

Not every program needs to be run at maximum priority. As you saw in Solution 5.6, one way of lowering the burden a program places on the system is by lowering the program's priority. Beyond that, you can reduce system loading by causing your program to "sleep" during noncritical times.

Linux is smart enough to sense when a program is waiting for some reason—user input, for example. Run a GUI application (**CrashTestDummy** is a good one for this), and while its dialog is displayed, awaiting an action from the user, open up a console and type the following:

```
ps -el
```

When you find the **CrashTestDummy** process on the list, you will see its status listed as "**S**" (sleeping).

The **TTimer** object provides an easy way to take care of tasks that require periodic attention, without a significant load on the CPU. As part of its event-driven nature, **TTimer** creates its own little world, where the code written to handle the timer event is executed each time it fires. There are occasions when coding this way becomes a distraction, and there are other times when you might like to avoid allocating the resources an event-driven object demands. In those cases, you might want to make use of the __sleep and **usleep** library calls.

Both __sleep and **usleep** suspend the process for a specified number of time intervals. For __sleep, those intervals are measured in seconds; for **usleep**, it's microseconds. The actual time elapsed will be at least the amount specified, and it may be significantly longer due to clock granularity or multitasking.

The __sleep and **usleep** functions return the number of time intervals of sleep remaining. When the number of intervals reaches zero, naptime is over. By placing a call to the appropriate function in a loop, your program can sleep for a period of time, be awakened, perform an action, and then once again be put to sleep.

The primary functional difference between the time delays generated by a **TTimer** object and the __sleep and **usleep** functions is this: programs continue to operate normally while waiting for the **TTimer** to fire—the user can operate buttons, choose menu items or whatever. When __sleep or **usleep** are called, however, the program simply stops running.

Getting the Right Kind of Sleep

One of the challenges involved in porting applications from one platform to another is identifying and making allowances for library routines that have the same name (or a very similar name) but a slightly different result—and **sleep** is one such function. In the Delphi for Windows and the Kylix system utilities, the **sleep** function pauses for a specified number of milliseconds. In Linux, however, the **sleep** function (renamed **__sleep** by Kylix, to avoid the duplicate name) pauses for a specified number of *seconds*.

Another **sleep** function is provided under Linux: **usleep**, which pauses for a specified number of *microseconds*. The Linux equivalent of the Delphi/Linux **sleep** function, then, is **usleep(1000 * timeval)**, where **timeval** is the number of milliseconds you specify using the Delphi/Kylix **sleep** routine.

Solution Example: The **Sleeper** Program

Figure 5.5 shows a simple demo program called **Sleeper**. This program incorporates both a timer and a sleep loop to show how causing a program to sleep affects even timed events.

The source code for **Sleeper** is shown in Listing 5.12. When **Sleeper**'s Start button is clicked, a **TTimer** object with a 12-second delay is enabled and then the program falls into a **for** loop that executes a 5-second delay four times, each time writing a message into a memo object before falling asleep again. When the **TTimer** object's delay has elapsed, the code in its event handler writes a message into another memo.

After the Start button is clicked, you will see a message each time the program reawakens; that is, after 5, 10, 15 and 20 seconds. You will notice, however, that the 12-second timer message doesn't appear until the 15-second "wake-up call," because the overall process had been put to sleep.

You can observe just a bit of the inner workings of this process by opening a console window and running **ps -el** periodically. The process status will always declare that it's sleeping (the status value displayed will be "S"), but an examination of the wait channel (**WCHAN**) value will reveal the actual wait state. Although the process is simply waiting for operator action, the **WCHAN** value will be **do_sel**. However, when you force the process to sleep, the value will change to **nanosl**.

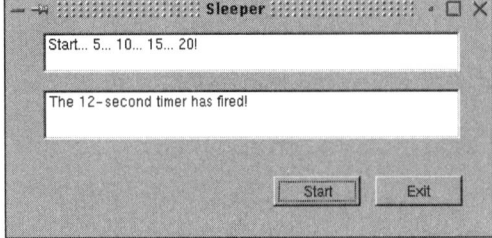

Figure 5.5
The **Sleeper** program.

Listing 5.12   Code for the Sleeper program.

```
{
  frmSleeper - Demonstrate the __sleep() library function
}
unit frmSleeper;

interface

uses
  SysUtils, Types, Classes, QGraphics, QControls, QForms, QDialogs,
  QExtCtrls, QStdCtrls, Libc;

type
  TSleeperMainForm = class(TForm)
    ExitBtn: TButton;
    StartBtn: TButton;
    SleepMemo: TMemo;
    TimerMemo: TMemo;
    Timer: TTimer;
    procedure SleepyBye;
    procedure ExitBtnClick(Sender: TObject);
    procedure StartBtnClick(Sender: TObject);
    procedure TimerTimer(Sender: TObject);
  private
    { Private declarations }
  public
    { Public declarations }
  end;

var
  SleeperMainForm: TSleeperMainForm;

implementation

{$R *.xfm}

procedure TSleeperMainForm.SleepyBye;
var
 i : Integer;
 s : String;
begin
 Timer.Enabled := True;
 SleepMemo.Clear;
 TimerMemo.Clear;
 s := 'Start... ';
 SleepMemo.Text := s;
```

```
    for i := 1 to 4 do
      begin
      Application.ProcessMessages;
      __Sleep(5);
      s := s + IntToStr(i * 5);
      if i < 4
        then s := s + '... '
        else s := s + '!';
      SleepMemo.Text := s;
      end; { for }
end;

procedure TSleeperMainForm.ExitBtnClick(Sender: TObject);
begin
  Close;
end;

procedure TSleeperMainForm.StartBtnClick(Sender: TObject);
begin
  SleepyBye;
end;

procedure TSleeperMainForm.TimerTimer(Sender: TObject);
begin
  Timer.Enabled := False;
  TimerMemo.Text := 'The 12-second timer has fired!';
end;

end.
```

Solution 5.8: Getting Process ID and User Information

Knowing the current process and who is running it is valuable information. Among other things, this information will help you determine what privileges the current user holds. Through the function library, Linux provides several routines that enable you to gather some good basic information, both about the process and the user. These functions are highlighted in Table 5.3.

The last two functions in Table 5.3 deserve comment. Each returns a **PPasswordRecord**, a pointer to a record object containing several pieces of information related to the user's password, including the user's name, encrypted password, user ID, group ID, real name, home directory, and chosen shell program.

Table 5.3   Functions that retrieve process and user information.

Function	Returns
getpid	Process ID of the current process
getppid	Process ID of the parent of the current process
getpgid	Process group ID of the specified process
getpgrpProcess	Group ID of the current process
getuid	Real user ID of the current process
getpwuid	Pointer to the password record for the specified user ID
getpwnam	Pointer to the password record for the specified username

Wait a minute—does this mean you could determine the user IDs of everyone using the system and then use those IDs to find their passwords? Yes and no. The password returned is the *encrypted* password, not the password itself. Whenever a user logs in, the password he or she enters is encrypted and compared to the value in this record; if it matches, the login is validated.

If you have browsed through the complete list of library functions, you might wonder why I didn't specify the **getlogin** function to retrieve the user ID. The reason is that **getlogin** has not been included in the library for all Linux distributions. For those distributions where it has not yet been implemented, calling **getlogin** returns a nil pointer, which does no one any good. Using **getpwuid** may seem a little clumsy, but it does work.

Solution Example: The **GetPID** Program

Figure 5.6 shows the **GetPID** program, a simple program that displays several pieces of information about both the process and the user. Listing 5.13 details the code, which simply calls several of the functions listed in Table 5.3 and displays the results in a **TMemo** object.

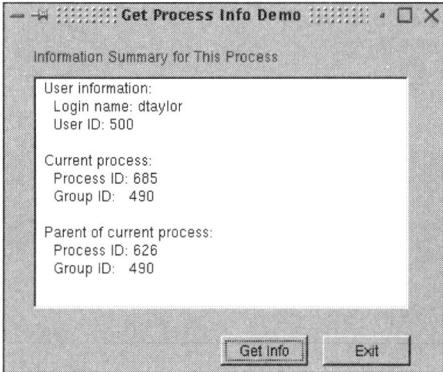

Figure 5.6
The **GetPID** program.

Listing 5.13 Code for the **GetPID** program.

```
{
  frmGetPID - Get and display summary information for
    this process
}
unit frmGetPID;

interface

uses
  SysUtils, Types, Classes, QGraphics, QControls, QForms, QDialogs, Libc,
  QStdCtrls;

type
  TGetPIDMainForm = class(TForm)
    InfoMemo: TMemo;
    InfoBtn: TButton;
    ExitBtn: TButton;
    Label1: TLabel;
    procedure ExitBtnClick(Sender: TObject);
    procedure InfoBtnClick(Sender: TObject);
  private
    { Private declarations }
  public
    { Public declarations }
  end;

var
  GetPIDMainForm: TGetPIDMainForm;

implementation

{$R *.xfm}

procedure TGetPIDMainForm.ExitBtnClick(Sender: TObject);
begin
 Close;
end;

procedure TGetPIDMainForm.InfoBtnClick(Sender: TObject);
var
  p        : PChar;
  PPWRec   : PPasswordRecord;
  pid      : Integer;
  uid      : Integer;
  ppid     : Integer;
```

```
 pgroup  : Integer;
 ppgroup : Integer;
begin
 pid := getpid;
 uid := getuid;
 ppid := getppid;
 pgroup := getpgid(pid);
 ppgroup := getpgid(ppid);
 PPWRec := getpwuid(uid);
 p := PPWRec^.pw_name;

 with InfoMemo.Lines do
  begin
   Clear;
   Add(' User information:');
   Add('   Login name: ' + p);
   Add('   User ID: ' + IntToStr(uid));
   Add('');
   Add(' Current process:');
   Add('   Process ID: ' + IntToStr(pid));
   Add('   Group ID:  ' + IntToStr(pgroup));
   Add('');
   Add(' Parent of current process:');
   Add('   Process ID: ' + IntToStr(ppid));
   Add('   Group ID:  ' + IntToStr(ppgroup));
  end; { with }
end;

end.
```

Solution 5.9: Getting Detailed Process Information

Linux provides a virtual filesystem (**/proc**) that contains information about the system and all the processes that are currently active. Each process that is currently active in the system has a directory (named with the process ID) in the **/proc** filesystem. In this section, we'll briefly touch on some of the information you can obtain from a process's **/proc** filesystem entry. For a full discussion of the **/proc** filesystem, see the **proc** man page (man 5 proc).

Within each process's **/proc** directory entry there are a number of different files and directories that contain the process's information. The most commonly used of these files are shown in Table 5.4. As you'll see in the following examples, your programs have to employ many different techniques in order to obtain process information in a useful form.

Table 5.4 Commonly used /proc filesystem files.

File	Description
cmdline	A text file that contains the full command line passed to the program on startup
cwd	A symbolic link to the process's current working directory
environ	A text file that contains all the process's environment strings
exe	A symbolic link to the process's executable image
fd	A directory that contains symbolic links to each of the files that the process currently has open
root	A symbolic link to the process's filesystem root
stat	A text file that contains information about the process's current state and runtime metrics

Solution Example: Enumerating Processes

To get a list of all processes that are currently running, you need to enumerate the files in the **/proc** directory and select those that have the directory attribute set and whose names are integers. This is fairly easy to accomplish using the **FindFirst** and **FindNext** functions from the **SysUtils** unit, as shown by the **EnumProcesses** procedure in Listing 5.14.

Listing 5.14 Enumerating processes.

```
procedure EnumProcesses (cb : TProcEnumCallback);
var
  sr : TSearchRec;
  findRslt : Integer;
  pid : __pid_t;
begin
  findRslt := FindFirst ('/proc/*', faDirectory or faAnyFile, sr);
  try
    while findRslt = 0 do
    begin
      if ((sr.Attr and faDirectory) <> 0) then
      begin
        {
          Try to convert directory name to an integer.
          If it fails, we know it isn't a process ID.
        }
        try
          pid := StrToInt (sr.Name);
        except
          // not a process ID, so set to -1
          pid := -1;
        end;
        if pid >= 0 then
          cb (pid);
      end;
```

```
      findRslt := FindNext (sr);
    end;
  finally
    FindClose (sr);
  end;
end;
```

This procedure finds each process and passes its process ID to the caller-supplied callback function. The callback function is of type **TProcEnumCallback**, which has this definition:

```
type
  // Procedure that receives process info from EnumProcesses
  TProcEnumCallback = procedure (pid: __pid_t) of object;
```

To use **EnumProcesses**, you simply call the procedure and pass it the address of your **callback** function. For example, the code fragment in Listing 5.15 enumerates the processes and puts their process IDs into a memo box.

Listing 5.15   Using the **EnumProcesses** procedure.

```
procedure TForm1.EnumProcessCB (pid: __pid_t);
begin
  Memo1.Lines.Add (IntToStr (pid));
end;

procedure TForm1.FormCreate (Sender: TObject);
begin
  EnumProcesses (EnumProcessCB);
end;
```

Solution Example: Obtaining a Process's Command Line

The **cmdline** file within a process's **/proc** filesystem directory contains the full command line used to invoke the process. The command line is terminated with a null character rather than a newline character. To obtain the command line, you simply read the file—except there's a catch. Because this (and the other **/proc** filesystem files) is a *virtual* file, the operations you can perform on it are somewhat limited. You can't, for example, obtain the file size. To read the file, you need to read the entire contents in a single gulp. The code shown in Listing 5.16 illustrates how this is done.

Listing 5.16   Reading the process's cmdline file.

```
{
  ProcReadFile reads the contents of the specified file
  for the passed process id, and returns the contents in the
  supplied buffer. On entry, length contains the size of
  the buffer. On exit, length contains the number of bytes
  read. The function returns 0 on success, -1 on error.
```

```
    }
    function  ProcReadFile (pid: __pid_t; const path: String;
      var buffer; var length: Integer): integer;
    var
      sFileName : String;
      fd : Integer;
    begin
      Result := -1;
      try
        sFileName := Format ('/proc/%d/%s', [pid, path]);

        fd := Libc.open (PChar (sFilename), O_RDONLY);
        if fd <> -1 then
        begin
          try
            Result := Libc.__read (fd, Buffer, length);
          finally
            Libc.__close(fd);
          end;
        end;
      except
        // swallow exception...
      end;
    end;


    {
      ProcReadFileString returns the entire contents of the specified
      file in a string.
    }
    function ProcReadFileString (pid: __pid_t;
      const path: String): String;
    var
      buffer : array [0..16000] of char;
      length : Integer;
    begin
      length := sizeof (buffer)-1;
      length := ProcReadFile (pid, path, buffer, length);
      if length = -1 then
        Result := ''
      else
      begin
        buffer[length] := #0;
        Result := buffer;
      end;
    end;
```

```
// ProcGetCmdline - return the command line that
// launched the process.
function ProcGetCmdline (pid: __pid_t) : String;
begin
  Result := ProcReadFileString (pid, 'cmdline');
end;
```

The **ProcReadFile** and **ProcReadFileString** functions are helpers that read an arbitrary **/proc** filesystem file and return its contents in a buffer (**ProcReadFile**) or a string (**ProcReadFileString**). You can use these helper functions to read other **/proc** filesystem files in addition to the **cmdline** file.

Solution Example: Obtaining a Process's Environment

A process's **environment** is stored as a series of null-terminated strings in the **environ** file. The **environ** file may contain (but doesn't always contain) a final null character that marks the end of the environment strings. To obtain the process's **environment**, you read the **environ** file into a buffer (by calling **ProcReadFile**) and then parse the individual strings into a string list. The **ProcGetEnvironment** function shown in Listing 5.17 illustrates how this is done.

Listing 5.17   Obtaining a process's environment.

```
// ProcGetEnvironment - return a string list that contains
// the process's environment strings.
function  ProcGetEnvironment (pid: __pid_t): TStringList;
var
  buffer : array[0..16000] of char;
  length : integer;
  lst : TStringList;
  p : PChar;
begin
  length := sizeof (buffer)-1;
  length := ProcReadFile (pid, 'environ', buffer, length);
  if length = -1 then
  begin
    Result := nil;
    exit;
  end;
  // make sure there's a terminating null character
  buffer[length] := #0;

  // returned environment is a series of 0-terminated strings
  lst := TStringList.Create;
  try
    p := buffer;
    while p^ <> #0 do
```

```
    begin
      lst.Add (p);
      p := StrEnd (p) + 1;
    end;
  except
    // if an exception occurs, free the list and re-raise
    lst.Free;
    raise;
  end;
  Result := lst;
end;
```

Solution Example: Getting a Process's Executable File, Root Directory, and Working Directory

Within a process's **/proc** filesystem folder, the **cwd**, **exe**, and **root** files are symbolic links to the process's current working directory, executable file, and root directory, respectively. To obtain these bits of information, you need to read the links by calling the **readlink** function in **Libc**. Listing 5.18 presents a helper function called **ProcReadLink**, which reads a process's link file. This listing also shows **ProcGetCwd**, **ProcGetRoot**, and **ProcGetExe**, which use the helper function.

Listing 5.18   The ProcReadLink helper function and the functions that use it.

```
// ProcReadLink - return the name of the file that the
// link points to.
function  ProcReadLink (pid: __pid_t; const sFile: String): String;
var
  buf : array [0..1024] of char;
  iLen : Integer;
  sFilename : String;
begin
  sFilename := Format ('/proc/%d/%s', [pid, sFile]);
  iLen := readlink (PChar(sFilename), buf, 1024);
  if iLen = -1 then
    iLen := 0;
  buf[iLen] := #0;
  Result := buf;
end;


// ProcGetCwd - return the process's current working directory.
function  ProcGetCwd (pid: __pid_t): String;
begin
  Result := ProcReadLink (pid, 'cwd');
end;
```

```
// ProcGetExe - return the name of the process's executable.
function  ProcGetExe (pid: __pid_t): String;
begin
  Result := ProcReadLink (pid, 'exe');
end;

// ProcGetRoot - return the process's root directory
function  ProcGetRoot (pid: __pid_t): String;
begin
  Result := ProcReadLink (pid, 'root');
end;
```

Solution Example: Obtaining Information about a Process's Open Files

The **fd** directory within a process's **/proc** filesystem directory contains symbolic links to all the files that the process currently has open. The file names within the **fd** directory are named with the file's integer descriptor. Typically (unless the program has redirected them), 0 is standard in, 1 is standard out, and 2 is standard error. From the Linux command line, you can see the links by entering the command

```
ls -l /proc/198/fd
```

where "198" is replaced by the process ID of the process you're interested in. Here's the output of such a command when I ran it on my system:

```
lrwx------    1 root     root        64 Mar 20 22:47 0 -> socket:[145]
l-wx------    1 root     root        64 Mar 20 22:47 1 -> /dev/tty10
lrwx------    1 root     root        64 Mar 20 22:47 2 -> /dev/xconsole
l-wx------    1 root     root        64 Mar 20 22:47 3 -> /var/log/mail
l-wx------    1 root     root        64 Mar 20 22:47 4 -> /var/log/news/news.crit
l-wx------    1 root     root        64 Mar 20 22:47 5 -> /var/log/news/news.err
l-wx------    1 root     root        64 Mar 20 22:47 6 -> /var/log/news/news.notice
l-wx------    1 root     root        64 Mar 20 22:47 7 -> /var/log/warn
l-wx------    1 root     root        64 Mar 20 22:47 8 -> /var/log/warn
l-wx------    1 root     root        64 Mar 20 22:47 9 -> /var/log/messages
```

This is a standard long format directory listing (see the manual page for the **ls** command for full information). This listing shows that the process has ten files open, on file descriptors 0 through 9. The names of the open files are to the right of the arrows.

If you want your program to enumerate all of a process's files, you need to enumerate the files in the process's **fd** directory, as shown in Listing 5.19.

Listing 5.19   Enumerating a process's files.

```
type
  // Process file enumeration callback.
  TProcFileEnumCallback = procedure (pid: __pid_t;
    fd: Integer) of object;

{
  ProcEnumFiles - Enumerate the files used by the process.
  If the calling process does not have permissions to
  access the fd directory for this process, no FDs will
  be enumerated.
}
procedure ProcEnumFiles (pid: __pid_t; cb: TProcFileEnumCallback);
var
  sr : TSearchRec;
  findRslt : Integer;
  sFilename : String;
  fd : Integer;
begin
  sFilename := Format ('/proc/%d/fd/*', [pid]);
  findRslt := FindFirst (sFilename, faAnyFile, sr);
  try
    while findRslt = 0 do
    begin
      try
        fd := StrToInt (sr.Name);
      except
        fd := -1;
      end;
      if fd <> -1 then
        cb (pid, fd);
      findRslt := FindNext (sr);
    end;
  finally
    FindClose (sr);
  end;
end;

// ProcGetFD - return the contents of the link for file fd.
function  ProcGetFD (pid: __pid_t; fd: Integer): String;
begin
  Result := ProcReadLink (pid, Format ('fd/%d', [fd]));
end;
```

The **ProcEnumFiles** function scans the specified process's **fd** directory and calls the supplied callback function for each of the file descriptors. . The callback function can then obtain the link text by calling **ProcGetFd**, as shown by the code fragments in Listing 5.20.

Listing 5.20   Using the ProcEnumFiles procedure.

```
procedure TForm1.EnumFilesCB (pid: __pid_t; fd: integer);
begin
  Memo1.Lines.Add (Format ('%d = %s', [fd, ProcGetFd (pid, fd)]));
end;

procedure TForm1.FormCreate (Sender: TObject);
begin
  ProcEnumFiles (EnumFilesCB);
end;
```

Solution Example: Obtaining Detailed Process Information

A process's **stat** file contains some very detailed information about the process, including the process name; process, group, and parent IDs; priority; and resource usage information. The **ps** program accesses this file to provide process information (type "**ps –ef**" for an example).

The information in this file is supplied as a series of values separated by spaces. If you were to list the contents of this file (**cat /proc/361/stat**), you would see something like this:

```
361 (sendmail) S 1 361 361 0 -1 320 422 2455 8 1665 1 1 29 53 0 0 0 180000
3596 2129920 96 2147483647 134512640 134956744 3221224848 0 0 0 0 4102
90625 3222473392 60 4 17 0
```

If you want to get this information into your program in a useful form, you need to read it into a string and then use the **sprintf** function to parse the individual fields. That's what the **ProcGetStat** function shown in Listing 5.21 does; it reads the **stat** file and returns the contents in a **TProcStat record**.

Listing 5.21   Reading a process's stat file.

```
type
  // The TProcStat record contains the information stored
  // in the process's stat file.
  // See "man 5 proc" for information on these fields.
  TProcStat = record
    pid        : __pid_t;  // process id
    comm       : String;   // Filename of executable
    state      : char;     // RSDZT
    ppid       : __pid_t;  // parent process ID
    pgrp       : __pid_t;  // process group ID
    session    : integer;  // session id
    tty        : integer;  // tty process uses
    tpgid      : __pid_t;  // pid of tty owner
    flags      : cardinal; //
    minflt     : cardinal; // # of minor faults for process
```

```
     cminflt      : cardinal; // # of minor faults for process
                               // and children
     majflt       : cardinal; // # of major faults for process
     cmajflt      : cardinal; // # of major faults for process
                               // and children
     utime        : cardinal; // time scheduled in user mode
     stime        : cardinal; // time scheduled in kernel mode
     cutime       : cardinal; // time scheduled in user mode,
                               // including children
     cstime       : cardinal; // time scheduled in kernel mode,
                               // including children
     counter      : integer;  // Next time slice
     priority     : integer;  // current priority, plus 15
     timeout      : cardinal; // time of next timeout
     itrealvalue  : cardinal; // next SIGALRM time
     starttime    : integer;  // time process started
     vsize        : cardinal; // Virtual memory size
     rss          : cardinal; // resident set size
     rlim         : cardinal; // RSS limit
     startcode    : cardinal; // start of code space
     endcode      : cardinal; // end of code space
     startstack   : cardinal; // start of stack address
     kstkesp      : cardinal; // current stack pointer
     kstkeip      : cardinal; // current instruction pointer
     signal       : integer;  // bitmap of pending signals
     blocked      : integer;  // bitmap of blocked signals
     sigignore    : integer;  // bitmap of ignored signals
     sigcatch     : integer;  // bitmap of caught signals
     wchan        : cardinal; // channel
   end;


// ProcGetStat - Return a TProcStat record that contains the
// information from the process's stat file.
function ProcGetStat (pid: __pid_t) : TProcStat;
const
  // scanf string for stat file
  StatScanfFormat =
    '%d %s %c %d %d %d %d %d %u %u %u %u %u %u %u %u %u %d %d %u '+
    '%u %d %u %u %u %u %u %u %u %u %d %d %d %d %u';
var
  s : TProcStat;
  pcomm : PChar;
  stat : String;
begin
  stat := ProcReadFileString (pid, 'stat');
  // allocate string for executable file name.
```

```
  // this is longer than absolutely necessary, but that's OK
  pcomm := StrAlloc (Length (stat));
  try
    sscanf (PChar (stat), StatScanfFormat,
      @s.pid, pcomm,     @s.state,        @s.ppid,
      @s.pgrp,           @s.session,      @s.tty,
      @s.tpgid,          @s.flags,        @s.minflt,
      @s.cminflt,        @s.majflt,       @s.cmajflt,
      @s.utime,          @s.stime,        @s.cutime,
      @s.cstime,         @s.counter,      @s.priority,
      @s.timeout,        @s.itrealvalue,  @s.starttime,
      @s.vsize,          @s.rss,          @s.rlim,
      @s.startcode,      @s.endcode,      @s.startstack,
      @s.kstkesp,        @s.kstkeip,      @s.signal,
      @s.blocked,        @s.sigignore,    @s.sigcatch,
      @s.wchan);
    s.comm := pcomm;
  finally
    StrDispose (pcomm);
  end;
  Result := s;
end;
```

A full discussion of the individual fields within the **TProcStat record** is beyond the scope of this book. Refer to the man page (man 5 proc) for detailed information.

Solution 5.10: Limiting a Process to a Single Instance

There are times when you want to keep a user from running your program concurrently with itself. The reasons are varied, ranging from licensing issues to the possible corruption of data files.

Under Windows there are several ways to accomplish the limiting of a program to a single instance, including setting up a file-mapping object. Under Linux, the most common way to accomplish this objective is with a *lock file*, which basically serves as a nonvolatile flag that stakes out the territory for a particular program for a particular user.

At this point you may find yourself in total disbelief, perhaps yelling "Stone knives and bearskins!" Certainly, lock files do seem a bit primitive, and they are far from perfect. But in case you're doubting their widespread use, just fire up the copy of Netscape 4.7 that undoubtedly came with your distribution of Linux. Then try to launch a second copy. Surprise—you'll get a message that a lock file has been detected, and you're given the opportunity to deal with that fact as you wish.

Is this the only way this task can be accomplished? Of course not! You can also use one of several Interprocess Communication (IPC) methods. You'll read more about IPC in Chapter 6. For now, I'm just going to keep this as simple as possible.

Solution Example: The **OneInst** Program

I'll create a specific example: a program that consists of a simple form that notifies you when it's the only instance, as shown in Figure 5.7.

To prevent the execution of the program itself, we have to jump to the Kylix project file and write our management code before the **TApplication** object gets initialized and executed. The strategy will follow this line of logic:

1. We'll look in the user's home directory for the lock file. We know he certainly has write permissions in that directory, and it's unlikely that anyone else but the superuser has those same permissions there.

2. If the file is not present, we presume the process is not already running, so we create the file, using a standard name and writing to it the process ID number for the current process. The instance is then free to execute.

3. When this instance of the program shuts down, we find the lock file and delete it.

   So far, so good. Now let's think about what should happen in the normal case when a second instance is attempted.

4. We look in the user's home directory and find the lock file. But does this prove it's really active? What if the previous instance of the program shut down unexpectedly, before it was able to delete the file?

5. We open the file and get the pid stored there and then begin a series of verifications:

   ◆ The pid must be on the current list of processes.

   ◆ The process for that pid must be active, and not a zombie process that has been abandoned and is not really doing anything.

Figure 5.7
The **OneInst** program.

♦ This active process must be the same program that we're attempting to execute. (If it's not, that's an indication that the process was shut down unexpectedly at an earlier time, and the system has reassigned the pid to another process.)

If we make it through every one of these tests, we really do have an active previous instance. However, if we fail any of the tests, we have a lock file artifact that can be safely deleted. In that case, we jump back to Step 2, where we write the file and let the program run. The logic for all this can be seen in the **OneInst** project file, shown in Listing 5.22. The program itself appears in Listing 5.23.

Listing 5.22   Contents of the **OneInst** project file.

```
program OneInst;

uses
  QForms,
  SysUtils,
  Libc,
  QDialogs,
  ProcStuff in 'ProcStuff.pas',
  frmOneInst in 'frmOneInst.pas' {OneInstMainForm};

const
  HOME_DIR : PChar = 'HOME';
  BaseLockFileName = '.oneinst.LCK';

var
  AlreadyRunning : Boolean;
  PID : Integer; { ID for this process }
  ProcStatus : String;
  UserName : String;
  CmdLine : String;
  LockPIDStr : String;
  LockFile : TextFile;
  HomeDirPtr : PChar;
  HomeDirName : String;
  LockFileName : String;

{$R *.res}

begin
  AlreadyRunning := False;
  CmdLine := '';
  PID := getpid;
  HomeDirPtr := getenv(HOME_DIR);
```

```
HomeDirName := StrPas(HomeDirPtr);
LockFileName := HomeDirName + '/' + BaseLockFileName;

if FileExists(LockFileName)
 then begin
        { Test the file's validity }
        AssignFile(LockFile, LockFileName);
        Reset(LockFile);
        readln(LockFile, LockPIDStr);
        CloseFile(LockFile);

        { Is that original process still running -- and
          is it this application? }
        if GetProcessStatus(StrToInt(LockPIDStr),
            ProcStatus, UserName, CmdLine)
          = NO_ERR
         then begin { It exists. Is it a Zombie? }
              if pos('Z', ProcStatus) = 0
                then begin
                      { It's running -- and it's not a Zombie. But
                        is it *this* application? }
                      if ExtractFileName(CmdLine) =
                         ExtractFileName(Application.ExeName)
                        then begin
                              AlreadyRunning := True;
                              MessageDlg('Sorry!', 'Sorry. Only '
                                 + 'one instance of this application '
                                 + 'is permitted to run at a time.',
                                 mtError, [mbOK], 0);
                             end;
                     end;
              end;
        end;

if not AlreadyRunning
 then begin
        { Create the lock file }
        if FileExists(LockFileName) then DeleteFile(LockFileName);
        AssignFile(LockFile, LockFileName);
        Rewrite(LockFile);
        writeln(LockFile, IntToStr(PID));
        CloseFile(LockFile);
```

```
           Application.Initialize;
           Application.CreateForm(TOneInstMainForm, OneInstMainForm);
           Application.Run;

           { Clean up }
           if FileExists(LockFileName) then DeleteFile(LockFileName);
         end;
end.
```

Listing 5.23   Code listing for the **frmOneInst** program.

```
unit frmOneInst;

interface

uses
  SysUtils, Types, Classes, QGraphics, QControls, QForms, QDialogs,
  QStdCtrls, QExtCtrls, Libc;

type
  TOneInstMainForm = class(TForm)
    Panel1: TPanel;
    ExitBtn: TButton;
    Label1: TLabel;
    Label2: TLabel;
    PIDLabel: TLabel;
    procedure ExitBtnClick(Sender: TObject);
    procedure FormActivate(Sender: TObject);
  private
    { Private declarations }
  public
    { Public declarations }
  end;

var
  OneInstMainForm: TOneInstMainForm;

implementation

{$R *.xfm}

procedure TOneInstMainForm.ExitBtnClick(Sender: TObject);
begin
 Close;
end;
```

```
procedure TOneInstMainForm.FormActivate(Sender: TObject);
begin
 PIDLabel.Caption := 'Process ID: ' + InttoStr(getpid);
end;

end.
```

Solution 5.11: Scheduling a Process

There are many situations when you may want to have your program run either at a specific time or on a periodic schedule. This would be especially true for programs such as disk defragmenters, backup utilities, and virus scanners. Under Windows, you could possibly add your program to the Task Scheduler, the built-in service always running in the background (although we're not aware of any Pascal interface libraries to Task Scheduler).

Linux has two versions of Task Scheduler: one called **atd** and another called **cron**. Like Task Scheduler, they both run as services in the background; using Linux terminology, they are *daemons*. Unlike a Windows service, these daemons require your program to use the command line to interface with them. The **at** utility (which uses the **atd** daemon) is especially suited for tasks that are scheduled one event at a time, such as 3:10 P.M. this afternoon. The **crontab** utility (which uses **cron**) is best used for repeated events—especially ones with complex schedules.

Solution Example: The **startdummy** Script

In this solution I'll show you how to establish interfaces with both at and **crontab**, using the **CrashTestDummy** program. But first I will need one bit of preparation. Linux command-line utilities are not able to run Kylix GUI-based programs directly, because they are missing two important pieces of information. First, they need to know where to find the path to any Kylix shared object libraries. Second, the X Window system needs to know which display to use.

Listing 5.24 is a shell script that contains all the necessary information. The first line informs the Linux command-line processor that this is a script and that it is to be executed by the standard shell specified by the user in his configuration. The two "export" lines provide the location information for the library path and the screen. The last line is a fully qualified path to the program to be executed.

Listing 5.24   The **startdummy** shell script.

```
#!/bin/sh
export LD_LIBRARY_PATH=/home/fred/kylix/bin:$LD_LIBRARY_PATH
export DISPLAY=:0
/home/fred/kylix_projects/Chapter06/CTD/CrashTestDummy
```

Solution Example: The **RunAt** Program

First I'll take on an interface with the command line utility **at**. The **at** utility works with its designated daemon, storing and retrieving schedule data. In its standard command-line mode, it is capable of processing information as text directly from the command line, or it can be given the name of an input file from which it will take its directions.

As with many Linux utilities, the use of **at** is subject to permissions granted by the superuser. If the superuser has created a file called **etc/at.allow**, a user can only run **at** if his username has been included in that file. On the other hand, if the superuser has created a file called **etc/at.deny** with his username in it, there is no way he can run **at**.

Figure 5.8 illustrates a simple graphical interface for **at**. As you can see, a task has been specified to run at 6:00 P.M. on February 14th, taking its instructions from the **startdummy** script. By clicking the radio button, the user can type in the command he would like to run. Listing 5.25 highlights the relevant routines from the **RunAt** program.

The two main routines in **RunAt** are **CreateCommandLine** and **WriteSchedule**. **CreateCommandLine** assembles a command line and a parameter string, based on the settings on the form. Notice that the **Parms** variable is set only if the **FileRB** radio button is not checked, meaning the parameters will be passed in on the command line and not pulled from a file.

The **WriteSchedule** routine's actions are also determined by the setting of the **FileRB** control. If **FileRB** is checked, a pipe (see Chapter 6) is created to read **stdout** and the **at** command is run, supplying **at** with the name of the file to read as its input. If **FileRB** is not checked, a pipe is created to write to **stdin**, and **WriteSchedule** executes the **at** command, supplying it with the input it requires, including both the newline (Ctrl+J) and end-of-text (Ctrl+D) characters that would be necessary to type when running **at** from the command line.

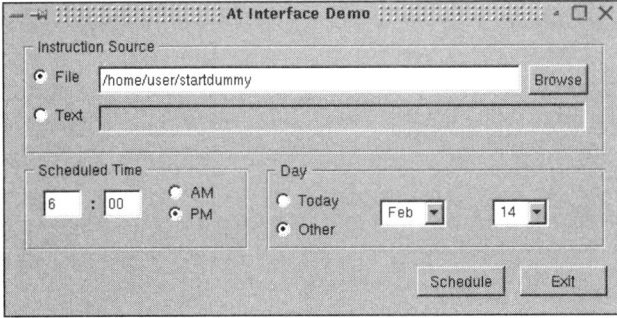

Figure 5.8
The **RunAt** program.

Listing 5.25   Snippets from frmRunAt.pas.

```
{
  frmRunAt - Demonstration of scheduling a task for
    running once at a later time
}
unit frmRunAt;

{ . . . }

function TRunAtMainForm.CreateCommandline(var Cmd : String;
                                    var Parms : String) : Boolean;
begin
 Cmd := '';
 Parms := '';
 Result := False;

 { Do the hours }
 if (StrToInt(HoursEdit.Text) > 0) and (StrToInt(HoursEdit.Text) < 13)
  then Cmd := HoursEdit.Text + ':'
  else begin
       ErrorMessage('Improper hours value');
       Exit;
       end;

 { Do the minutes }
 if (StrToInt(MinsEdit.Text) >= 0) and (StrToInt(MinsEdit.Text) < 60)
  then Cmd := Cmd + MinsEdit.Text
  else begin
       ErrorMessage('Improper minutes value');
       Exit;
       end;

 { Do AM/PM }
 if AMRB.Checked
  then Cmd := Cmd + 'am '
  else Cmd := Cmd + 'pm ';

 { Do Day/Month }
 if not TodayRB.Checked
  then begin
       Cmd := Cmd + MonthCombo.Items[MonthCombo.ItemIndex];
       Cmd := Cmd + ' ' + IntToStr(DayCombo.ItemIndex + 1) + ' ';
       end;

 if FileRB.Checked
  then begin { pass everything on command line }
```

```
        if (Length(FileNameEdit.Text) > 0) and
           (FileExists(FileNameEdit.Text))
         then begin
                Cmd := Cmd + '< ' + FileNameEdit.Text;
              end
         else begin
                ErrorMessage('Specified file doesn''t exist');
                Exit;
              end;
      end
  else begin { pass manual parameters separately }
        Parms := TextEdit.Text;
      end;

 Result := True;
end;

procedure TRunAtMainForm.WriteSchedule;
const
 READ_IOMode = 'r'; { read mode from pipe }
 WRITE_IOMODE = 'w'; { write mode from pipe }
var
 Command : array[0..128] of char;
 CmdLineArr : array[0..512] of char;
 CmdLine : String;
 ParamArr : array[0..512] of char;
 Params : String;
 F : PIOFile;
 ErrNum : Integer;
begin
 CmdLine := '';
 Params := '';
 if CreateCommandline(CmdLine, Params)
  then begin
        if FileRB.Checked
         then begin { pass the file name on the command line }
            errormessage(CmdLine);
              StrCopy(Command, 'at ');
              StrPCopy(CmdLineArr, CmdLine);
              StrCat(Command, CmdLineArr);

              F := popen(Command, READ_IOMode);
              ErrNum := pclose(F);
              if ErrNum <> -1
               then MessageDlg('Success', 'Your event has been '
                    +'scheduled', mtInformation, [mbOK], 0)
```

```
                        else ErrorMessage('Error encountered while trying to '
                                + 'close pipe to "at" utility');
                    end
          else begin { Send the params via stdin }
                    StrCopy(Command, 'at ');
                    StrPCopy(CmdLineArr, CmdLine);
                    StrCat(Command, CmdLineArr);
                    StrPCopy(ParamArr, Params);
                    F := popen(Command, WRITE_IOMode);
                    fputs(ParamArr, F);   { write the params line }
                    fputc(ord(LF), F);    { write the newline }
                    fputc(ord(EOT), F);    { write the EOT }
                    ErrNum := pclose(F);
                    if ErrNum <> -1
                      then MessageDlg('Success', 'Your event has been '
                            +'scheduled', mtInformation, [mbOK], 0)
                      else ErrorMessage('Error encountered while trying to '
                              + 'close pipe to "at" utility');
                    end;
          end
    else ErrorMessage('Unable to schedule the event');

end;
```

Solution Example: The **RunScheduled** Program

When you want to schedule the periodic execution of your program, the logical choice is **crontab**. The **crontab** utility (short for *cron table*) coordinates the data used by the **cron** daemon, storing the event schedules in files located in separate subdirectories **within /etc**. Each user can determine his or her own **crontab** schedule, subject to the permission of the superuser. (If the superuser determines that your scheduled tasks are consuming too much processor time, he can deny your ability to use **crontab**.)

Figure 5.9 shows a running version of the **RunScheduled** demo program. As you can see, **crontab**'s ability to deal with complex schedules is extensive. In Figure 5.9, you see that our old friend **CrashTestDummy** is about to be scheduled to run at 2:15 A.M., 6:15 A.M., and 2:15 P.M. on every weekday of every month. Clicking the Overwrite button will write out this schedule to **crontab**; clicking the Kill button will eliminate all **crontab** entries for this user.

Warning

*The **RunScheduled** demo is exactly that—a demo. It is not intended to be a full-fledged interface to **crontab**. As such, it is not able to read the current **crontab** entries and writes out only the event schedule created on the form. When that happens, any current **crontab** entries for the user will be replaced by the single event scheduled with **RunScheduled**.*

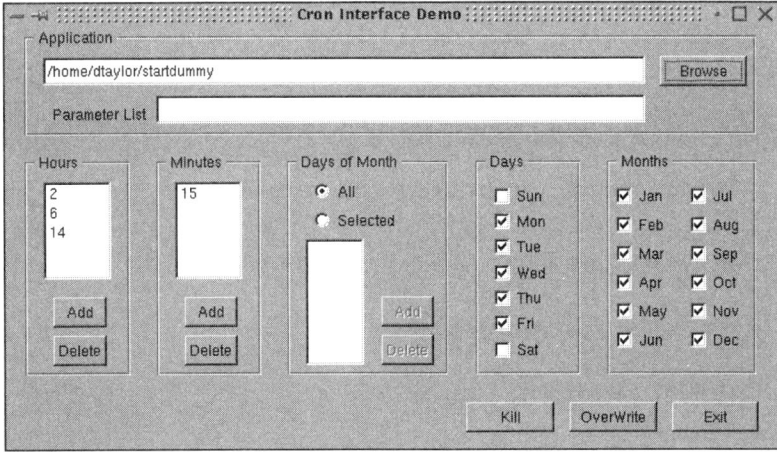

Figure 5.9
The **RunScheduled** program.

*To determine whether you have **crontab** events on record, bring up a console and type the following command:*

```
crontab -l
```

This will list any events on file for the current user. If it returns nothing, you're safe to run the demo and schedule an event.

Relevant snippets from the **RunScheduled** program's source code are shown in Listing 5.26. The **CreateCronSpec** function creates the standard data string that **crontab** requires, using the settings on the form. **KillCronFile** simply creates a pipe that reads from **stdout** and runs **crontab** with the "**-r**" parameter, telling it to kill any **crontab** entries for this user.

The **WriteCronFile** procedure has some points of interest. Because **crontab** can only take its input from a file, we have to first write our data to a file and then tell **crontab** to read it. **WriteCronFile** uses a call to the library function **tmpnam** to get a unique name for the file so we won't clobber any existing files. The specification created by **CreateCronSpec** is then written to this file, and then we pass that filename to **crontab** as a parameter on the command line. The temporary file is then deleted. At the appointed time, **CrashTestDummy** pops onto the screen.

Listing 5.26   Snippets from **frmRunScheduled.pas**.

```
{
  frmRunSCheduled - A demo visual interface to the
    crontab scheduling daemon
}
unit frmRunScheduled;
```

```
{ . . . }

const
 NumDOW = 7;
 NumMonths = 12;

{ . . . }

procedure TRunScheduledMainForm.WriteCronFile;
const
 IOMode = 'r'; { read mode from pipe (not used) }
var
 Command : array[0..128] of char;
 CronFile : TextFile;
 CronFileName : array[0..128] of char;
 CronSpec : String;
 F : PIOFile;
 ErrNum : Integer;
begin
 CronSpec := '';
 if CreateCronSpec(CronSpec)
  then begin
        tmpnam(CronFileName);
        StrCopy(Command, 'crontab ');
        StrCat(Command, CronFileName);

        AssignFile(CronFile, CronFileName);
        Rewrite(CronFile);
        Writeln(CronFile, CronSpec);
        CloseFile(CronFile);

        F := popen(Command, IOMode);
        ErrNum := pclose(F);
        if ErrNum <> -1
         then MessageDlg('Success', 'Your schedule has been '
          +'implemented', mtInformation, [mbOK], 0)
         else ErrorMessage('Error encountered while trying to '
          + 'close pipe to cron utility');

        DeleteFile(CronFileName);
       end
  else ErrorMessage('Unable to create the Cron specification file.');
end;

procedure TRunScheduledMainForm.KillCronFile;
const
 IOMode = 'r'; { read mode from pipe (not used) }
```

```
var
 Command : array[0..128] of char;
 F : PIOFile;
 ErrNum : Integer;
begin
 StrCopy(Command, 'crontab -r');
 F := popen(Command, IOMode);
 ErrNum := pclose(F);
 if ErrNum <> -1
 then MessageDlg('Success', 'All scheduled events have been killed',
         mtInformation, [mbOK], 0)
 else ErrorMessage('Error encountered while trying to '
         + 'close pipe to cron utility');
end;

function TRunScheduledMainForm.CreateCronSpec(var Spec : String) : Boolean;
var
 s : String;
 i : Integer;
 AllChecked : Boolean;
begin
 Result := False;
 Spec := '';

 { Do the minutes }
 if MinsListBox.Items.Count = 0
  then begin
        ErrorMessage('No minute times specified');
        Exit;
       end;

 for i := 0 to MinsListBox.Items.Count - 1 do
  Spec := Spec + MinsListBox.Items[i] + ',';
 if Spec[Length(Spec)] = ',' then Delete(Spec, Length(Spec), 1);
 Spec := Spec + ' ';

 { Do the hours }
 if HoursListBox.Items.Count = 0
  then begin
        ErrorMessage('No hourly times specified');
        Exit;
       end;

 for i := 0 to HoursListBox.Items.Count - 1 do
  Spec := Spec + HoursListBox.Items[i] + ',';
 if Spec[Length(Spec)] = ',' then Delete(Spec, Length(Spec), 1);
 Spec := Spec + ' ';
```

```
{ Do the Days }
if AllDaysSelected
 then Spec := Spec + '* '
 else if DOMListBox.Items.Count = 0
        then begin
                ErrorMessage('No days selected');
                Exit;
             end
        else begin
                for i := 0 to DOMListBox.Items.Count - 1 do
                  Spec := Spec + DOMListBox.Items[i] + ',';
                if Spec[Length(Spec)] = ','
                  then Delete(Spec, Length(Spec), 1);
                Spec := Spec + ' ';
             end;

{ Do the months }
UpdateMonthsArray;
AllChecked := True;
for i := 1 to NumMonths do
 AllChecked := AllChecked and MonthsBoolArray[i];

if AllChecked
 then Spec := Spec + '*'
 else begin
        for i := 1 to NumMonths do
          if MonthsBoolArray[i] then Spec := Spec + IntToStr(i) + ',';
        if Spec[Length(Spec)] = ','
          then Delete(Spec, Length(Spec), 1);
      end;
 Spec := Spec + ' ';

{ Do the DOW }
UpdateDOWArray;
AllChecked := True;
for i := 0 to NumDOW - 1 do
 AllChecked := AllChecked and DOWBoolArray[i];

if AllChecked
 then Spec := Spec + '*'
 else begin
        for i := 0 to NumDOW - 1 do
          if DOWBoolArray[i] then Spec := Spec + IntToStr(i) + ',';
        if Spec[Length(Spec)] = ','
          then Delete(Spec, Length(Spec), 1);
      end;
 Spec := Spec + ' ';
```

```
{ Do the command }
s := AppNameEdit.Text;
Spec := Spec + s;
if not FileExists(s)
 then begin
        ErrorMessage('Invalid application name');
        Exit;
      end;

{ Add any parameters }
if Length(ParamEdit.Text) > 0
 then s := s + ' ' + ParamEdit.Text;

Result := True;
end;

end.
```

Solution 5.12: Running a Program as the Superuser

There are activities your program may require that just can't be accomplished by an ordinary user. System administration utilities fall under this heading, because ordinary users don't have the permissions required to accomplish work such as configuring a piece of hardware. When these activities are required, you have no choice: You must increase your permissions—you must run as the superuser, or *root*.

Running an application as root can take several forms. The most obvious form is simply to log in as root and run the application. Although this may be practical on single-user systems (where you personally have control of the entire system), it frequently will not be an option. On administered systems, the system administrator will likely be reluctant to hand over the root password to just anyone—and rightfully so, because the root user has ultimate power (and responsibility) on the system. Fortunately there are other options that are less far reaching. We can draw on another aspect of the file permission mask to create what are called *setuid programs* and *setgid programs*.

Setuid programs run as the owner of the application's executable file. Consider, for example, an imaginary program we'll call **dwim** (short for *Do What I Mean*). To achieve this lofty goal, however, **dwim** frequently needs permissions to do things barred to ordinary users. To enable those permissions, we can ask the administrator to install the application *setuid root*, meaning the **dwim** application file (**/bin/dwim**) will be owned by root and will have its setuid bit set in the file permission mask. To set this bit, the root user will use the **chmod** command as follows:

```
chmod 4755 /bin/dwim
```

When the **ls** utility is used to examine this particular file, the screen output will be:

```
-rwsr-xr-x    1 root     root         13424 Jan 18 00:21 dwim
```

Notice the **"s"** replacing the execute permission. This indicates that the file's setuid bit has been enabled. Whenever this program is executed, it will run under the effective user ID of the root user, with all the permissions belonging to that user, regardless of the identity of the user who actually ran the program.

Naturally, none of this happens without risk. Programs executed in this way should be carefully written to prevent access to any other program on the system. For example, setuid programs should never start other processes, because those processes will also be running with root permissions. Alas, setuid programs running as root may actually cause more problems than they solve. But fortunately, there is another bit in the file permission mask that can be used to give us flexibility with less risk—the **setgid** bit.

Setgid programs run much like **setuid** programs, except the group the file belongs to is substituted for the group its current user belongs to. Whoever runs the program then inherits the permissions attributed to the file itself. Let's say that **dwim** needs to access raw disk information, but it doesn't need full root permissions. Simply running with the effective group "disk" will likely be enough. To do this, the system administrator will install **dwim** and then use the **chgrp** command to change **dwim**'s group ownership to the *disk* group, as follows:

```
chgrp disk /bin/dwim
```

He will then set the **setgid** bit in the application's permission mask, similar to what you saw for the **setuid** program, once again using the **chmod** command:

```
chmod 2755 /bin/dwim
```

The **ls** output for this application will be:

```
-rwxr-sr-x    1 root     disk         13424 Jan 18 00:21 dwim
```

Both the **setuid** and **setgid** methods work, enabling ordinary users to run applications with elevated permissions while not requiring them to know the root password. Cooperation is required from the system administrator to install applications this way, however. So be ready to explain (and justify) why your application needs special permissions to do its job.

Handling Interprocess Communication

In Chapter 5, we saw how to create, track, and destroy processes. It is when we enable processes to communicate with one another that we really begin to reap serious benefits. In this chapter, we will explore several means our Kylix applications have of communicating with other Kylix applications, other processes running on the system, and even the system itself.

While presenting several solutions in Chapter 5, we promised to go into more detail. In this chapter, we'll keep that promise. As we present solutions to various programming challenges here, you'll discover the inner workings of and uses for signals, pipes, semaphores, message queues, and memory mapping—which together achieve a wide variety of communication methods between processes.

What about Sockets?

In this chapter, we discuss mechanisms that allow processes on the same computer to communicate with each other. One mechanism we aren't going to cover is sockets.

Although the Linux socket API is most often associated with network communications, it also includes facilities for local interprocess communication. The Internet Direct component suite (Indy) that ships with Kylix provides components that implement TCP socket communications, as well as common socket protocols such as FTP, HTTP, SMTP, Telnet, and many others. The demonstration programs supplied with Indy (installed in your Kylix/Demos/internetdirect directory) provide many excellent examples of using sockets to communicate with both local and remote processes. For detailed information on sockets and their use, we suggest you study these sample programs.

Solution 6.1: Basic Messaging with Signals

If we were to pick the most fundamental interprocess communication mechanism in Linux, it would without doubt be signaling. The Linux system itself uses a defined set of signals to communicate with and control processes. Imagine for a moment the Linux kernel as a little switchboard, with a wire running out to every process running on the system. Over that connection the system can send information to processes, and processes can communicate with other processes, by sending signals through the switchboard. (Note: It's not always possible to send a signal to another process; this most commonly happens when the target process is owned by another user. Of course, if you're running as the superuser, there's no such restriction.)

The actual collection of signals available is implementation-dependent, although many of the signals are standard. Some signals cannot be ignored; others can be ignored or held by processes for later handling. Table 6.1 contains a list of the most common signals.

Table 6.1 Summary of system signals.

Name	Default Action	Description
SIGHUP	Terminate	Hangup detected from a terminal
SIGINT	Terminate	Interrupt (Ctrl+C) from keyboard
SIGQUIT	Terminate	Quit issued from keyboard
SIGILL	Terminate	Illegal instruction
SIGTRAP	Dump core	Trace/breakpont trap*
SIGABRT	Dump core	Abort
SIGUNUSED	Terminate	Unused signal
SIGFPE	Dump core	Floating-point exception
SIGKILL	Terminate	Termination signal (can't be caught or ignored)
SIGSEGV	Dump core	Invalid memory reference
SIGPIPE	Terminate	Write to pipe with no readers
SIGALRM	Terminate	Timer signal from alarm
SIGTERM	Terminate	Termination signal
SIGSTKFLT	Terminate	Stack fault on coprocessor*
SIGCHLD	Ignore	Child terminated
SIGCONT	-	Continue if stopped, otherwise ignore
SIGTSTOP	Stop process	Stop process (can't be caught or ignored)
SIGTSTP	Stop process	Stop typed at tty
SIGTTIN	Stop process	tty input for background process
SIGTTOU	Stop process	tty output for background process
SIGIO	Terminate	I/O error*
SIGXCPU	Terminate	CPU time limit exceeded*
SIGXFSZ	Terminate	File size limit exceeded*
SIGVTALRM	Terminate	Virtual time alarm*
SIGPROF	Terminate	Profile signal*
SIGWINCH	Ignore	Window resize signal*
SIGUSR1	Terminate	User-defined signal #1
SIGUSR2	Terminate	User-defined signal #2

*Not POSIX.1 conformant.

Killing with Kindness

It might at first seem strange that the **kill** function would be used for any purpose other than to terminate a process with extreme prejudice, but it is the standard function used for transmitting signals around the system. Perhaps it got its name because the default action for most of the signals received is termination of the process. Perhaps not.

In an effort to accurately report why the **kill** function was given its name, we did some serious research in the historical archives, but we came up empty-handed. So here is our speculation of how it came about (which will undoubtedly become a new urban legend):

One day, while designing the original Unix system, a developer needed a function to terminate a process by sending it a signal. Not surprisingly, he named that function "kill." A few days later the guy in the next cubicle shouted over the wall, "Hey—we need to create a general-pupose function that will send signals across the system. Maybe we ought to call it 'broadcast'."

"Nope," insisted the first guy. We've already got a function that does that. It's called 'kill'."

So it was. And everyone lived happily ever after. But they always wondered about the strange name.

As identified in Table 6.1, each signal has associated with it a default action taken by a process receiving it. You can change the action by creating a signal handler, or just trapping or ignoring the signal, if permitted. We'll show how to accomplish that when we cover the reception of signals in Solution 6.3.

Signals are sent using the **kill** library function, which takes as its arguments the process ID of the target process and the signal to be sent. By now you may have noticed that as communication devices, signals are truly primitive—although they are fast, they can carry no information in addition to the meaning inferred by the signals themselves. Unlike Windows, Linux does not provide a ready-made messaging system with thousands of unique ID numbers for messages and the ability to transmit data or pointers as part of a message. Linux does, however, provide two user-defined signals (**SIGUSR1** and **SIGUSR2**) that can be used for minimal signaling.

> **Tip**
>
> It's never a good idea to send **SIGUSR1** and **SIGUSR2** to a process, unless you are certain what the process will do when it receives them. At a minimum, the process might just terminate (the default action), but it's possible that it could wreak some havoc. For the protection of your own programs, we suggest that you add code to your programs that causes these two user-defined signals to be ignored by default.

> **Tip**
>
> If you read the man page for the **kill** function, you'll discover a special library function—**raise**—that enables a process to send signals to itself. (Note: To avoid duplicate identifiers, the libc **raise** function has been renamed **__raise** within Kylix.) Although using this function may at first seem convenient, be aware that **raise** is based on an ANSI C standard and is not POSIX compatible. Some "interesting"

*(read: unexpected) side effects may result from its use. When sending signals within a process, we recommend that you use the standard **kill** equivalent:*

```
kill(getpid, SIGNALNAME);
```

Solution Example: The **SigSender** Program

The **SigSender** program, shown in Figure 6.1, demonstrates the use of the **kill** function as a generic transmitter of signals. **SigSender** presumes you are running the **CrashTestDummy** program introduced in Chapter 5. The controls on the **SigSender** dialog box enable you to perform two signal-sending experiments. In the first, you can select one of three signals (**SIGINT**, **SIGCHLD**, or **SIGUSR1**) and send it to **CrashTestDummy**. Based on the information presented in Table 6.1 (and the fact that **CrashTestDummy** exhibits the default signal handling), you would likely expect that the receipt of the **SIGINT** and **SIGUSR1** signals by **CrashTestDummy** would cause it to terminate. That's exactly what happens. By the same logic, sending **SIGCHLD**, which by default is ignored, will have no effect.

The second function provided by **SigSender** is an attempt to send a signal that the program has no authority to send: It attempts to shut down the X Window server. If you click the Attempt To Shut Down X button, you will receive an error message.

Warning
If you run as the superuser, you actually will have permission to shut down the X Window server (or just about anything else your heart desires). That would not be wise, however, unless you enjoy trying to fumble around in a dark room, trying to find the light switch. Once again, run as the superuser only when performing system maintenance, and you'll live a much happier life.

Code from **SigSender** is presented in Listing 6.1 (edited for brevity). **SigSender** makes use of the **ProcStuff** unit presented in Chapter 5 to fetch a list of named processes executing on the system. In Chapter 5, we used the **kill** function to send a **SIGTERM** signal to **CrashTestDummy**. In the **SendBtnClick** event handler of **SigSender**, we use **kill** in a more general sense to send one of three possible signals. In the **ShutdownXBtn**

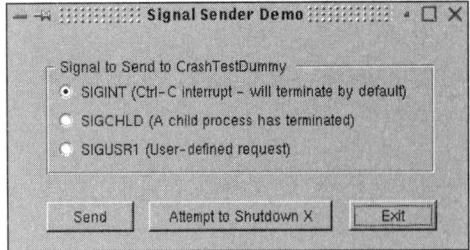

Figure 6.1
The **SigSender** Program.

event handler, we send the **SIGTERM** signal to the X process (after first making sure we're not running as the superuser).

Listing 6.1   Excerpts from **SigSendMain.pas**.

```
procedure TSigSendMainForm.SendBtnClick(Sender: TObject);
var
 i : Integer;
 ErrResult : Integer;
 SigValue : Integer;
 L : TList;
 PRec : PProcInfoRec;
begin
 ErrResult := 0;
 SigValue := -1;

 { Determine the signal value to send }
 case SigRBGroup.ItemIndex of
  0 : SigValue := SIGINT;
  1 : SigValue := SIGCHLD;
  2 : SigValue := SIGUSR1;
 end; { case }

 { Get the CTD process info if executing }
 L := GetProcessListByName('CrashTestDummy');
 if L.Count > 0
  then for i := 0 to L.Count - 1 do
   begin
    PRec := L.Items[i];
    with PRec^ do
     begin
      if MessageDlg('Sending Signal',
        'Process ' + IntToStr(i + 1) + ' of ' + IntToStr(L.Count)
        + LF + LF
        + 'Send to this process?' + LF + LF
        + 'Process ID: ' + IntToStr(PID) + LF,
        mtConfirmation, [mbYes, mbNo], 0) = mrYes
       then ErrResult := kill(PID, SigValue);
       if ErrResult <> 0
        then MessageDlg('Error', 'Unable to perform this '
          + 'operation!', mtError, [mbOK], 0);

     end; { with }
   end { for }
  else MessageDlg('Error', 'CrashTestDummy not running',
       mtError, [mbOK], 0);
 L.Free;
end;
```

```
procedure TSigSendMainForm.ShutdownXBtnClick(Sender: TObject);
var
 L : TList;
 PRec : PProcInfoRec;
 ErrResult : Integer;
begin
 ErrResult := 0;
 if (getuid = 0) { root }
  then begin
        MessageDlg('Error', 'We told you not to run this as "root"',
         mtError, [mbOK], 0);
         Exit;
        end;

 { Get the X Window process info }
 L := GetProcessListByName('X');
 if L.Count > 0
  then begin
        PRec := L.Items[0];
        with PRec^ do
         begin
          if MessageDlg('Sending Signal',
              'Send to this process?' + LF + LF
              + 'Process ID: ' + IntToStr(PID) + LF,
              mtConfirmation, [mbYes, mbNo], 0) = mrYes
            then ErrResult := kill(PID, SIGTERM);
            if ErrResult <> 0
             then MessageDlg('Error', 'Not allowed to perform this '
              + 'operation!', mtError, [mbOK], 0);
          end; { with }
        end
  else MessageDlg('Error', 'X Windows not running',
        mtError, [mbOK], 0);
 L.Free;
end;
```

Solution 6.2: Obtaining Descriptions of Valid System Signals

If you think the names given the various signals are just a bit vague, you're not alone. Wouldn't it be nice to have a way to pull up a description of any signal—a description written in plain English?

Solution Example: The **SigNames** Program

Thankfully Linux has provided a library function called **strsignal** exactly for the purpose of retrieving signal descriptions. The **strsignal** function accepts a numerical signal value for an argument, and it returns a string describing the signal. Figure 6.2 shows **SigNames**, a simple utility that makes use of the **strsignal** function.

Listing 6.2 details the operation of the event handler for the combo control in the **SigNames** program. As you can see, getting the string describing the signal is merely a matter of passing the signal value to **strsignal**. Note the system constant **NSIG**, which is defined as the maximum signal number plus one.

Listing 6.2   Combo event handler from SigNameMain.pas.

```
procedure TSigNamesForm.SigValComboClick(Sender: TObject);
var
 SigVal : Integer;
begin
 SigVal := -1;
 NamePanel.Caption := '';
 if SigValCombo.ItemIndex >= 0
  then begin
       try
        SigVal := SigValCombo.ItemIndex + 1;
       except
        on Exception do MessageDlg('Error', 'Invalid value',
            mtError, [mbOK], 0);
       end; { try }

       if (SigVal >= 0) and (SigVal < NSIG)
        then NamePanel.Caption := ' ' + strsignal(SigVal)
        else MessageDlg('Error', 'Signal value out of range', mtError,
               [mbOK], 0);
      end;
end;
```

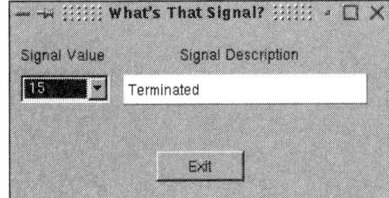

Figure 6.2
The **SigNames** program.

Solution 6.3: Creating Signal-Handling Routines

Until now, we've talked about sending signals to processes, and we've mentioned the default signal-handling behavior. If we were stuck with that default behavior, life would be pretty dull. But Linux offers us the option to write our own handlers, making the use of signals a much more powerful means of communication. For this solution, we will create a simple sender application that sends a variety of signals to a receiver application.

Solution Example: The **HndSender** Program

First, we'll concentrate on the sender application, **HndSender**. It appears in Figure 6.3. **HndSender** provides three buttons that send unique signals to another program (**HndRecvr**, which we'll discuss shortly).

Listing 6.3 details the relevant routines within **HndSender**. No surprises will be found here—we're merely using buttons to send **SIGUSR1**, **SIGUSR2**, and **SIGINT** to **HndRecvr**, assuming we find it running. We intend **SIGUSR1** to change a display's color to green and **SIGUSR2** to change it to red. **SIGINT** will be used to demonstrate some other aspects of signal handling.

Listing 6.3   Excerpts from HndSendMain.pas.

```
function SendCommand(ProcName : String;
                     SigValue : Integer) : Boolean;
var
 i : Integer;
 L : TList;
 PRec : PProcInfoRec;
 ErrResult : Integer;
begin
 ErrResult := 0;

 { Get the process info if executing }
 L := GetProcessListByName(ProcName);
 if L.Count > 0
  then for i := 0 to L.Count - 1 do
   begin
    PRec := L.Items[i];
    with PRec^ do
     begin
      if MessageDlg('Sending Signal',
        'Process ' + IntToStr(i + 1) + ' of ' + IntToStr(L.Count)
        + LF + LF
        + 'Send to this process?' + LF + LF
```

```
          + 'Process ID: ' + IntToStr(PID) + LF,
           mtConfirmation, [mbYes, mbNo], 0) = mrYes
         then ErrResult := kill(PID, SigValue);
         if ErrResult <> 0
           then MessageDlg('Error', 'Unable to perform this '
             + 'operation!', mtError, [mbOK], 0);


    end; { with }
  end { for }
 else begin
       ErrResult := -1;
       MessageDlg('Error', ProcName + ' not running',
       mtError, [mbOK], 0);
       end;

 L.Free;
 Result := ErrResult = 0;
end;

procedure THndSenderForm.GreenBtnClick(Sender: TObject);
begin
 SendCommand('HndRecvr', SIGUSR1);
end;

procedure THndSenderForm.RedBtnClick(Sender: TObject);
begin
 SendCommand('HndRecvr', SIGUSR2);
end;

procedure THndSenderForm.IntBtnClick(Sender: TObject);
begin
 SendCommand('HndRecvr', SIGINT);
end;
```

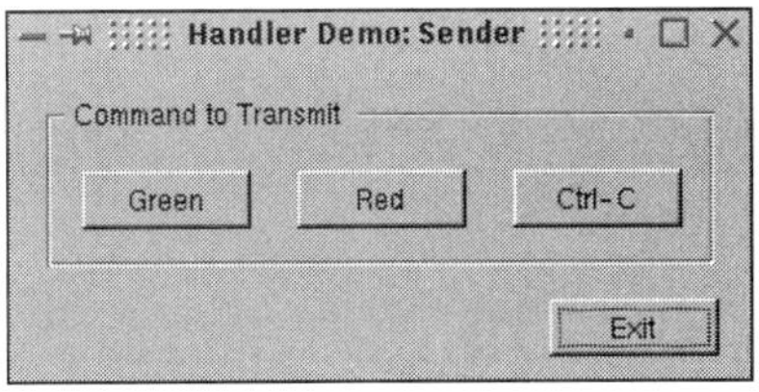

Figure 6.3
The **HndSender** program.

The **sigaction** Function and the **TSigAction** Object

The interplay of a signal handler is a bit involved, so we'll spend a little time examining it. Signal handling is controlled by the **sigaction** library function and its associated data record, wrapped into a **TSigAction** object in Kylix. The fields within a **TSigAction** object are described in Table 6.2.

The **sigaction** function takes the following form:

```
function sigaction(sig : Integer;
  action : PSigAction;
  old_action : PSigAction) : Integer;
```

If you provide a pointer to a second **TSigAction** object as its __old_action argument, **sigaction** will automatically preserve the current **TSigAction** object by copying it to __old_action. This makes it very easy to swap handlers in and out.

The **sa_mask** field contains a set of signal numbers that are to be added to the process's signal mask before __sigaction_handler is called. The signal mask blocks designated signals before they can be delivered to the process. Blocked signals are not ignored but are instead queued up so they can be detected and processed by the program in an orderly manner. This mechanism prevents the possibility of another signal being received before its handler has completed its processing. The **sa_flags** field can be used to modify how a signal is processed. Table 6.3 lists the possible values for **sa_flags**.

Table 6.2   Description of TSigAction fields.

Field Name	Description
__sigaction_handler	This field can contain either a reference to a procedure (of type **TsigActionHandler**) or one of two system constants. If a procedure is specified, it must take a single integer argument that specifies the signal number to be handled. The two acceptable constants which may be used in place of the procedure reference are **SIG_DFL** and **SIG_IGN**. **SIG_DFL** causes the specified signal to be handled with its default handler; **SIG_IGN** simply causes the signal to be ignored, if possible.
sa_mask	A set containing the signals to be blocked and not delivered to the process.
sa_flags	An integer used as a flag to modify the action of the signal handler.

Table 6.3   Valid sa_flags values.

Constant	Behavior
SA_NODEFER	Specifies not to add captured signals to the signal mask
SA_RESTART	Restarts the interruptible functions
SA_RESETHAND	Restores the default handling when the signal is received
SA_NOCLDSTOP	Suppresses the transmission of **SIGCHLD**

signal or *sigaction?*

The **signal** library function was originally used to install a signal handler. Unfortunately, **signal** leaves handlers open to "race conditions," where signals that arrive while other signals are being processed can cause unpredictable (and unpleasant) results.

The X/Open and POSIX specifications recommend using the newer **sigaction** function. With its abilities to dynamically change signal sets and change the behavior of how signals are handled, **sigaction** provides a much more robust capability for signal handling. When writing new applications, always use **sigaction** instead of **signal**.

A little explanation is in order. Normally, a signal is added to the signal mask when it's received, as a means of blocking the signal so that the handler can complete its action before being presented with the newly received signal—a situation that can cause problems if you're not careful. **SA_NODEFER** eliminates the blocking, so the handler will see a second signal when it is received.

Many system calls can be interrupted during their execution, causing them to return an error condition. Specifying **SA_RESTART** will instead cause the system call to be restarted as soon as the handler completes its action.

Once a handler is installed with **sigaction**, it remains until replaced—unless **sa_flags** has been set to **SA_RESETHAND**. In this case, the handler returns to the default behavior the next time the signal is received.

Finally, any child process will automatically generate a **SIGCHLD** signal when it terminates. Setting **sa_flags** to **SA_NOCLDSTOP** suppresses this action.

Signal Set Management

Linux provides us with an array of library routines for managing the process signal mask. Table 6.4 describes these functions. We'll be using several of the signal-management functions in our **HndRecvr** example.

Table 6.4 Signal-management functions.

Function Name	Description
sigemptyset	Creates an empty set
sigfillset	Creates a set containing all valid signals
sigaddset	Adds a specified signal to a specified set
sigdelset	Removes a specified signal from a specified set
sigismember	Returns 1 if a specified signal is a member of a specified set, returns 0 if it is not, and returns -1 if the specified signal was invalid
sigprocmask	Allows signals to be added or removed from the process signal mask or the signal mask to be set from a specified set
sigpending	Creates a set containing all the currently pending signals for a process
sigsuspend	Suspends execution of a process until one of a specified set of signals is received

Safe Signaling

Not all library functions can be used safely within signal handlers because they may not be reentrant or they may, themselves, raise signals. To avoid problems, make certain you call only those library functions listed here:

access	**alarm**	**cfgetispeed**	**cfgetospeed**	**cfsetispeed**
cfsetospeed	**chdir**	**chmod**	**chown**	**__close**
creat	**dup2**	**dup**	**execle**	**execve**
__exit	**fcntl**	**fork**	**fstat**	**getegid**
geteuid	**getgid**	**getgroups**	**getpgrp**	**getpid**
getppid	**getuid**	**kill**	**link**	**lseek**
mkdir	**mkfifo**	**open**	**pathconf**	**pause**
pipe	**read**	**rename**	**rmdir**	**setgid**
setpgid	**setsid**	**setuid**	**sigaction**	**sigaddset**
sigdelset	**sigemptyset**	**sigfillset**	**sigismember**	**sigpending**
sigprocmask	**sigsuspend**	**__sleep**	**stat**	**sysconf**
tcdrain	**tcflow**	**tcflush**	**tcgetattr**	**tcgetpgrp**
tcsendbreak	**tcsetattr**	**tcsetpgrp**	**time**	**times**
umask	**uname**	**ulink**	**utime**	**wait**
waitpid	**write**			

Solution Example: The **HndRecvr** Program

We're now ready to create our signal receiver, **HndRecvr**, which is shown in Figure 6.4. It requires **HndSender** to be running at the same time.

HndRecvr was created to respond to three signals: **SIGUSR1** turns the colored panel from yellow (its default color) to green. **SIGUSR2** changes it to red, and the receipt of **SIGINT** pops up a dialog box informing us that a Ctrl+C interrupt has been received. In addition, **HndRecvr** also affords us some tools to experiment with signal handling. The radio button group lets us determine how signals will be handled (via a special handler, the default handler, or just ignored), and a checkbox lets us block **SIGINT**.

The relevant code portions of **HndRecvr** are shown in Listing 6.4. Because a handler is of a standard format, you can either write a separate handler for each signal to be handled or use a single handler for several signals. Here, we've chosen to write a single handler (called **Handler**) for all three signals, assigning the specific action for each through a **case** statement.

The three possible handler configurations are set up by **InstallHandlers**, **DefaultHandlers**, and **IgnoreHandlers**. In each case, the same methodology is used to create values for the fields in **SigActionRec**. First, the __sigaction_handler field is set to the name of the handler (or, in the cases of **DefaultHandlers** and **IgnoreHandlers**, to predefined constants).

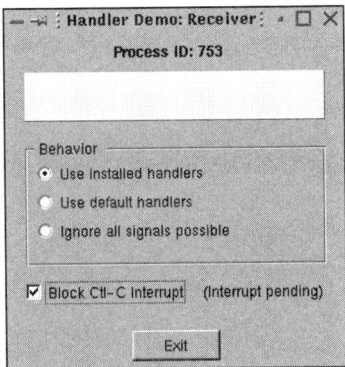

Figure 6.4
The **HndRecvr** program.

The **sa_mask** is then assigned to an empty set, and **sa_flags** is cleared. Finally, **sigaction** is called for each signal to be assigned to **SigActionRec**.

When **HndRecvr** is executed with **Handler** installed, it exhibits the behavior previously described. Selecting "Use default handlers" causes **HndRecvr** to terminate when any signal is received from **HndSender**. Also, switching to "Ignore all signals possible" does exactly that—clicking the buttons on **HndSender** has no effect on **HndRecvr**.

Checking the Block Ctl+C Interrupt box puts another mechanism in motion, creating an empty set in **ProcMask** and then adding **SIGINT** to that set. The **sigprocmask** function is then used to establish the set as the signal process mask, telling it to either block or unblock the signals within it, based on the setting of the checkbox. If a **SIGINT** signal arrives and blocking has been enabled, the signal will be captured. A timer examines the set of pending signals every 250ms, and if **SIGINT** is found to be a member of that set, a pending message is displayed. (Unchecking the box while a signal is listed as pending will immediately release the signal, causing the "Received a Ctrl+C Interrupt!" message to pop up.

Listing 6.4   Excerpts from HndRecvrMain.pas.

```
var
  HndRecvrForm: THndRecvrForm;
  SigActionRec: TSigAction;


procedure Handler(Sig : Integer); cdecl;
begin
 case Sig of
  SIGUSR1 : HndRecvrForm.ColorPanel.Color := clGreen;
  SIGUSR2 : HndRecvrForm.ColorPanel.Color := clRed;
  SIGINT  : ShowMessage('Received a Ctrl+C Interrupt!');
 end; { case }
end;
```

```
procedure InstallHandlers;
begin
 with SigActionRec do
  begin
   __sigaction_handler := Handler;
   sigemptyset(sa_mask);
   sa_flags := 0;
   sigaction(SIGUSR1, @SigActionRec, nil);
   sigaction(SIGUSR2, @SigActionRec, nil);
   sigaction(SIGINT, @SigActionRec, nil);
  end; { with }
end;

procedure DefaultHandlers;
begin
 with SigActionRec do
  begin
   __sigaction_handler := TSigActionHandler(SIG_DFL);
   sigemptyset(sa_mask);
   sa_flags := 0;
   sigaction(SIGUSR1, @SigActionRec, nil);
   sigaction(SIGUSR2, @SigActionRec, nil);
   sigaction(SIGINT, @SigActionRec, nil);
  end; { with }
end;

procedure IgnoreHandlers;
begin
 with SigActionRec do
  begin
   __sigaction_handler := TSigActionHandler(SIG_IGN);
   sigemptyset(sa_mask);
   sa_flags := 0;
   sigaction(SIGUSR1, @SigActionRec, nil);
   sigaction(SIGUSR2, @SigActionRec, nil);
   sigaction(SIGINT, @SigActionRec, nil);
  end; { with }
end;

procedure THndRecvrForm.BlockIntCBClick(Sender: TObject);
var
 ProcMask : sigset_t;
begin
 sigemptyset(ProcMask);
 sigaddset(ProcMask, SIGINT);
```

```
  if BlockIntCB.Checked
    then sigprocmask(SIG_BLOCK, @ProcMask, nil)
    else sigprocmask(SIG_UNBLOCK, @ProcMask, nil);
end;

procedure THndRecvrForm.MonitorTimerTimer(Sender: TObject);
var
 PendingMask : sigset_t;
begin
 sigpending(PendingMask);
 if sigismember(PendingMask, SIGINT) <> 0
   then StatusLabel.Caption := '(Interrupt pending)'
   else StatusLabel.Caption := '';
end;
```

Solution 6.4: Preventing Zombie Processes

In Solution 5.2 we briefly discussed "zombies" and promised to discuss them later in more depth. It's time to keep that promise. With the exception of **init**, every process running under Linux is a child that at some point in time was started by a parent process. The Linux system keeps track of this genealogy, which can be traced by running the **ps** command and examining the output. When a process is terminated, it may leave behind parents, children, or both, and some cleanup of the process tables needs to take place so the system retains the correct genealogy.

As the process terminates, the system determines if the process has one or more children; if so, the children are "adopted" by the **init** process—it becomes their new parent. The system issues a **SIGCHLD** signal to the parent of the terminating process. If the process's parent is **init**, everything is finished, because **init** will take care of any cleanup. But if the terminating process has a real parent still running, the terminating process leaves an entry in the process table. If that continued day and night, the table could get pretty large.

The intent of **SIGCHLD** is to give the parent an opportunity to react to the termination of a process it started, but the default is for processes to ignore **SIGCHLD**. The result is that "zombies" languish in the process table until the parent terminates and **init** takes over their management. To make sure zombies are automatically taken care of, then, we simply need to process **SIGCHLD**, which means creating a handler for it. The system expects the parent to use some variation of the **wait** function to process **SIGCHLD**, so that's what we'll do.

Solution Example: The **KillAllZombies** Program

Figure 6.5 displays a simple test program called **KillAllZombies**, which terminates an executing copy of **CrashTestDummy** and cleans up the resulting zombie. To run this program, you'll need to have **CrashTestDummy** installed in your home directory. When the Launch CTD button is pressed, it launches a copy of **CrashTestDummy**. When **CrashTestDummy**

Figure 6.5
The **KillAllZombies** program.

is terminated with the **SIGCHLD** handler Installed radio button selected, a dialog box pops up, informing you that the child process has completed. If you run a terminal window alongside the program and monitor the process table with **ps**, you will just see **CrashTestDummy** disappear from the table. If you instead select the Use default handler radio button, no message will be displayed—but you'll see the **CrashTestDummy** process turn into a zombie in **ps**.

Relevant routines from **KillAllZombies** are contained in Listing 6.5. **CrashTestDummy** is "forked and exec'd" in the **onClick** event handler for **LaunchBtn**, and the combination of a timer and a flag variable detect whether or not the **SIGCHLD** signal has been processed by the **Handler** procedure.

If the installed **Handler** detects a **SIGCHLD** signal, the **waitpid** function is called, using the process ID of the child as well as the constant **WNOHANG** (so **KillAllZombies** won't freeze, just in case the process ID associated with the signal doesn't match that of the child). On success, the **ChildDone** flag is set, and the monitor timer soon detects the change in status and disables itself, displays the "Child process completed" message, and reenables the Launch button.

Listing 6.5   Excerpts from KillZombiesMain.pas.

```
const
 LF = ^J; { ASCII linefeed/newline }
var
  KillAllZombiesForm: TKillAllZombiesForm;
  SigActionRec : TSigAction;
  ChildDone : Boolean;
  ChildPID : pid_t;
…
procedure Handler(Sig : Integer); cdecl;
begin
 case Sig of
  SIGCHLD : begin
```

```pascal
                    if waitpid(ChildPID, nil, WNOHANG) = ChildPID
                      then ChildDone := True;
                  end;
   end; { case }
 end;

 procedure InstallHandlers;
 begin
  with SigActionRec do
   begin
     __sigaction_handler := Handler;
     sigemptyset(sa_mask);
     sa_flags := 0;
     sigaction(SIGCHLD, @SigActionRec, nil);
   end; { with }
 end;

 procedure DefaultHandlers;
 begin
  with SigActionRec do
   begin
     __sigaction_handler := TSigActionHandler(SIG_DFL);
     sigemptyset(sa_mask);
     sa_flags := 0;
     sigaction(SIGCHLD, @SigActionRec, nil);
   end; { with }
 end;

 procedure TKillAllZombiesForm.RefreshForm;
 begin
  case BehaviorRBGroup.ItemIndex of
   0 : InstallHandlers;
   1 : DefaultHandlers;
  end; { case }
 end;

 procedure TKillAllZombiesForm.LaunchBtnClick(Sender: TObject);
 var
  i : Integer;
  FName : String;
  argv : array[0..1] of PChar;
  open_max : Integer;

 begin
  FName := 'CrashTestDummy';
```

```
    argv[0] := PChar(FName);
    argv[1] := nil;

    if not FileExists(FName)
     then begin
           MessageDlg('Error', 'Cannot locate the file ' + FName + '.' + LF
             + 'Make sure a copy is present in your' + LF
             + 'home directory.',
             mtError, [mbOK], 0);
            Exit;
          end;

    ChildPID := fork;
    case ChildPID of
     -1 : { This is still the parent }
          MessageDlg('Error', 'Could not launch child process.',
            mtError, [mbOK], 0);

      0 : begin { This is the child }
           { Close the open files }
           open_max := sysconf(_SC_OPEN_MAX);
           for i := stderr + 1 to open_max - 1 do
            fcntl(i, F_SETFD, FD_CLOEXEC);

            FName := 'CrashTestDummy';
            execlp(PChar(FName), @argv, nil);

            { If execlp failed then bail the child }
            __exit(-1);
          end;
     else { This is the parent, so disable the button }
      LaunchBtn.Enabled := False;
      ChildDone := False;
      MonitorTimer.Enabled := True;
     end { case }
    end;

procedure TKillAllZombiesForm.MonitorTimerTimer(Sender: TObject);
begin
 if ChildDone
  then begin
        MonitorTimer.Enabled := False;
        ShowMessage('Child process completed.');
        LaunchBtn.Enabled := True;
       end;
end;
```

Solution 6.5: Communicating with Console Applications via Pipes

One powerful method for communicating between processes is through the use of pipes. As you would expect from its name, a *pipe* connects a supply to its consumer, typically passing content in a single direction. In this and the following two solutions, we'll talk about three different variations of pipes, demonstrating how each one can be used to communicate between processes. In this solution, we will concentrate on the use of the **popen** function and how it can be used to connect Kylix GUI applications to command line–driven programs.

Figure 6.6 presents one way to visualize a generic Linux process. As you can see, the process has one input and two outputs (here made to resemble conventional pipe fittings) with which it directs data. In Linux, nearly everything is treated as a file, including directories and even hardware devices. (Remember the **mount** command? It attaches a hardware device such as a CD-ROM drive to a "mount point" in the filesystem structure.)

Even though there are subtle variations in the way some specialized files are handled, casting data-transfer mechanisms as files provides an overall consistency to Linux's handling of data. You can pretty much deal with any "file" with only five functions: **open**, **__close**, **__read**, **__write**, and **ioctl**. As you'll soon see, pipes are yet another special type of file (are you surprised?), and you'll find yourself using four of those five functions, depending on the type of pipe you're using.

Accessing a file requires a *file descriptor*—a unique number (represented by a small integer) that identifies a file. The **popen** call and other calls are made using this descriptor as an argument. Each process can have several descriptors, but three are provided by default: *stdin* (the standard file from which input is received), *stdout* (the standard file on which output is written), and *stderr* (the file where error messages are written). Unless specified otherwise, stderr is connected to stdout.

Figure 6.7 illustrates the "plumbing" for a typical console process. Input is received from the keyboard, and output is sent to the console. In this case, we've plumbed stderr to a log file.

Using the **popen** function establishes a one-way pipe between one process and either the stdin or stdout of another. Because stdin and stdout are not typically used by GUI processes, at least one of the two processes connected with **popen** must be a console process. Figure 6.8 is a representation of a GUI process using a pipe to the stdout file of a console process.

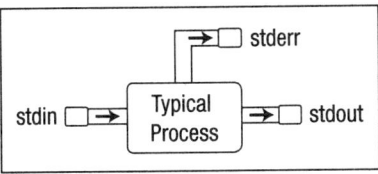

Figure 6.6
Representation of a typical Linux process.

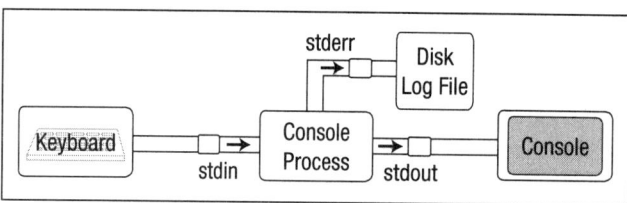

Figure 6.7
Representation of a typical console process.

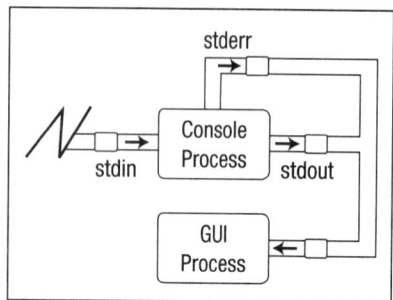

Figure 6.8
Representation of a pipe between a GUI process and a console process.

Solution Example: The **PipeRead** Program

Figure 6.9 shows **PipeRead**, a simple Kylix application that provides information on the processes currently running on a machine through the use of the **ps** command-line utility. The combo box provides several combinations of command-line arguments that are passed to **ps** when it is started with the button at the bottom of the dialog box.

To pull off its magic, **PipeRead** must be set up similar to the configuration shown in Figure 6.8. Listing 6.6 contains the relevant excerpt from **PipeRead**, showing how the piping process is set up and operated. As you can see, the **popen** function is called by providing it two pieces of information—a pointer to a character array containing the command you would issue at the command line, and a mode flag. For the command, we start with **ps** and then add the arguments selected in the combo box. Because we will be reading the output of the **ps** command, we use the **r** value for the mode flag.

If successful, the **popen** function returns a pointer to a file stream (**PIOFile**); this pointer is then used with the various Linux stream read/write functions. As you can see, we're using the **fgets** function to read strings of up to 1,023 characters (allowing one extra character for the terminating newline). When the pointer returned from **fgets** returns nil, we've read everything there is to read, and **pclose** is called to close the pipe (the stream). Although we have ignored it in this example, the **pclose** function returns an integer value: 0 if there were no errors or –1 if an error occurred. Should an error occur, the variable **errno** can be tested for a specific error description.

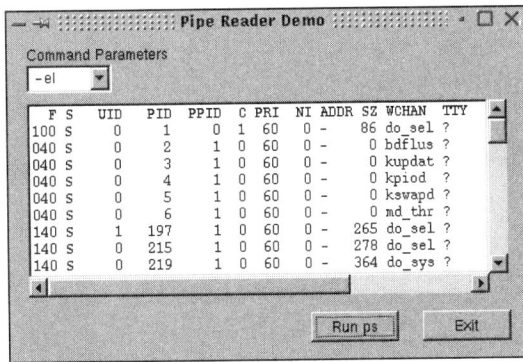

Figure 6.9
The **PipeRead** program.

Listing 6.6   Excerpt from **PipeReadMain.pas.**

```pascal
procedure TPipeReadMainForm.RunPSBtnClick(Sender: TObject);
const
  LF = ^J; { ASCII linefeed/newline }
  READ_IOMode = 'r'; { read mode from pipe }
var
  CmdArr : array[0..512] of char;
  StrArr : array[0..1024] of char;
  F : PIOFile;
  pPipeStr : Pointer;
  s : String;
begin
  psMemo.Clear;

  { Set up to run the ps command }
  StrCopy(CmdArr, 'ps');

  if ParamCombo.ItemIndex > 0
    then begin
         { Add a selected parameter }
         s := ' ' + ParamCombo.Items[ParamCombo.ItemIndex];
         StrPCopy(StrArr, s);
         StrCat(CmdArr, StrArr);
         end;

  { Open a pipe for reading from ps's output }
  F := popen(CmdArr, READ_IOMode);
  if assigned(F)
    then begin
         repeat
           { Read a complete line from the ps output stream }
```

```
      pPipeStr := fgets(StrArr, 1024, F);
      if Assigned(pPipeStr)
       then begin
             s := StrPas(pPipeStr);
             if pos(LF, s) > 0 then delete(s, pos(LF, s), 1);
             psMemo.Lines.Add(s);
           end;
     until not Assigned(pPipeStr);
     { Close the pipe - don't try to catch errors }
     pclose(F);
   end;
end;
```

Solution Example: The **RunAt** Program (Revisited)

Although not often required, it is also a simple exercise to "plumb" a GUI process to a console application in such a way that the output of a file stream from the GUI process is directed to the **stdin** file of the console application. This was actually accomplished in Solution 5.11, with the **RunAt** program. The relevant code portion from that example is reproduced in Listing 6.7.

Depending on the setting of the FileRB radio button, the code in Listing 6.7 will either read a stream back from the **at** command or will write a stream to it. The procedures used to open and close the stream for writing are identical to those for reading. But once opened, the stream can be written to with **fputs** (write out a string) and **fputc** (write out a character). As you can see here, we've used a combination of these two functions to write out a parameter string, followed by newline and end-of-text characters. It's important to send to the console process exactly what it would expect if you were sitting at a keyboard. For all practical purposes, we have completely hoodwinked the console process by setting up the pipe, and the process has no idea where its data is coming from.

Listing 6.7   Excerpt from frmRunAt.pas.

```
procedure TRunAtMainForm.WriteSchedule;
const
 READ_IOMode = 'r'; { read mode from pipe }
 WRITE_IOMODE = 'w'; { write mode from pipe }
var
 Command : array[0..128] of char;
 CmdLineArr : array[0..512] of char;
 CmdLine : String;
 ParamArr : array[0..512] of char;
 Params : String;
 F : PIOFile;
 ErrNum : Integer;
begin
 CmdLine := '';
```

```
Params := '';
if CreateCommandline(CmdLine, Params)
 then begin
        if FileRB.Checked
          then begin { pass the file name on the command line }
             errormessage(CmdLine);
                StrCopy(Command, 'at ');
                StrPCopy(CmdLineArr, CmdLine);
                StrCat(Command, CmdLineArr);

                F := popen(Command, READ_IOMode);
                ErrNum := pclose(F);
                if ErrNum <> -1
                  then MessageDlg('Success', 'Your event has been '
                          +'scheduled', mtInformation, [mbOK], 0)
                  else ErrorMessage('Error encountered while trying to '
                          + 'close pipe to "at" utility');
             end
          else begin { Send the params via stdin }
                StrCopy(Command, 'at ');
                StrPCopy(CmdLineArr, CmdLine);
                StrCat(Command, CmdLineArr);
                StrPCopy(ParamArr, Params);
                F := popen(Command, WRITE_IOMode);
                fputs(ParamArr, F);  { write the params line }
                fputc(ord(LF), F);   { write the newline }
                fputc(ord(EOT), F);  { write the EOT }
                ErrNum := pclose(F);
                if ErrNum <> -1
                  then MessageDlg('Success', 'Your event has been '
                          +'scheduled', mtInformation, [mbOK], 0)
                  else ErrorMessage('Error encountered while trying to '
                          + 'close pipe to "at" utility');
             end;
        end
   else ErrorMessage('Unable to schedule the event');

end;
```

Solution 6.6: Piping Data between Parent and Child GUI Processes

The **pipe** function from the Linux library enables us to construct a data pipe between a parent process and a child process. Unlike the type of pipe created with the **popen** function, this data pipe is treated as a *file*, not a file stream, so it uses the usual **read** and **write** library functions (renamed **__read** and **__write** for Kylix, to avoid duplicate identifiers). It does

---

Two-Way Piping

Although a data pipe is strictly a one-way device, two-way communications can be established by creating *two* pipes—one reserved for communications from the parent to the child, and the other strictly for child-to-parent messaging. As an example of this technique, we've created bidirectional versions of the **PipeParent** and **PipeChild** programs used in this solution. Both programs are available in source code format at the book's Web site, **www.kylixpowersolutions.com**.

---

not, however, use the **open** function because the pipe function performs that task automatically. Also, the pipe connection is not normally made to the stdin or stdout of a process, although that can be accomplished (if you are working with console processes). Here we will devote our attention to GUI applications on both ends of the pipe.

Figure 6.10 illustrates the pipe concept. Because this type of pipe is treated as a file, the read/write functions require a file descriptor as an argument. This assignment is made through the use of a **TPipeDescriptors** object, a packed record containing a descriptor for each end of the pipe. As shown in Figure 6.10, data for a pipe with a **TPipeDescriptors** variable of **MyPipe** is written to the pipe as **MyPipe.WriteDes** and read from the pipe as **MyPipe.ReadDes**. If you were to roll marbles down a water pipe, you would expect the first one out the other end would be the first one inserted; the same is true here—the data transmission is first in, first out (FIFO).

We're going to present two program examples that demonstrate the writing of data to a pipe by a parent GUI process and the reading of the data from a child process. To share a pipe in this manner, it must first be created by the parent; once this has been accomplished, the parent can pass one or both of the file descriptors to the child via command-line arguments.

Solution Example: **PipeParent**

Figure 6.11 shows the parent program (**PipeParent**) in action. When the user keys some text into the edit control and then clicks the Send button, the entered text is transmitted to a child process (described later) that will display it in a memo field.

Listing 6.8 contains most of the code for **PipeParent**. As you have come to expect from other functions, **pipe** returns the value 0 if successful and –1 if not. The call to **pipe** is

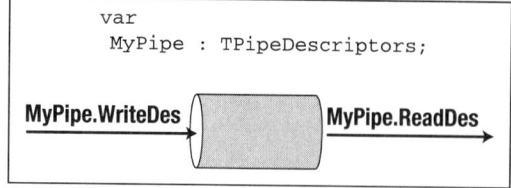

Figure 6.10
Representation of a pipe created with the **pipe** command.

Figure 6.11
The **PipeParent** program.

performed in the **onCreate** event handler. If it is successful, **PipeOpen** is assigned a value of True and the pipe is ready for use, and **PipeParent** launches **PipeChild** through the standard fork-and-exec procedure, this time passing the **ReadDes** file descriptor as a command-line argument to the child. (Note also that although files opened as part of the fork process are closed, the new pipe file descriptors are exempted from this procedure, as are **stdin**, **stdout** and **stderr**.)

We're going to allow the child to be exited by a button-press on the part of the user. If that hasn't happened when **PipeParent** is about to close, we want it to close the child automatically. So, as part of the handling of **SIGCHLD**, PipeParent keeps track of its child's status and closes it, if necessary, at program termination.

The **onClick** event handler for the Sent button sends the message. Because message lengths will vary, the child will need some way of discovering the length of the message it will be reading. This could be accomplished in a number of ways, but here we've prepended the transmitted string with a four-character string that specifies the string length. The entire string is then written to the **WriteDes** end of the pipe, and a **SIGUSR1** signal is sent to the child to let it know a message has been transmitted. Sending the signal is not absolutely necessary, but it does free the recipient from having to be blocked on a read operation, as will be discussed in Solution 6.7.

One final note: **PipeParent** relies on the system to close the pipe automatically. This might seem a bit messy, but the system closes all the files when a program terminates, and we certainly don't want to close the pipe before termination—we would lose communication with the child.

Listing 6.8   Excerpts from PipeParentMain.pas.

```
const
  StrIndexLen = 4;
  LF = ^J; { ASCII linefeed/newline }

var
  PipeParentMainForm: TPipeParentMainForm;
  SigActionRec : TSigAction;
  PipeOpen : Boolean;
  ParentPipe : TPipeDescriptors;
```

```
    PReadDesStr : String;
    ChildPID : pid_t;
    ChildDone : Boolean;

implementation

{$R *.xfm}

procedure Handler(Sig : Integer); cdecl;
begin
 case Sig of
  SIGCHLD : ChildDone := waitpid(ChildPID, nil, WNOHANG) = ChildPID;
 end; { case }
end;

procedure InstallHandler;
begin
 with SigActionRec do
  begin
   __sigaction_handler := Handler;
   sigemptyset(sa_mask);
   sa_flags := 0;
   sigaction(SIGCHLD, @SigActionRec, nil);
  end; { with }
end;

procedure LaunchChild;
var
 i : Integer;
 FName : String;
 open_max : Integer;
begin
 ChildDone := True;
 PReadDesStr := IntToStr(ParentPipe.ReadDes);
 FName := 'PipeChild';
 if not FileExists(FName)
  then begin
        MessageDlg('Error', 'Cannot locate the file ' + FName + '.' + LF
          + 'Make sure a copy is present in your' + LF
          + 'home directory.',
          mtError, [mbOK], 0);
        Exit;
       end;

 ChildPID := fork;
 case ChildPID of
```

```
  -1 : { This is still the parent }
       MessageDlg('Error', 'Could not launch child process.',
        mtError, [mbOK], 0);

   0 : begin { This is the child }
        { Close the open files }
        open_max := sysconf(_SC_OPEN_MAX);
        for i := stderr + 1 to open_max - 1 do
         if (i <> ParentPipe.ReadDes) and (i <> ParentPipe.WriteDes)
          then fcntl(i, F_SETFD, FD_CLOEXEC);

        execlp(PChar(FName), PChar(FName), PReadDesStr, nil);

        { If execlp failed then bail the child }
        __exit(EXIT_FAILURE);
       end;
  else ChildDone := False;
 end { case }
end;

procedure TPipeParentMainForm.ExitBtnClick(Sender: TObject);
begin
 if not ChildDone then kill(ChildPID, SIGTERM);
 Close;
end;

procedure TPipeParentMainForm.FormCreate(Sender: TObject);
begin
 InstallHandler;
 PipeOpen := pipe(ParentPipe) = 0;
 if PipeOpen then LaunchChild;
end;

procedure TPipeParentMainForm.FormActivate(Sender: TObject);
begin
 if PipeOpen then Label1.Caption := '[ Pipe is open ]';
end;

procedure TPipeParentMainForm.SendBtnClick(Sender: TObject);
var
 StrBuf : array[0..BUFSIZ] of Char;
 s : String;
 slen : String;
begin
 if PipeOpen
  then begin
```

```
            s := MsgEdit.Text;
            slen := IntToStr(Length(s));
            while Length(slen) < StrIndexLen do slen := '0' + slen;
            s := slen + s;
            StrPCopy(StrBuf, s);
            __write(ParentPipe.WriteDes, StrBuf, Length(s));
            kill(ChildPID, SIGUSR1);
         end;
end;
```

Solution Example: **PipeChild**

The **PipeChild** program is shown in Figure 6.12. It is a simple message receiver that places each message it receives on a new line in a **TMemo** object.

The relevant code from **PipeChild** is shown in Listing 6.9. Not surprisingly, this process is simpler than its parent—all it has to do is wake up and be able to handle a **SIGUSR1** signal to read the pipe and display the message string.

The **onCreate** event handler takes care of fetching the pipe's file descriptor and assigning it to **ParentReadPipe**. The **Handler** routine is installed to process a **SIGUSR1** signal when it is received, by executing the **ReadPipe** procedure. The pipe is read twice using **__read**—first to retrieve the 4-byte length string and then to read in the message string.

Listing 6.9   Excerpts from **PipeChildMain.pas**.

```
const
 StrIndexLen = 4;
 LF = ^J; { ASCII linefeed/newline }

var
  PipeChildMainForm: TPipeChildMainForm;
  ParentReadPipe : Integer;
  SigActionRec : TSigAction;

implementation

{$R *.xfm}

procedure Handler(Sig : Integer); cdecl;
begin
 case Sig of
  SIGUSR1 : PipeChildMainForm.ReadPipe;
 end; { case }
end;

procedure InstallHandler;
begin
```

```
 with SigActionRec do
  begin
   __sigaction_handler := Handler;
   sigemptyset(sa_mask);
   sa_flags := 0;
   sigaction(SIGUSR1, @SigActionRec, nil);
  end; { with }
end;

procedure TPipeChildMainForm.ReadPipe;
var
 ReadBuf : array[0..BUFSIZ] of Char;
 s : String;
 len : Integer;
begin
 { Get the length of the string }
 __read(ParentReadPipe, ReadBuf, StrIndexLen);
 ReadBuf[StrIndexLen] := chr(0);
 len := StrToInt(ReadBuf);

 { Get the string }
 __read(ParentReadPipe, ReadBuf, len);
 ReadBuf[len] := chr(0);
 s := ReadBuf;
 MsgMemo.Lines.Add(s);
end;

procedure TPipeChildMainForm.FormCreate(Sender: TObject);
begin
 InstallHandler;
 ParentReadPipe := StrToInt(ParamStr(1));
end;
```

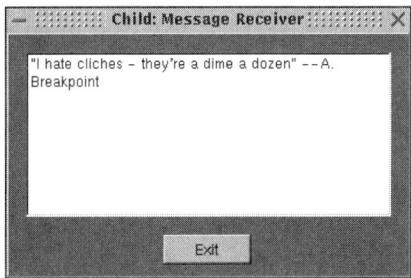

Figure 6.12
The **PipeChild** program.

Solution 6.7: Piping Data between Independent GUI Processes

In previous solutions, we have covered how to send information between a console or GUI process and a console process, and between two GUI processes that have a parent-child relationship. But what if you want to use pipes to communicate between two GUI processes that have no such relationship?

The answer is—you guessed it—another variation of the pipe. The FIFO (short for "first in, first out") is a special pipe that truly looks, acts, and smells like a file. It is frequently referred to as a *named pipe* because it is actually visible by name as a file in the Linux filesystem. Its strong point and its weak point are the same: it can be read or written to by any program that knows its name. By locating a FIFO in the /tmp directory, anyone running on a computer with access to that directory can see it, read it, or write to it. If the FIFO is created in a user's home directory, only that user (and of course, the venerable superuser) will have access to it. It's common practice to use a FIFO to enable several programs (or several instances of a single program) acting as clients to send requests to a single reader acting as a server. FIFOs are therefore a good choice for client/server applications. Including the pid of the requesting process along with requests and responses makes managing the data traffic between a server and its clients a straightforward task.

You can create a FIFO either programmatically or from the command line with the **mkfifo** command. By entering the following code, you can create a FIFO named **KYLIX_FIFO** in the **/tmp** directory:

```
mkfifo /tmp/KYLIX_FIFO
```

You can see details on the named pipe by using the **ls** command, with the –l switch:

```
prwxr-xr-x    1 ace    users        0 Feb 24  10:22  /tmp/KYLIX_FIFO
```

Notice the "p" on the left end of that line—it indicates that the "file" is actually a pipe. (Then again, the pipe is actually a file. Go figure.) A FIFO can be deleted using the **rm** command.

A FIFO is created programmatically with the **mkfifo** library function, which takes as its arguments a **PChar** to a string containing the file name, and a mode flag that contains the desired permissions for the file. (Note: the permissions specified will be altered by the user mask setting—typically 022. Specifying permissions of 777 will, with that user mask, result in a pipe with permissions of 755.) A FIFO is removed programmatically with the **unlink** system call.

As with other Linux files, access to a FIFO is obtained with the **open**, **__read**, and **__write** functions. But the way reading and writing is handled can be modified by the way the **open** function is called. The **open** function takes two arguments. The first is a **PChar** to a string containing the file name to open. The second is called the *open flag*.

A pipe can be opened for reading by specifying the system constant **O_RDONLY** as the open flag, and it can be opened for writing by specifying **O_WRONLY**. A pipe is not allowed to use the **O_RDWR** constant (open for read/write) intended for standard files (nor would you want it to be—that would be totally confusing!). Under certain circumstances, however, you can modify the open flag by performing a logical **or** on it with the constant **O_NONBLOCK**.

Normally, opening a file (including a pipe) for reading or writing will block the main program thread, so the program will halt until data can be read or written. Although this pause is very efficient in terms of CPU cycles, it still brings a program to a screeching halt as far as the user is concerned. By performing a logical **or** on **O_RDONLY** with **O_NONBLOCK**, a call to open will succeed and return immediately, even if another process has not opened the FIFO for writing. A similar effect can be achieved by performing a logical **or** on **O_WRONLY** with **O_NONBLOCK**, but this time the open call fails (returning a value of –1).

For an overall example of using named pipes for interprocess communication between two GUI processes, we will create two separate processes. **FIFOSender** will attempt to send 10 million characters to **FIFORecvr**, using the named pipe **/tmp/FIFODEMO_FIFO**.

Solution Example: **FIFOSender**

FIFOSender is a simple program that sends a large block of characters to a designated FIFO. The program is shown in operation in Figure 6.13.

Relevant portions of the program listing are shown in Listing 6.10. The **onCreate** event handler calls the routine **CreateFIFOIfNecessary**, which creates the named pipe if it can't be found. A delay mechanism is incorporated with a **TTimer** object, allowing the **onClick** handler for the Send button to complete its action (and it's able to pop back up) even if the open call blocks the thread because no reader has yet opened the named pipe. The **TTimer** handler calls the **SendIt** procedure.

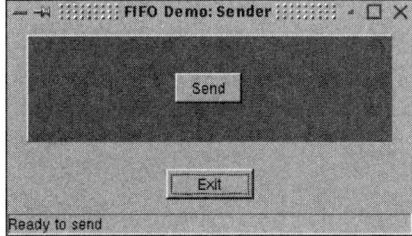

Figure 6.13
The **FIFOSender** program.

SendIt opens the pipe for writing in the blocking mode. When the accompanying **FIFORecvr** program opens the pipe for reading, the **open** function succeeds and a buffer is written out with the __**write** function until a count of at least 10 million has been reached. (For the purposes of this demo program, we don't care what the characters are—just *how many* there are.) When all characters have been written, the FIFO is closed, and the number of bytes written is displayed.

Listing 6.10   Excerpts from **FIFOSendMain.pas.**

```
const
 MIN_BYTES_TO_SEND = 10000000; { 10 million }
 FIFO_Name = '/tmp/FIFODEMO_FIFO';

var
  FIFOSendForm: TFIFOSendForm;
  FIFOOpen : Boolean;

implementation

{$R *.xfm}

procedure CreateFIFOIfNecessary;
begin
 FIFOOpen := access(FIFO_Name, F_OK) = 0;
 if not FIFOOpen
   then FIFOOpen := mkfifo(FIFO_Name, 511) = 0; { octal 777 }
end;

procedure TFIFOSendForm.SendIt;
var
 FileDesc : Integer;
 BytesSent : Integer;
 TotalBytesSent : Longint;
 Buf : array[0..BUFSIZ] of char;
begin
  FileDesc := open(FIFO_Name, O_WRONLY);
  if FileDesc <> -1
    then begin
         TotalBytesSent := 0;
         while TotalBytesSent < MIN_BYTES_TO_SEND do
           begin
             BytesSent := __write(FileDesc, Buf, BUFSIZ);
             if BytesSent = -1
               then begin
                    MessageDlg('Error', 'Error writing to FIFO!',
                      mtError, [mbOK], 0);
```

```
                         StatusBar.SimpleText := 'Ready to send';
                         Exit;
                       end;

               TotalBytesSent := TotalBytesSent + BytesSent;
             end; { while }
             __close(FileDesc);
             StatusBar.SimpleText := IntToStr(TotalBytesSent)
               + ' bytes sent';
           end
    else begin
           MessageDlg('Error', 'Unable to access FIFO!', mtError,
            [mbOK], 0);
           StatusBar.SimpleText := 'Unable to access FIFO';
         end;

end;

procedure TFIFOSendForm.FormCreate(Sender: TObject);
begin
 CreateFIFOIfNecessary;
 StatusBar.SimpleText := 'Ready to send';
end;

procedure TFIFOSendForm.FormActivate(Sender: TObject);
begin
 if not FIFOOpen
  then begin
         SendBtn.Enabled := False;
         MessageDlg('Error', 'FIFO is not open!',
          mtError, [mbOK], 0);
       end;
end;

procedure TFIFOSendForm.SendBtnClick(Sender: TObject);
begin
 SendBtn.Enabled := False;
 StatusBar.SimpleText := 'Waiting to send data to FIFO...';
 SendMonitor.Enabled := True;
end;

procedure TFIFOSendForm.SendMonitorTimer(Sender: TObject);
begin
 SendMonitor.Enabled := False;
 SendIt;
end;
```

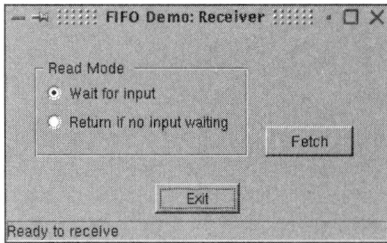

Figure 6.14
The **FIFORecvr** program.

Solution Example: **FIFORecvr**

The receiver program, **FIFORecvr**, is shown in Figure 6.14. When the Fetch button is clicked, **FIFORecvr** will attempt to read characters from the named pipe until the writing program closes the pipe on its end. A set of radio buttons enables the demo to run in either of two modes, attempting to open the pipe in blocked or unblocked mode. If the Fetch button is clicked and the Wait for input radio button is selected, the blocked mode will be specified, and the program will halt until it receives input. If the Return if no input waiting radio button is selected and the pipe has not been opened for writing, **FIFORecvr** will remain in its "ready" mode. But if the pipe is open for writing, **FIFORecvr** will immediately begin to transfer the data. When complete, the number of bytes read is displayed.

A mostly complete listing of **FIFORecvMain** appears in Listing 6.11. It duplicates much of the "mechanics" of **FIFOSendMain**, ensuring the existence of the named FIFO and using a **TTimer** to avoid some ugly repercussions of blocking.

The real work of **FIFORecvr** is performed by the **FetchIt** procedure. After the open call appropriate to the setting of the radio buttons is issued, a **repeat** loop is used to pull in characters with the **__read** function until none remain in the pipe. The **__close** function is then called to shut down the pipe.

Listing 6.11   Excerpts from FIFORecvMain.pas.

```
const
 FIFO_Name = '/tmp/FIFODEMO_FIFO';

var
  FIFORecvrForm: TFIFORecvrForm;
  FIFOOpen : Boolean;

implementation

{$R *.xfm}
```

```
procedure CreateFIFOIfNecessary;
begin
 FIFOOpen := access(FIFO_Name, F_OK) = 0;
 if not FIFOOpen
  then FIFOOpen := mkfifo(FIFO_Name, 511) = 0; { octal 777 }
end;

procedure TFIFORecvrForm.FetchIt;
var
 FileDesc : Integer;
 BytesRead : Integer;
 TotalBytesRead : Longint;
 Buf : array[0..BUFSIZ] of char;
begin
 if ReadTypeRBGroup.ItemIndex = 0
  then FileDesc := open(FIFO_Name, O_RDONLY)
  else FileDesc := open(FIFO_Name, O_RDONLY or O_NONBLOCK);

  if FileDesc <> -1
   then begin
         TotalBytesRead := 0;
         repeat
          BytesRead := __read(FileDesc, Buf, BUFSIZ);
          TotalBytesRead  := TotalBytesRead + BytesRead;
         until BytesRead = 0;
         __close(FileDesc);
         StatusBar.SimpleText := IntToStr(TotalBytesRead)
           + ' bytes read';
        end
   else begin
         MessageDlg('Error', 'Unable to access FIFO!', mtError,
          [mbOK], 0);
         StatusBar.SimpleText := 'Unable to access FIFO';
        end;

end;

procedure TFIFORecvrForm.FormCreate(Sender: TObject);
begin
 CreateFIFOIfNecessary;
 StatusBar.SimpleText := 'Ready to receive';
end;
```

```
procedure TFIFORecvrForm.FormActivate(Sender: TObject);
begin
 if not FIFOOpen
  then begin
       FetchBtn.Enabled := False;
       MessageDlg('Error', 'FIFO is not open!',
         mtError, [mbOK], 0);
      end;
end;

procedure TFIFORecvrForm.FetchBtnClick(Sender: TObject);
begin
 FetchBtn.Enabled := False;
 ReadTypeRBGroup.Enabled := False;
 StatusBar.SimpleText := 'Fetching data from FIFO...';
 RecvMonitor.Enabled := True;
end;

procedure TFIFORecvrForm.RecvMonitorTimer(Sender: TObject);
begin
 RecvMonitor.Enabled := False;
 FetchIt;
end;
```

Solution 6.8: Coordinating Processes with Semaphores

In this and the two following solutions, we're going to discuss the Unix System V interprocess communications facilities that are implemented in Linux. These facilities (semaphore sets, shared memory, and message queues) all appeared in the same Unix release (AT&T System V.2) and are commonly referred to as *System V IPC*. These facilities also have similar programming interfaces and share some common structures and commands.

Warning

*The **Libc.pas** module in the initial shipping version of Kylix contains incorrect definitions for many of the IPC data structures. By the time you read this, Borland will likely have issued a patch release that addresses this problem. At the time of this writing, programs that use the incorrect data structures will not work correctly. You can obtain a file that has the correct data structures from this book's Web site (**www.kylixpowersolutions.com**). The incorrectly defined IPC data structures are **TIpcPermission**, **TSemaphoreIdDescriptor**, **TSharedMemIdDescriptor**, and **TMsgQueueIdDescriptor**.*

Working with IPC Objects

An individual semaphore set, shared memory, or message queue is referred to as an *IPC object*. IPC objects are global system objects managed by the Linux kernel. As global system objects, they're accessible to all processes that have sufficient permissions, and they remain active until they're explicitly deleted or until the kernel is restarted.

Each individual IPC object is identified by a unique operating system–supplied ID that you obtain by passing a *key* to the object's creation function. The key is a long integer value mutually agreed upon by all applications that will use a particular IPC object. Think of the key as the index value in a lookup table. The process that creates an IPC object passes the key to the creation function. The Linux kernel creates a new IPC object, maps the key to the new object's ID, and returns the new ID to the calling process. Other processes that want to access the same object pass the same key to the creation function and receive the ID of the object to which the key was previously mapped.

Key selection is somewhat problematic. You can hard-code a key into your program, but by doing so you run the risk of your key conflicting with the key for another program. There's no way to guarantee that these conflicts won't occur, but conventions can help. In the Linux world, a very common convention is to use the **ftok** function to create a key. The **ftok** function takes a path name and a byte value as parameters and returns a key value. This doesn't guarantee a unique key, but the chances of collision are reasonably small. The path name that you pass to **ftok** can be the name of a data file that's common to the programs that will be using the IPC object or perhaps the application's installation directory. You'll see examples of using **ftok** in the solutions that follow.

Two operating system commands, **ipcs** and **ipcrm**, are used to manage the IPC objects. The **ipcs** command provides information about currently active IPC objects, and **ipcrm** removes IPC objects. Except during development, when you're likely to forget to delete an IPC object before your program exits, you won't very often need **ipcrm**. See the man pages (**man ipcs** and **man ipcrm**) for more information on these commands.

Semaphores

A *semaphore* is a counter used to control access to a shared resource. For example, on a computer with a single printer and no printing queue, it's imperative that processes cooperate when accessing the printer. The results, if they fail to cooperate, aren't pretty. How would you like your latest program listing interleaved with the Accounting department's end of year reports?

To prevent this ugliness, processes that access the printer could agree to use a semaphore to control access to the printer. The first process to access the printer attempts to *lock* the semaphore. Because the printer isn't busy, the lock succeeds. The first process then begins sending its output to the printer. Meanwhile, the second process comes along and tries to lock the semaphore. Because the first process already has the semaphore locked, the second process's lock attempt fails. The second process must then either wait for the first process to *release* the semaphore (*wait*) or come back later and try again (*poll*). When the first process has finished sending its output to the printer, it unlocks the semaphore so other processes can use it.

Semaphores aren't limited to simple binary (locked or unlocked) states. Perhaps a particular resource can accept up to three connections. In that case, you can create a semaphore with an initial value of 3 so that the first three processes that attempt to lock the semaphore will succeed, but if a fourth comes along, it will have to wait until one of the first three is finished using the resource and releases the semaphore.

In System V IPC, semaphores are implemented as sets, where a set can contain one or more (up to a kernel-defined limit) semaphores. This makes it easy to create a single set of semaphores for controlling multiple similar objects. For example, a computerized telephone switching system might control five outside lines. Because it's controlling five different devices rather than a single device that can accept five connections, the switch would create a set of five semaphores. When requested to make an outgoing call, the switch examines the semaphore set to find one that is not currently locked. If it finds one, it locks the semaphore and places the call, unlocking the semaphore when the call is completed.

The Semaphore Functions

Programs use three functions to operate on semaphore sets. The functions and their descriptions are shown in Table 6.5.

All these functions return –1 in the case of an error. If an error occurs, the error number will be in the global variable **errno**.

You'd think that with only three API functions, semaphores would be simple to understand and easy to use. Nothing could be further from the truth. Those three functions can do a lot. We won't go into a full discussion of all those functions here. For that, you should refer to the man pages (**man semget**, and so on). Instead, we'll focus on describing how these functions are typically used in a program.

Table 6.5   The semaphore functions.

Function	Description
semget	function **semget (key: key_t; nsems: integer; flags: integer): integer;** Creates or opens a semaphore set.
semctl	function **semctl (semid: integer; semnum: integer; cmd: integer; arg:TSemUnion): integer;** Performs control commands on individual semaphores or an entire semaphore set.
semop	function **semop (semid: integer; sops: PSemaphoreBuffer; nsops: size_t): integer;** Performs the operations specified in the **sops** pointer. The number of operations is supplied in **nsops**.

Creating and Opening Semaphore Sets

Before you can do anything else with a semaphore set, it must be created. Typically, the semaphore set is created by a server application when it starts. Client applications then open the semaphore set by passing the agreed-upon key. In cases where there is no clear client/server distinction (cooperating processes, for example), the first process that needs to use the semaphore set creates it.

When calling **semget**, the **key** parameter is the agreed-upon key you assign to the semaphore set—it's either a constant number or a value generated by a call to **ftok**. The **nsems** parameter is the number of semaphores you want the set to contain. This number must be greater than zero and less than the kernel's maximum semaphores number (currently 500).

If you want to create a semaphore set that is private to your application, you can specify **IPC_PRIVATE** for the **key** parameter. This is useful if you don't need to share your semaphores with other processes and want to ensure that a unique semaphore set is created for your application. You might use this feature in a multithreaded application, for example.

The **flags** parameter specifies creation flags and the access mode bits. The access mode bits take up the lower nine bits and are similar to file-access mode bits. Table 6.6 lists creation flags that can be specified.

You **OR** the values together in order to create a single **flags** parameter. For example, to open an existing semaphore set, or create it if it doesn't already exist, you would use code like this:

```
const
  { Give read and write permissions to User and Group. No access to others }
  AccessMode = S_IREAD or S_IWRITE or S_IRGRP or S_IWGRP;
  KeyValue = 1234;
  NumSems = 10;
var
  semid : Integer;
begin
  semid := semget (KeyValue, NumSems, IPC_CREAT or AccessMode);
  if semid = -1 then
    // Some error occurred. Error value is in errno.
```

This code attempts to open the semaphore set identified by key 1234. If no such semaphore set exists, it will be created.

Table 6.6   Creation flags.

Flag	Function
IPC_CREAT	Creates the semaphore set if it doesn't exist
IPC_EXCL	Fails if the semaphore set already exists (used with **IPC_CREAT**)

If you just want your program to open an existing semaphore set and fail if it doesn't exist, you don't need to specify the number of semaphores or the access mode. In that case, the code would look like this:

```
semid := semget (KeyValue, 0, 0);
```

The return value will be –1 if the semaphore set wasn't previously created.

If you want your program to create the semaphore set and fail if it already exists, you need to include **IPC_EXCL** in the **flags** parameter:

```
semid := semget (KeyValue, NumSems, IPC_CREAT or IPC_EXCL or AccessMode);
```

If your program creates a semaphore set, it has to set the initial values of the semaphores. That is one of the tasks performed by the **semctl** function.

Controlling Semaphores with **semctl**

The **semctl** function is used to perform many different semaphore control tasks, including removing (deleting) the semaphore set, getting the value of one or all semaphores, setting the value of one or all semaphores, getting status information, and setting options. The command to perform these tasks is specified in the **cmd** parameter. Table 6.7 lists commonly used commands. See the man page (**man semctl**) for a full listing of all the **semctl** command values.

The **arg** parameter to **semctl** is of type **TSemUnion**. This type is not defined in the Libc module or any other Kylix-supplied unit. Users are expected to define it themselves. In fact, because some **semctl** commands don't require the structure, it's actually optional. If you look in Libc.pas, the declaration of **semctl** looks like this:

```
function semctl(__semid: Integer; __semnum: Integer; __cmd: Integer):
  Integer; cdecl; varargs;
```

Table 6.7 Commonly used semctl commands.

Command	Description
IPC_STAT	Returns information from the semaphore set data structure
IPC_SET	Sets values from the semaphore set data structure
IPC_RMID	Removes (deletes) the semaphore set
GETVAL	Returns the value of the semaphore specified by **semnum**
SETVAL	Sets the value of the semaphore specified by **semnum**

How's *that* for confusing? It gets better. The type of the last argument depends on the value of **cmd**. The Linux documentation and the sem.h header file define a variant record (a *union* in C parlance) that looks like this:

```
TSemUnion = record
  case integer of
    0: (val: Integer);                    // value for SETVAL
    1: (buf: PSemaphoreIDDescriptor);     // buffer for IPC_STAT and IPC_SET
    2: (ary: PWord);                      // array for GETALL and SETALL
    3: (__buf: PSemaphoreInfo);           // buffer for IPC_INFO
end;
```

The convention is to declare a variable of this type, set the appropriate member based on the command value, and then pass the variable to **semctl**. Perhaps some examples will clarify things.

Getting and Setting a Semaphore's Value

The first thing you need to do after you create a semaphore set is set the individual semaphores' values. For that, you need to call **semctl** and pass it a value of **SETVAL** for each semaphore. The **SemSetValue** procedure, shown here, will set the value of a given semaphore in the semaphore set identified by the **semid** parameter:

```
procedure SemSetValue (semid: Integer; semnum: Integer; aVal: Integer);
var
  arg: TSemUnion;
begin
  arg.val := aVal;
  if semctl (semid, semnum, SETVAL, arg) = -1 then
    raise Exception.Create (strerror (errno));
end;
```

Similarly, if you want to retrieve the value of an individual semaphore, you specify the **GETVAL** command, as shown in the **SemGetValue** function:

```
function SemGetValue (semid: Integer; semnum: Integer): Integer;
begin
  Result := semctl (semid, semnum, GETVAL);
  if Result = -1 then
    raise Exception.Create (strerror (errno));
end;
```

Note that this function doesn't supply a fourth parameter to **semctl**, because it's not needed for the **GETVAL** command.

Getting and Setting the Semaphore Data Structure

The semaphore data structure, **TSemaphoreIDDescriptor** (defined in Libc.pas), contains a wealth of information about the semaphore data set. Most of the information isn't generally useful to typical programs, but one field in particular, the **sem_nsems** member, is critical. If you open an existing semaphore set, you need to check this value to see how many semaphores are in the set. The **SemGetNumSems** function will return that value:

```
function SemGetStat (semid: Integer): TSemaphoreIDDescriptor;
var
  arg: TSemUnion;
  ds: TSemaphoreIDDescriptor;
begin
  arg.buf := @ds;
  if semctl (semid, 0, IPC_STAT, arg) = -1 then
    raise Exception.Create (strerror (errno));
  Result := ds;
end;

function SemGetNumSems (semid: Integer): Integer;
begin
  Result := SemGetStat (semid).sem_nsems;
end;
```

Note that in this case we're working with the semaphore set rather than an individual semaphore within the set, so the **semnum** parameter is ignored. The convention is to pass 0 in this case.

Applications are allowed to change a handful of fields in the semaphore data structure. This is accomplished by getting the data structure (as shown previously), setting the new values in the data structure, and then applying the changes by calling **semctl** again with the command **IPC_SET**. Of the fields that applications are allowed to change, the most commonly used is the access mode. The following **SemGetAccessMode** and **SemSetAccessMode** functions get and set the access mode value in the semaphore set's data structure:

```
function SemGetAccessMode (semid: Integer): Integer;
begin
  Result := SemGetStat (semid).sem_perm.mode;
end;

procedure SemSetStat (semid: Integer; const ds: TSemaphoreIDDescriptor);
var
  arg : TSemUnion;
begin
  arg.buf := @ds;
  if semctl (semid, 0, IPC_SET, arg) = -1 then
    raise Exception.Create (strerror (errno));
end;
```

```
procedure SemSetAccessMode (semid: Integer; aMode: Integer): Integer;
var
  ds : TSemaphoreIDDescriptor;
begin
  ds := SemGetStat (semid);
  ds.sem_perm.mode := aMode;
  SemSetStat (semid, ds);
end;
```

Removing a Semaphore Set

When a semaphore set is no longer needed (that is, before the last process using it exits), you should remove it from the system. IPC objects take up valuable global resources, so they should be removed when they're no longer required. To remove a semaphore set, you call **semctl** with the command **IPC_RMID**, like this:

```
procedure SemRemoveSet (semid: Integer);
begin
  if semctl (semid, 0, IPC_RMID) = -1 then
    raise Exception.Create (strerror (errno));
end;
```

There is no locking mechanism to prevent a semaphore set from being removed while other processes are using the semaphores. Applications that use semaphore sets must agree to "play nice" so that one doesn't pull the rug out from underneath the other. In the case of a client/server application, the server application is tasked with creating and deleting the semaphore set. The semaphore access function (**semop**) described in the next section returns an error if the semaphore set has been removed.

Locking and Releasing Semaphores

The **semop** function allows you to increment and decrement the value of a particular semaphore within a semaphore set. The function's interface allows you to perform multiple operations on one or more semaphores with a single call so that you could, for example, release one semaphore and lock another in a single operation. The most common usage, though, is to perform a single increment or decrement operation to lock or release a semaphore.

The first argument to **semop** is the semaphore set id that was returned by **semget**. The second argument is a pointer to a **TSemaphoreBuffer** structure (or an array of those structures) that defines the operations to be performed. The last argument specifies the number of operations to be performed (the number of items in the array pointed to by the second parameter). The **TSemaphoreBuffer** structure looks like this:

```
TSemaphoreBuffer = record
  sem_num : Smallint;  { semaphore number }
  sem_op: Smallint;    { operation to perform }
  sem_flg: Smallint;   { operation flags }
end;
```

Here, **sem_op**, the operation to perform, is the value by which you want to increment or decrement the semaphore. In most cases, this will be 1 (release) or –1 (lock). It is possible, however, to increment or decrement by more than 1.

To lock or release a semaphore, you declare and populate a variable of type **TSemaphore-Buffer** and pass the address of that variable to **semop**, as shown in the following **SemDoOp** function:

```
function SemDoOp (semid, semnum, op, flags: Integer): boolean;
var
  buf : TSemaphoreBuffer;
begin
  buf.sem_num := semnum;
  buf.sem_op := op;
  buf.sem_flg := flags;
  if sem_op (semid, @buf, 1) = -1 then
    if (errno = EINTR) or (errno = EAGAIN) then
      Result := false
    else
      raise Exception.Create (strerror (errno))
  else
    Result := true;
end;
```

The default behavior of **semop** is to attempt the operation and to block (wait) if it can't complete the operation. If you're incrementing the semaphore value (releasing the semaphore), it will never block. If you're attempting to lock the semaphore (decrease its value), and the value is already zero, **semop** will wait until some other process releases the semaphore.

If the value of **sem_op** is zero, the process blocks until the value of the semaphore goes to zero. This is useful if you want your program to wait for a semaphore to be locked. Like the other semaphore functions, **semop** returns –1 if it's unsuccessful. But "unsuccessful" in this case doesn't necessarily mean "error." There are two cases in which the function can fail, but they aren't really errors. If **semop** returns –1 and the global variable **errno** is set to **E_INTR**, it means that your program was waiting on a semaphore (that is, you tried to lock and were unable to) but had to stop waiting because a signal came through that the program had to handle. The other case is similar. If you specify **IPC_NOWAIT** in the **sem_flg** member, **semop** attempts the operation and returns immediately if it's unable to. In that case, it returns –1 and **errno** is set to **EAGAIN**. This allows you to try for a semaphore lock without having to wait if the semaphore isn't available. **IPC_NOWAIT** has no effect when you're incrementing a semaphore's value (releasing the semaphore).

One other flag, **SEM_UNDO**, lets the system clean up after processes that terminate without releasing semaphores that they have locked. It's considered good practice to always specify **SEM_UNDO**, unless you have a very good reason not to. There are four functions that you will typically perform with **semop**: lock a semaphore, try to lock a semaphore, release a semaphore, and wait for a semaphore's value to go to zero. The following code fragments show an example of each:

```
// lock a semaphore
SemDoOp (semid, semnum, -1, SEM_UNDO);

// try to lock a semaphore
if SemDoOp (semid, semnum, -1, SEM_UNDO or IPC_NOWAIT) then
  // semaphore locked
else
  // failed to lock

// release a semaphore
SemDoOp (semid, semnum, 1, SEM_UNDO);

// wait for 100% resource utilization
SemDoOp (semid, semnum, 0, SEM_UNDO);
```

Tip

*A common problem that occurs in applications that use semaphores is semaphore deadlock. This occurs when one process locks a semaphore and then doesn't release it. Other processes then will never be able to lock the semaphore. You can alleviate this to some extent by using the **SEM_UNDO** flag when you perform semaphore operations. That, at least, will prevent your process from leaving a semaphore locked when it exits.*

Another type of semaphore deadlock occurs when two semaphores try to control multiple resources. Suppose Process A has a lock on Semaphore 1, and Process B has a lock on Semaphore 2. Process A needs to lock Semaphore 2 before it can release Semaphore 1. Similarly, Process B needs to lock Semaphore 1 before it can release Semaphore 2. You have a deadlock because each process is waiting on the other to release a semaphore. Although this is less common than simply forgetting to release a semaphore, this type of thing does occur if you're not careful when writing your applications. The most reliable way to prevent this problem is to write your code so that processes always acquire locks in the same order. If a process wants to lock Semaphore 2, it must first lock Semaphore 1. Then, after it has acquired a lock on Semaphore 2, it can release Semaphore 1. If a process that has a lock on Semaphore 2 wants to lock Semaphore 1, it must first release Semaphore 2 and start over.

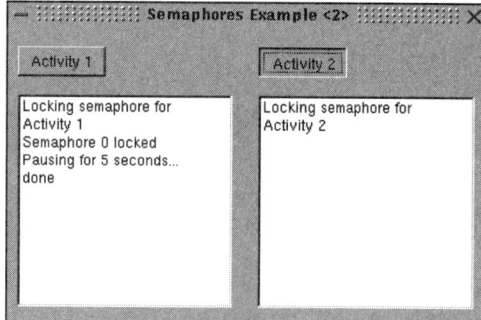

Figure 6.15
The **OneAtATime** program.

Solution Example: The **OneAtATime** Program

As an example of using semaphores to control resources, consider the **OneAtATime** program shown in Figure 6.15. This program uses a semaphore set to ensure that only one instance of the program is performing the same activity at a particular time. So, if you start two instances of the program, only one at a time may be performing Activity 1 (in the memo box on the left), and only one at a time may be performing Activity 2 (in the memo box on the right).

The activities in this program just sleep for a few seconds, but they simulate performing an activity that requires a lock on a shared resource. The source code for the program's main form is shown in Listing 6.12. The **SemFuncs** unit to which it refers contains the semaphore functions shown in the previous code examples. You can download the **SemFuncs** unit from the book's Web site.

Listing 6.12   The OneAtATime program's main form.

```
unit frmOnce;

interface

uses
  SysUtils, Libc, Types, Classes, Variants, QGraphics, QControls,
  QForms, QDialogs, QStdCtrls,
  SemFuncs;

type
  TForm1 = class(TForm)
    Button1: TButton;
    Button2: TButton;
    Memo1: TMemo;
    Memo2: TMemo;
    procedure FormCreate(Sender: TObject);
```

```
    procedure FormDestroy(Sender: TObject);
    procedure Button1Click(Sender: TObject);
    procedure Button2Click(Sender: TObject);
  private
    FSemID : Integer;
    FOwnSems : boolean;
    procedure DoActivity (mm: TMemo; sem: Integer);
  public
    { Public declarations }
  end;

var
  Form1: TForm1;

implementation

{$R *.xfm}

const
  AccessMode = S_IREAD or S_IWRITE or S_IRGRP or S_IWGRP;

procedure TForm1.FormCreate(Sender: TObject);
var
  Key : Integer;
begin
  Key := ftok (PChar(GetModuleName (0)), 1);
  // try to create a new semaphore set
  FSemID := semget (Key, 2, IPC_CREAT or IPC_EXCL or AccessMode);
  if FSemID = -1 then
  begin
    // create failed, try to open it...
    FOwnSems := false;
    FSemID := semget (Key, 0, 0);
    if FSemID = -1 then
      raise Exception.Create (strerror (errno));
  end
  else
  begin
    // created semaphores...set values
    FOwnSems := true;
    SemSetValue (FSemID, 0, 1);
    SemSetValue (FSemID, 1, 1);
  end;
end;
```

```
procedure TForm1.FormDestroy(Sender: TObject);
begin
  if FOwnSems then
    SemRemoveSet (FSemid);
end;

function SetScreenCursor (cur: TCursor): TCursor;
begin
  Result := Screen.Cursor;
  Screen.Cursor := cur;
end;

procedure TForm1.DoActivity (mm: TMemo; sem: Integer);
var
  curSave : TCursor;
begin
  curSave := SetScreenCursor (crHourGlass);
  try
    mm.Clear;
    mm.Lines.Add (Format ('Locking semaphore for Activity %d', [sem+1]));
    SemDoOp (FSemID, sem, -1, SEM_UNDO);
    try
      mm.Lines.Add (Format ('Semaphore %d locked', [sem]));
      mm.Lines.Add ('Pausing for 5 seconds...');
      __sleep (5);
      mm.Lines.Add ('done');
    finally
      SemDoOp (FSemID, sem, 1, SEM_UNDO);
    end;
  finally
    SetScreenCursor (curSave);
  end;
end;

procedure TForm1.Button1Click(Sender: TObject);
begin
  DoActivity (Memo1, 0);
end;

procedure TForm1.Button2Click(Sender: TObject);
begin
  DoActivity (Memo2, 1);
end;

end.
```

Solution 6.9: Achieving High Performance Communication with Shared Memory

The good news is that semaphores are the most complicated of the System V IPC facilities. Although the shared memory API is similar to that for semaphores, it's much simpler.

System V shared memory allows multiple processes to access the same memory, providing a very efficient way to transfer information between processes. Typically, one process will create a shared memory object and map that memory into the process's address space. Other processes can then "attach" the shared memory object to their own address spaces. Information written to the shared memory is immediately visible to all processes that are attached.

The shared memory API doesn't provide any process synchronization, so it's possible for two processes sharing memory to "step on each other" by writing to the same memory block at the same time. Typically, programs that need to synchronize access to shared memory will provide that synchronization with semaphores.

Shared Memory Functions

There are four shared memory API functions that programs use to create and control shared memory objects. These functions and their descriptions are shown in Table 6.8.

As the names imply, the **shmget** and **shmctl** functions are very similar to the semaphore functions **semget** and **semctl**. All these functions return –1 in the case of an error. If an error occurs, the error number will be in the global variable **errno**. You may think it's strange to have a function that returns a pointer (**shmat**) return an integer error value, but there you have it. Welcome to the weird world of C-centric API functions. As you'll see, we can handle that oddity with a simple typecast.

Table 6.8   The shared memory functions.

Function	Description
shmget	function **shmget (key: key_t; size: size_t; flags: Integer): Integer;** Creates or opens a shared memory object
shmat	function **shmat (shmid: Integer; shmaddr: Pointer; flags: Integer): Pointer;** Attaches a shared memory object to the process's address space
shmdt	function **shmdt (shmaddr: Pointer): Integer;** Detaches a shared memory object
shmctl	function **shmctl (shmid: Integer; cmd: Integer; buf: PSharedMemIDDescriptor): Integer;** Performs shared memory control operations

Warning

The first shipping release of Kylix contained an incorrect shared memory structure in **Libc.pas**. *Programs that use that structure will not work correctly. See the warning under Solution 6.8 for more information.*

Creating and Opening Shared Memory Objects

You create and open shared memory objects by calling the **shmget** function, which works in much the same way as the **semget** function. You create a key and then pass that key and the desired size and flags to **shmget**, which returns the shared memory ID or –1 if it was unable to perform the operation. As with semaphores, you can pass a key value of **IPC_PRIVATE** if you want a private shared memory object. The **IPC_CREAT** and **IPC_EXCL** flags also work just like they do for semaphores. Here's a code fragment that creates a new shared memory object:

```
const
  { Give read and write permissions to User and Group. No access to others }
  AccessMode = S_IREAD or S_IWRITE or S_IRGRP or S_IWGRP;
  SegmentSize = 1024;  // size of memory block to create
  KeyValue = 1234;
var
  shmid : Integer;
begin
  shmid := shmget (KeyValue, SegmentSize,
    IPC_CREAT or IPC_EXCL or AccessMode);
  if shmid = -1 then
    // Some error occurred. Error value is in errno.
```

If you want to open an existing shared memory object, you don't need to specify the size or the access mode:

```
shmid := shmget (KeyValue, 0, 0);
```

Once you've created or opened a shared memory object, you need to attach that shared memory to your process. You do this with the **shmat** function.

The **shmat** function takes the shared memory identifier, an address, and flags, and then returns a pointer through which you can access the shared memory block. The **shmaddr** parameter allows you to specify an address into which the memory should be mapped. Specifying such an address would likely make your program very hardware dependent, so it's recommended that you pass **nil** for this value, which instructs Linux to find an unmapped region of physical memory into which to map the memory.

The **flags** parameter can contain **SHM_RND** to force the address to be page aligned (normally used only when specifying a memory address), or it can contain **SHM_RDONLY** if you want your program to have read-only access to the shared memory. Here are two examples:

```
var
  pShared : Pointer;
begin
  // attach with normal permissions
  pShared := shmat (shmid, 0, 0);
  if Integer(PShared) = -1 then
    // Some error occurred. Error value is in errno.
  // attach memory with read only
  pShared := shmat (shmid, 0, SHM_RDONLY);
  if Integer(PShared) = -1 then
    // Some error occurred. Error value is in errno.
```

When your program is finished working with a shared memory block, it should detach by passing the pointer value returned from **shmat** to the **shmdt** function:

```
// Done using shared memory. Detach.
if shmdt (pShared) = -1 then
    // Some error occurred. Error value is in errno.
else
    pShared := nil;
```

It's a good idea to set your shared memory pointer to **nil** after detaching. Doing so allows you easily to test whether the pointer is referencing a valid memory block.

Controlling Shared Memory Objects

The **shmctl** function lets you perform three functions on shared memory objects: retrieve the object's data structure, set values in the data structure, and remove the shared memory object. The first parameter to **shmctl** is the shared memory identifier returned by shmget. The command that specifies which function to perform is specified in the **cmd** parameter (the second parameter) to **shmctl**. The command values are listed in Table 6.9. The third parameter to **shmctl** is a pointer to a shared memory identifier record, **TSharedMemoryIdDescriptor**, defined in **Libc.pas**.

Table 6.9 Commonly used shmctl commands.

Command	Description
IPC_STAT	Returns information from the shared memory data structure
IPC_SET	Sets values in the shared memory data structure
IPC_RMID	Removes (deletes) the shared memory object

Getting and Setting Shared Memory Information

The shared memory data structure contains information about the shared memory object, including its size, the number of currently attached processes, and other information. It also contains as its first member a **TIpcPermission** record that contains operating permissions. Programs are allowed to change the access mode field of this record. The following functions and procedures show how to manipulate the shared memory data structure using **shmctl**:

```
function ShmGetStat (shmid: Integer): TSharedMemoryIdDescriptor;
var
  ds : TSharedMemoryIdDescriptor;
begin
  if shmctl (shmid, IPC_STAT, @ds) = -1 then
    raise Exception.Create (strerror (errno));
  Result := ds;
end;

procedure ShmSetStat (shmid: Integer; const ds: TSharedMemoryIdDescriptor);
begin
  if shmctl (shmid, IPC_SET, @ds) = -1 then
    raise Exception.Create (strerror (errno));
end;

function ShmGetAccessMode (shmid: Integer): Integer;
begin
  Result := ShmGetStat (shmid).shm_perm.mode;
end;

procedure ShmSetAccessMode (shmid: Integer; aMode: Integer);
var
  ds: TSharedMemoryIdDescriptor;
begin
  ds := ShmGetStat;
  ds.shm_perm.mode := aMode;
  ShmSetStat (ds);
end;
```

Removing a Shared Memory Object

When the last process detaches from the shared memory object, the process should remove the shared memory in order to free system resources. To accomplish this, simply call **shmctl** with the command value **IPC_RMID**, like this:

```
if shmctl (shmid, IPC_RMID, nil) = -1 then
  // Some error occurred. Error is in errno.
```

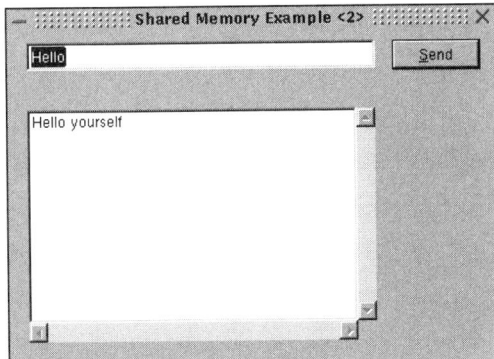

Figure 6.16
The **shmTalk** program.

Solution Example: The **shmTalk** Program

In order to illustrate using shared memory, We've created the **shmTalk** program shown in Figure 6.16. If you run two separate instances of this program, every time you type something into the edit box of one and press the Send button, the text that you typed will appear in the memo box of the other program. The code for the program's main form is shown in Listing 6.13.

Listing 6.13   The shmTalk program's main form.

```
unit frmTalk;

interface

uses
  SysUtils, Libc, Types, Classes, Variants, QGraphics, QControls,
  QForms, QDialogs,  QStdCtrls, QTypes, QExtCtrls;


const
  AccessMode = S_IREAD or S_IWRITE or S_IRGRP or S_IWGRP;
  BufSize = 508;

type
  PComBuffer = ^TComBuffer;
  TComBuffer = record
    bMsg : boolean;  // set when a message is available
    aMsg : Array[0..BufSize] of char;
  end;
```

```
const
  SegmentSize = 2*sizeof (TComBuffer);

type
  TForm1 = class(TForm)
    Button1: TButton;
    Memo1: TMemo;
    Edit1: TEdit;
    Timer1: TTimer;
    procedure FormCreate(Sender: TObject);
    procedure FormDestroy(Sender: TObject);
    procedure Button1Click(Sender: TObject);
    procedure Timer1Timer(Sender: TObject);
  private
    FShmId : Integer;
    FOwnShm : boolean;
    FSharePtr : Pointer;
    FSendBuf : PComBuffer;
    FRecvBuf : PComBuffer;
  public
    { Public declarations }
  end;

var
  Form1: TForm1;

implementation

{$R *.xfm}

procedure TForm1.FormCreate(Sender: TObject);
var
  Key : Integer;
begin
  // create key
  Key := ftok (PChar(GetModuleName(0)), 1);

  // try to open existing shared memory
  FShmId := shmget (Key, 0, 0);
  if FShmId = -1 then
  begin
    // doesn't exist, create it
    FShmId := shmget (Key, SegmentSize,
      IPC_CREAT or IPC_EXCL or AccessMode);
```

```
    if FShmId = -1 then
      raise Exception.Create (strerror (errno));
    FOwnShm := true;
  end
  else
    FOwnShm := false;

  // attach to shared memory
  FSharePtr := shmat (FShmId, nil, 0);
  if Integer(FSharePtr) = -1 then
  begin
    FSharePtr := nil;
    raise Exception.Create (strerror (errno));
  end;

  // set up buffers
  if FOwnShm then
  begin
    FSendBuf := FSharePtr;
    FRecvBuf := PComBuffer(PChar(FSharePtr) + sizeof (TComBuffer));
    FRecvBuf^.bMsg := false;
  end
  else
  begin
    FRecvBuf := FSharePtr;
    FSendBuf := PComBuffer(PChar(FSharePtr) + sizeof (TComBuffer));
  end;
  FSendBuf^.bMsg := false;
  Timer1.Enabled := true;
end;

procedure TForm1.FormDestroy(Sender: TObject);
begin
  Timer1.Enabled := false;
  if Assigned (FSharePtr) then
    shmdt (FSharePtr);
  if FOwnShm then
    if shmctl (FShmId, IPC_RMID, nil) = -1 then
      raise Exception.Create (strerror (errno));
end;

procedure TForm1.Button1Click(Sender: TObject);
var
  s : String;
```

```
begin
  // copy the text from the edit box to the shared memory
  s := Edit1.Text;
  StrCopy (@FSendBuf^.aMsg, PChar(s));
  // set flag to indicate that a message is there
  FSendBuf^.bMsg := true;
end;

procedure TForm1.Timer1Timer(Sender: TObject);
begin
  if FRecvBuf^.bMsg then
  begin
    // read the message
    Memo1.Lines.Add (FRecvBuf^.aMsg);
    // and clear the flag
    FRecvBuf^.bMsg := false;
  end;
end;

end.
```

How the Program Works

When the program starts, it tries to open an existing shared memory object. If that fails, it creates the shared memory. After getting the shared memory object, the program attaches and sets up pointers for a send buffer and a receive buffer. The program that creates the shared memory ends up with its send buffer at the head of the shared memory area and its receive buffer at the tail. The second instance of the program has its buffers reversed. The result is that each program sends into the other's receive buffer.

When you type something into the edit box and press the Send button, the program copies what you typed into its send buffer and sets the send buffer's message flag to indicate that new text has been written into the buffer. A **TTimer** object set to fire every half second checks the receive buffer's message flag to see whether new text has been written. If the message flag is set to true, the timer's message handler copies the text from the buffer into the memo box and then clears the message flag.

This program is hardly bulletproof. If a third instance of the program is started, it will start stepping on the second program's send and receive buffers. In addition, because there is no synchronization of access to the shared memory, it's possible for the receiver to "miss" a message. For example, suppose that the receiver determines that a message is available and copies it. Then, before it can clear the message flag, the sender's process gets a time slice (Linux *is* a preemptive multitasking system) and at that moment writes a new message to the buffer. When the receiver's process wakes up again, the first thing it does is clear the message flag. It just "deleted" a message that it never read.

You can prevent these problems by using a semaphore to control access to the shared memory. A semaphore works well if you have only two processes accessing the memory, or if you have multiple processes that perform read and write operations frequently. However, if you have an application in which multiple processes read the memory frequently and few processes write infrequently, you'll want a more robust synchronization scheme, such as a reader/writer lock.

Solution 6.10: Communicating with Message Queues

Message queues, the third of the System V IPC facilities, are like named pipes in some ways, but with additional functionality. The general idea is that one process will add messages to the queue while another process takes messages from the queue in the order they were added. There *are*, however, ways to get messages from the queue out of order.

Every message added to a message queue has an associated type (an integer) that readers can search for. The types allow you to create "bins" or "buckets" within a message queue. Readers can ask for the next message in a queue or the next message of a particular type. The types are entirely application defined.

You can also use message types to create a priority queue. For example, you may decide that messages of type 1 are considered urgent, and all other types are normal messages. If you want to read all the urgent messages before you read anything else, you can.

A message queue isn't a bottomless pit, though. The maximum size of an individual message is defined by the **MSGMAX** value in the Linux kernel. That value is currently 4,080 bytes. There are also limits on the size of a message queue and on the total number of message queues in the system. You can obtain the maximum size of a message queue from the **msg_qbytes** member of the message queue's data structure. There is no convenient way to obtain the maximum number of message queues.

Message Queue Functions

There are four message queue API functions that programs use to create and control message queue objects. These functions and their descriptions are shown in Table 6.10.

As the names imply, the **msgget** and **msgctl** functions are very similar to the semaphore functions **semget** and **semctl**. All these functions return –1 in the case of an error. If an error occurs, the error number will be in the global variable **errno**.

> **Warning**
>
> *The first shipping release of Kylix contained an incorrect message queue structure in **Libc.pas**. Programs that use that structure will not work correctly. See the warning under Solution 6.8 for more information.*

Table 6.10 The shared memory functions.

Function	Description
msgget	function **msgget (key: key_t; flags: Integer): Integer;** Creates or opens a message queue
msgctl	function **shmctl (msqid: Integer; cmd: Integer; buf: PMsgQueueIdDesc): Integer;** Performs message queue control operations
msgsnd	function **msgsnd (msqid: Integer; const msgp; msgsize: size_t; flags: Integer): Integer;** Sends a message to the message queue
msgrcv	function **msgrcv (msqid: Integer; var msg; msgsize: size_t; msgtype: Longint; flags: Integer): Integer;** Receives a message from the message queue

Creating and Opening Message Queues

You create and open message queues by calling the **msgget** function, which works in much the same way as the **semget** function. You create a key and then pass that key and the desired flags to **msgget**, which returns the message queue ID or –1 if it was unable to perform the operation. As with semaphores, you can pass the key value **IPC_PRIVATE** if you want a private message queue. The **IPC_CREAT** and **IPC_EXCL** flags also work just like they do for semaphores. Here's a code fragment that creates a new message queue object:

```
const
  { Give read and write permissions to User and Group. No access to others }
  AccessMode = S_IREAD or S_IWRITE or S_IRGRP or S_IWGRP;
  KeyValue = 1234;
var
  msqid : Integer;
begin
  msqid := msgget (KeyValue, IPC_CREAT or IPC_EXCL or AccessMode);
  if msqid = -1 then
    // Some error occurred. Error value is in errno.
```

If you want to open an existing message queue, you don't need to specify the access mode:

```
  msqid := msgget (KeyValue, 0);
```

Controlling Message Queues

The **msgctl** function lets you perform three functions on shared memory objects: retrieve the object's data structure, set values in the data structure, and remove the message queue. The command to perform these functions is specified in the **cmd** parameter to **msgctl**. The command values are shown in Table 6.11.

The third parameter to **msgctl** is a pointer to a message queue identifier record, **TMsgQueueIdIdDesc**, defined in **Libc.pas**.

Table 6.11   Commonly used msgctl functions.

Command	Description
IPC_STAT	Returns information from the message queue data structure
IPC_SET	Sets values in the message queue data structure
IPC_RMID	Removes (deletes) the message queue

Getting and Setting Message Queue Information

The message queue data structure contains information about the message queue, including its current and maximum size, the number messages currently on the queue, and some other information. It also contains as its first member a **TIpcPermission** record that contains operating permissions. Programs are allowed to change the access mode field of this record. The following functions and procedures show how to manipulate the message queue data structure using **msgctl**:

```
function MsgGetStat (msqid: Integer): TMsgQueueIdDesc;
var
  ds: TMsgQueueIdDesc;
begin
  if msgctl (msqid, IPC_STAT, @ds) = -1 then
    raise Exception.Create (strerror (errno));
  Result := ds;
end;

procedure MsgSetStat (msqid: Integer; const ds: TMsgQueueIdDesc);
begin
  if msgctl (msqid, IPC_SET, @ds) = -1 then
    raise Exception.Create (strerror (errno));
end;

function MsgGetAccessMode (msqid: Integer): Integer;
begin
  Result := MsgGetStat (msqid).msg_perm.mode;
end;

procedure MsgSetAccessMode (msqid: Integer; aMode: Integer);
var
  ds: TMsgQueueIdDesc;
begin
  ds := MsgGetStat;
  ds.msg_perm.mode := aMode;
  MsgSetStat (ds);
end;

function MsgGetNumMsgs (msqid: Integer): Integer;
begin
```

```
  Result := MsgGetStat (msqid).msg_qnum;
end;

function MsgGetSize (msqid: Integer): msgnum_t;
begin
  Result := MsgGetStat (msqid).__msg_cbytes;
end;

function MsgGetMaxSize (msqid: Integer): msglen_t;
begin
  Result := MsgGetStat (msqid).msg_qbytes;
end;
```

Removing a Message Queue

When the last process is done using the message queue, the process should remove the shared memory in order to free system resources. Simply call **msgctl** with the command value **IPC_RMID**, like this:

```
if msgctl (msqid, IPC_RMID, nil) = -1 then
  // Some error occurred. Error is in errno.
```

Sending Messages

To send a message, you package the data that you want to send into a message record and then pass that record and the record's size to the **msgsnd** function. The message record has two constraints: it must not be longer than the system's maximum message size (4,080 bytes), and the first member of the message record must be a LongWord that contains the message type. For example, suppose you wanted to send this **TActorRec** structure in a message:

```
TActorRec = record
  FirstName: String[20];
  LastName: String[20];
  BirthDate: TDateTime;
end;
```

In this case, you would have to add a **MessageType** field as the first field in the record or create a new record type that has a **MessageType** field as its first field, followed by a **TActorRec** structure, like this:

```
TMovieMessage = record
  MessageType: LongWord;
  Actor: TActorRec;
end;
```

Before you send the message, you should set the **MessageType** field to indicate the type of message. **MessageType** must be a positive number greater than zero; otherwise, **msgsnd** will fail.

The last parameter to **msgsnd**, the **flags** parameter, controls what happens if the message queue is full or the system-wide limit on message queue size has been reached. If the **flags** parameter is zero, **msgsnd** will block until the message can be sent (that is, until space is available in the message queue). If **flags** is **IPC_NOWAIT**, then **msgsnd** will fail immediately if it is unable to send the message. Here's an example of initializing a **TActorRec** structure and sending it to an existing message queue:

```
function MsgSend (msqid: Integer; const Msg; msgSize: size_t;
  flags: Integer): boolean;
begin
  if msgsnd (msqid, Msg, msgSize, flags) = -1 then
    if (errno = EAGAIN) or (errno = EINTR) then
      Result := false
    else
      raise Exception.Create (strerror (errno))
  else
    Result := true;
end;


const
  mtActor = 1;


var
  MovieMsg: TMovieMessage;
begin
  MovieMsg.MessageType := mtActor;
  MovieMsg.Actor.FirstName := 'Helen';
  MovieMsg.Actor.LastName := 'Hunt';
  MovieMsg.Actor.BirthDate := StrToDate ('07/15/1963');
  try
    if MsgSend (msqid, MovieMsg, sizeof (MovieMsg), IPC_NOWAIT) then
      ShowMessage ('Message sent')
    else
      ShowMessage ('Message send failed');
  except
    on E:Exception do
      ShowMessage (Format ('Exception "%s" sending message', [E.Message]));
  end;
```

Receiving Messages

Receiving a message is very similar to sending a message: You pass a message record and the size of the record to **msgrcv**, which gets the next message from the message queue, puts the data into the message structure, and returns the number of bytes copied to the message buffer. As with the other IPC functions, **msgrcv** returns –1 on error.

Two parameters, **msgtype** and **flags**, control how messages are received from the queue. The **msgtype** parameter specifies the type of message you want to get from the queue. If **msgtype** is zero, then **msgrcv** retrieves the first message on the queue, regardless of the message type. If **msgtype** is greater than zero, the first message of the requested type is returned, unless **IPC_EXCEPT** is included in the **flags** parameter. If **IPC_EXCEPT** is included in **flags** and **msgtype** is greater than zero, then **msgrcv** retrieves the first message on the queue whose message type is *not* equal to the requested type.

If **msgtype** is less than zero, the first message on the queue with the lowest type less than or equal to the absolute value of **msgtype** is retrieved. So, if the queue has messages of types 3, 4, 1, 3, 2, and 4, in that order, and **msgtype** is –2, then **msgrcv** will retrieve the third message (type 1) from the queue.

If the **flags** parameter includes **IPC_NOWAIT**, then **msgrcv** will check the queue for a message, and if it doesn't find one of the appropriate type, it will return –1. If **IPC_NOWAIT** is not included, then **msgrcv** blocks until an appropriate message is received. If **MSG_NOERROR** is not included in **flags**, then **msgrcv** will return with an error if the message to be received is longer than the size specified by the **msgsize** parameter. If **MSG_NOERROR** is included in **flags**, the message will be truncated if it's too long.

Here's an example that receives an actor message from a message queue:

```
function MsgRecv (msqid: Integer; var Msg; var msgsize: size_t;
  msgtype: Longint; flags: integer): boolean;
begin
  msgsize := msgrcv (msqid, Msg, msgsize, msgtype, flags);
  if msgsize = -1 then
    if (errno = EINTR) or (errno = EAGAIN) then
      Result := false
    else
      raise Exception.Create (strerror (errno))
  else
    Result := true;
end;

var
  MovieMsg : TMovieMessage;
  msgsize: Integer;
begin
  try
    msgsize := sizeof (MovieMsg);
    if MsgRecv (msqid, MovieMsg, msgsize, mtActor, 0) then
      ShowMessage (Format ('%s %s', [MovieMsg.Actor.FirstName,
        MovieMsg.Actor.LastName]))
    else
      ShowMessage ('Error receiving message');
```

```
except
  on E:Exception do
    ShowMessage (Format ('Exception "%s" sending message', [E.Message]));
end;
```

In this example, the **msgsize** parameter to the **MsgRecv** function is a **var** parameter. When you call **MsgRecv**, the **msgsize** variable that you pass should contain the maximum size of the message buffer. When **MsgRecv** returns, **msgsize** will contain the number of bytes actually copied into the message buffer.

Working with Different Message Types

If you always pass the same size message to your queue, then sending and receiving messages is very easy, as we just illustrated. But if you are sending messages that have varying sizes, things get a little more complicated. For example, suppose you added a new record, **TFilmRec**, to the data structures in the previous examples:

```
const
  mtFilm = 2;

type
  TFilmRec = record
    Name: String[50];
    Year : Shortint;
  end;
```

And suppose you turned the **TMovieMessage** structure into a variant record, like this:

```
TMovieMessage = record
  case MessageType: LongWord of
    0: (Actor: TActorRec);
    1: (Film: TFilmRec);
end;
```

You now have two problems. When sending a message, you want to put as few bytes as possible onto the message queue; there's no sense in filling the message queue with unnecessary data. In this particular case, a **TActorRec** structure takes 50 bytes, and a **TFilmRec** structure takes 55 bytes. The **MessageType** field requires four more bytes, giving you 54 bytes for an actor and 59 bytes for a film. When you send a **TActorRec** (message type 1), you want to send only 54 bytes. But if you write the code

```
MsgSend (msqid, MovieMsg, sizeof (MovieMsg), 0);
```

then 59 bytes (the size of a **TMovieMessage** record) will be placed on the message queue. Granted, four extra bytes probably wouldn't make a big difference in this particular case, but if the difference in message sizes were 100 bytes, you can see how that wasted space could cause problems. Perhaps the easiest solution to this problem is to provide a wrapper for the **MsgSend** function that knows about the different message types and sets the size accordingly, like this:

```
function MessageSendWrapper (msqid: Integer; const Msg: TMovieMessage;
  flags: Integer): boolean;
var
  sendSize: Integer;
begin
  case Msg.MessageType of
    mtActor: sendSize := sizeof (TActorRec);
    mtFilm: sendSize := sizeof (TFilmRec);
  end;
  sendSize := sendSize + sizeof (Msg.MessageType);
  Result := MsgSend (msqid, Msg, sendSize, flags);
end;
```

You have exactly the opposite problem when you're receiving different-sized messages. In that case, the buffer you pass to **MsgRecv** has to be at least as big as the largest message that you expect to receive. Otherwise, you run the risk of having your message truncated (if you specify the **MSG_NOERROR** flag) or getting a runtime error. You'll also need code to process the message based on its type. The following code fragment shows one way to handle receiving different-sized messages:

```
var
  MovieMsg: TMovieMessage;
begin
  try
    if MsgRecv (msqid, MovieMsg, sizeof (MovieMsg), 0, MSG_NOERROR) then
    begin
      case MovieMsg.MessageType of
        mtActor: // process Actor
        mtFilm: // process film
        else
          ShowMessage (Format ('Unknown message type %d',
            [MovieMsg.MessageType]));
      end;
    end
    else
      ShowMessage ('No message received');
  except
    on E:Exception do
      ShowMessage (strerror (E.Message));
  end;
```

Pointers and Message Queues

In general, you can't pass pointers in message queue messages. Well, you can pass the pointer, but unless the receiving process is the same process that sent the message, dereferencing the pointer will likely result in an access violation, or worse. Pointers reference memory on a per-process basis, so a pointer that addresses a string in one process will access something different (or nothing at all) in another process.

This means that you can't pass *any* type of pointer value through a message queue and expect it to work correctly on the other side. This includes objects and AnsiString types, both of which are implemented using pointers.

Solution Example: A Simple Debug Log

Source-level debuggers are nice, but when you're developing programs that talk to each other, it's often difficult to use a debugger to locate problems because you don't know where to look. Is the problem with the client's request, the server's processing of the request, the server's response, or the client's handling of the response? Perhaps the problem is somewhere else entirely. When you're debugging these types of problems, the tried and true log file is often the most effective tool. Whenever a process does anything significant, it writes a message to a log file. You can then examine the log file to see what went wrong. The problem with log files is that you can't see messages as they're coming in. What you really need is a tool that can examine the debug message stream in real time. The **dbglog** program, shown in Figure 6.17, implements a very simple debug log with a message queue.

When you start the **dbglog** program, it opens a message queue and starts a timer that empties the message queue every 100 milliseconds and displays the message contents in a memo box. The program expects messages to be simple text strings that are less than 2,000 bytes in length. The code for the program's main form is shown in Listing 6.14.

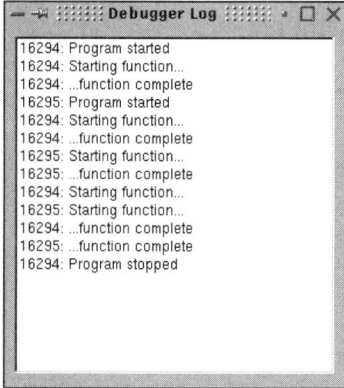

Figure 6.17
The **dbglog** program.

Listing 6.14 The dbglog program's main form.

```
unit frmDebug;

interface

uses
  SysUtils, Libc, Types, Classes, Variants, QGraphics, QControls,
  QForms, QDialogs, QStdCtrls, QTypes, QExtCtrls;

type
  TForm1 = class(TForm)
    Memo1: TMemo;
    Timer1: TTimer;
    procedure FormCreate(Sender: TObject);
    procedure Timer1Timer(Sender: TObject);
  private
    FQueueId : Integer;
  public
    { Public declarations }
  end;

var
  Form1: TForm1;

implementation

{$R *.xfm}

const
  KeyStr = './dbglog';
  AccessMode = S_IREAD or S_IWRITE or S_IRGRP or S_IWGRP;

procedure TForm1.FormCreate(Sender: TObject);
begin
  FQueueId := msgget (ftok (KeyStr, 1), IPC_CREAT or AccessMode);
  if FQueueID = -1 then
    raise Exception.Create (strerror (errno));
  Timer1.Enabled := true;
end;

procedure TForm1.Timer1Timer(Sender: TObject);
type
  mqMessage = record
    mtype: LongWord;
    msg: array [0..2000] of char;
  end;
```

```
var
  msg: mqMessage;
  len: Integer;

begin
  repeat
    len := msgrcv (FQueueId, msg, sizeof (msg), 0,
      IPC_NOWAIT or MSG_NOERROR);
    if len <> -1 then
      Memo1.Lines.Add (msg.msg);
  until len = -1;
end;

end.
```

If you want your program to write messages to the debug log, all you have to do in your program is open the message queue with the proper key and start sending messages to it. The code to open the message queue is the same as the code used in the **dbglog** program. In this example, we used a value of '**./dbglog**' for the key value. That will work if the dbglog program and the program being debugged are in the same directory. If they aren't, you'll need some other way to determine the key. You may want to use the **dbglog** program's full path name or just pick a number and hope that no other program is using that number for its message queue.

Here's some code that will send a message to the queue. It adds the process ID to the beginning of the message so that you can tell which process sent the message when you see it in the debugger log:

```
procedure TForm2.MsgSend (const msgText: String);
type
  mqMessage = record
    mtype: LongWord;
    msg: array [0..200] of char;
  end;

var
  msg: mqMessage;
  len: Integer;
  sMessage: String;

begin
  if FQueueID <> -1 then
  begin
    msg.mtype := 1;
    sMessage := Format ('%d: %s', [getpid, msgText]);
```

```
    StrCopy (msg.msg, PChar(sMessage));
    len := sizeof (msg.mtype) + Length(sMessage) + 1;
    msgsnd (FQueueId, msg, len, IPC_NOWAIT);
  end;
end;
```

Note that the **MsgSend** procedure doesn't do any error checking on the value returned from **msgsnd**. If the message can't be put into the queue, it just gets dropped. There's no reason to have the debug logging code crash the program.

If the **dbglog** program isn't running when the client program starts, the client can still put messages into the queue. When you start **dbglog**, it will display all the messages that are currently in the queue. Of course, if the queue fills up before you start **dbglog**, you'll start losing messages.

Note that the **dbglog** program doesn't remove the message queue when it exits. You'll need to use the **ipcrm** program to remove the message queue from the system.

Chapter 7
Using the Filesystem

Kylix provides the same wide range of file-access procedures and functions available in Delphi. As we have shown in previous chapters, however, the Linux filesystem differs somewhat from that of Windows. This chapter delves into some challenges and solutions unique to Linux files.

Solution 7.1: Getting the Permission Settings for a File

Linux is a true multiuser operating system. As such, it maintains detailed permission settings for each file on the system. Sometimes applications need to obtain these permission settings as part of working with directories and files. Fortunately, obtaining these settings from the filesystem is simple.

The **stat** system call is the standard Unix/Linux system call for obtaining information about a file. One of the pieces of information returned by the **stat** function is the permission mask of the file being examined. The **stat** system calls fills in a record of type **TStatBuf**. We'll look more closely at the other fields of **TStatBuf** in Solution 7.5; right now, though, we're interested only in the **st_mode** field. This field is a bit-mapped value that contains (among other information) the permission mask itself.

To make any sense out of the permission mask, I'll make use of bitwise operations against several constants provided in the **Libc** unit. These constants are contained in Table 7.1.

Table 7.1 File permission constants.	
Constant	**Description**
S_IRUSR	Read by owner.
S_IWUSR	Write by owner.
S_IXUSR	Execute by owner.
S_IRGRP	Read by group.
S_IWGRP	Write by group.
S_IXGRP	Execute by group.
S_IROTH	Read by others.
S_IWOTH	Write by others.
S_IXOTH	Execute by others.
S_ISUID	Program will run **setuid**.
S_ISGID	Program will run **setgid**.
S_ISVTX	The famous "sticky bit".

By using the bitwise **and** operation, you can easily compare the file permission mask against any combination of the constants listed in Table 7.1.

Solution Example: The **GetPermissions** Program

The **GetPermissions** program, shown in Figure 7.1, demonstrates the use of the **stat** call to obtain permission settings for an arbitrary file.

The **GetPermissions** program allows you to browse the system for a specific file using the Open File dialog box. Once you have selected a file, **GetPermissions** then simply uses bitwise **and** operations to update the numerous checkboxes so they reflect the current permission mask for the file. Relevant code from the **GetPermissions** application is presented in Listing 7.1.

The Sticky Bit

In days past (all right, *years* past), systems didn't have the performance or memory capacity of present-day systems. Having to cope with limited system resources led to numerous attempts at system optimization, among them was the *sticky bit*. The whole idea behind the sticky bit was this: applications with this bit set would save their executable image (their "text area," which explains the "SVTX" in the constant **S_ISVTX** in Table 7.1) in the system's swap space after the program finished execution. This would speed the loading process the next time the program was executed. Needless to say, this was intended only for programs that were frequently used.

With the amount of system resources typically available today, the sticky bit is seldom used for its original purpose. Instead, it serves as another layer of protection on files in world-writable directories. Unix file permissions are interpreted by the system as allowing anyone to delete or rename files that are inside a world-writable directory, regardless of the owner of the file. If the sticky bit is set on the directory, however, only the file owner, directory owner, or superuser will be able to delete or rename files in that directory. The /tmp directory is a prime candidate for this treatment.

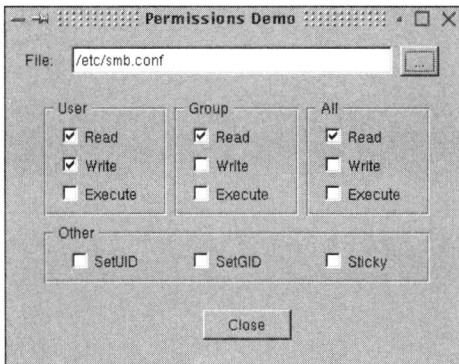

Figure 7.1
The **GetPermissions** program.

Listing 7.1   Excerpts from **GetPermissions.pas**.

```
procedure TfrmPermissions.getPermissions;
var
      rv: Integer;
      perms: Cardinal;
      statBuf: TStatBuf;
      filename: String;
begin
   cbSetUID.Checked := false;
   cbSetGID.Checked := false;
   cbSticky.Checked := false;
   cbUserRead.Checked := false;
   cbUserWrite.Checked := false;
   cbUserExecute.Checked := false;
   cbGroupRead.Checked := false;
   cbGroupWrite.Checked := false;
   cbGroupExecute.Checked := false;
   cbAllRead.Checked := false;
   cbAllWrite.Checked := false;
   cbAllExecute.Checked := false;

   filename := tbFileName.Text;
   rv := stat( PChar( filename ), statBuf );
   if ( rv = -1 ) then
       ShowMessage( 'Unable to stat file.' )
   else
       begin
       perms := statBuf.st_mode;

       if ( perms And S_ISUID <> 0 ) then
           cbSetUID.Checked := true;
       if ( perms And S_ISGID <> 0 ) then
           cbSetGID.Checked := true;
```

```
        if ( perms And S_ISVTX <> 0 ) then
            cbSticky.Checked := true;
        if ( perms And S_IRUSR <> 0 ) then
            cbUserRead.Checked := true;
        if ( perms And S_IWUSR <> 0 ) then
            cbUserWrite.Checked := true;
        if ( perms And S_IXUSR <> 0 ) then
            cbUserExecute.Checked := true;
        if ( perms And S_IRGRP <> 0 ) then
            cbGroupRead.Checked := true;
        if ( perms And S_IWGRP <> 0 ) then
            cbGroupWrite.Checked := true;
        if ( perms And S_IXGRP <> 0 ) then
            cbGroupExecute.Checked := true;
        if ( perms And S_IROTH <> 0 ) then
            cbAllRead.Checked := true;
        if ( perms And S_IWOTH <> 0 ) then
            cbAllWrite.Checked := true;
        if ( perms And S_IXOTH <> 0 ) then
            cbAllExecute.Checked := true;
        end;
    end;
```

Solution 7.2: Setting the Permission for a File

Simply reading permission settings is a useful activity, but sometimes you'll need to set permissions as well. Setting permissions is easy, thanks to the Linux **chmod** system call.

Sometimes the default file permission settings just aren't enough. Sometimes you'll want to keep file information from your kid sister or keep source code from that annoying new intern that likes to take your source and claim it as his own. Perhaps your application creates a file so valuable that you don't even want yourself to have the permission to delete it. In all these cases, you've got a job for file permissions (or cryptography, but that's another subject altogether).

To set a file permission mask, you can either read the existing permission setting from a file (see Solution 7.1) and modify it, or you can create a new one that meets your needs. A *file permission mask* is simply a cardinal value whose bits have been set using the bitwise **or** operator and one or more of the permission values from Table 7.1. This mask is then applied to a specific file using the **chmod** system call.

Solution Example: The **SetPermissions** Program

The solution application presented here is based on the example in Solution 7.1. By simply adding a button and a little bit of code to that application, we've created **SetPermissions**, an application that both gets and sets file permissions (see Figure 7.2).

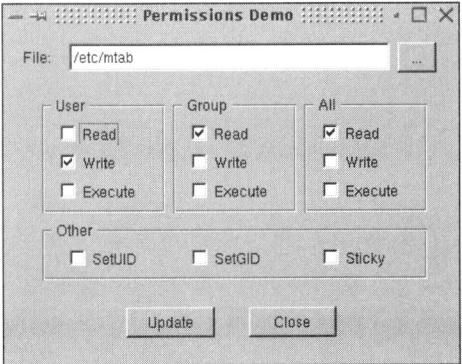

Figure 7.2
The **SetPermissions** program.

Listing 7.2 details the use of the **chmod** system call, which is used to set the file permissions according to the settings in the application's checkboxes.

Warning
*Although this program allows you to set the **setuid** and **setgid** bits in a file's permission mask, you run the risk of opening a security hole on your system if you do so. Remember that **setuid** and **setgid** programs run as their owner or as their group, with all the system privileges that belong to that user or group. Leaving a world-writable file lying around with its **setuid** bit set isn't asking for trouble—it's dropping to your knees and begging for it. Use this technique with caution.*

Listing 7.2   Permission-setting method from the SetPermissions application.

```
procedure TfrmPermissions.updatePermissions;
var
    perms: Cardinal;
    filename: String;
    rv: Integer;
begin
    filename := tbFileName.Text;
    perms := 0;

    if ( cbSetUID.Checked ) then
        perms := perms Or S_ISUID;
    if ( cbSetGID.Checked ) then
        perms := perms Or S_ISGID;
    if ( cbSticky.Checked ) then
        perms := perms Or S_ISVTX;
    if ( cbUserRead.Checked ) then
        perms := perms Or S_IRUSR;
    if ( cbUserWrite.Checked ) then
        perms := perms Or S_IWUSR;
```

```
    if ( cbUserExecute.Checked ) then
        perms := perms Or S_IXUSR;
    if ( cbGroupRead.Checked ) then
        perms := perms Or S_IRGRP;
    if ( cbGroupWrite.Checked ) then
        perms := perms Or S_IWGRP;
    if ( cbGroupExecute.Checked ) then
        perms := perms Or S_IXGRP;
    if ( cbAllRead.Checked ) then
        perms := perms Or S_IROTH;
    if ( cbAllWrite.Checked ) then
        perms := perms Or S_IWOTH;
    if ( cbAllExecute.Checked ) then
        perms := perms Or S_IXOTH;

    rv := chmod( PChar( filename ), perms );
    if ( rv = -1 ) then
        begin
        ShowMessage( 'Unable to chmod file.' );
        getPermissions;
        end;
end;
```

Solution 7.3: Implementing File-Level Locking for Data Files

You would expect that any multiuser, multitasking operating system worth its salt would offer a way for programs to safely share data files. For that to happen, a program must be assured that it will be the *only* one allowed to modify a file at a given moment. Conversely, a program reading a data file must be certain that the data will not be changing as it is being read. Failure to adhere to either of these two principles will invariably result in corrupted data.

Linux does offer file-locking mechanisms. That's the good news. However, if you're expecting *mandatory* file locking, you're in for a disappointment, because Linux provides only *cooperative* (or *advisory*) locking. If programs do cooperate, however, the Linux file-locking mechanisms work perfectly. In this section, I will present a solution for locking an entire file. I'll tackle regional (record-level) locking in Solution 7.4.

Before we take one more step, I must make something clear: We do not actually operate directly on the data files we want to protect. Instead, a lock file is used merely as an *indicator* to cooperating programs—a traffic light of sorts—that lets those programs know on a continuous basis their permission to write to or read from a specific file.

In the general case, two or more programs (or instances of a single program) can simultaneously read a data file, but only one program at a time can have write access. You saw a

---

Lock Files: Just for Data Files?

Although in this solution you're seeing a lock file used to direct traffic to a data file, a lock file can be used to control access to any resource—including devices (which in Linux are, of course, *files*). As one example, when a modem is in use, Linux creates a lock file in the /usr/spool/uucp directory. The existence of this file (or the lack thereof) can be used to determine the availability of the modem.

---

lock file used in Chapter 5 (Solution 5.10) as part of a simple way to prevent two instances of a process from running. There, the mere existence of the file was an indicator to the program that another identical process was already running. It's time to ratchet that concept up just one notch and give it a little "industrial strength" in the process.

Basically, we will assume that a program has a critical section within it that requires exclusive access to a data file (or some other resource). That process will attempt to create the lock file. When its critical operations are complete, it will delete the lock file, indicating to other programs that a lock can be obtained.

Here's how the cooperative part works: the process owning the lock file owns all rights to the associated data file. Any other process has no rights whatsoever, so it must wait around until it can obtain ownership. Even though several processes *might* technically be able to read the data file simultaneously without harm, we're just stubbornly not going to allow them.

That would seem to settle everything, but there is one nasty little detail that involves exactly how ownership is to be determined. How can we ensure that nothing else can happen while the lock is being created? The answer lies in the use of the low-level **open** command, coupled with one of its optional flags: **O_EXCL**. The **O_EXCL** flag specifies that the file is to be exclusive to its creator. By using the **O_CREAT** and **O_EXCL** flags together, we are also guaranteed that the creation of the lock file will be *atomic*, that is, it will be one smooth operation that will not be interrupted.

Solution Example: The **LockFile** Program

Figure 7.3 displays **LockFile**, a program that demonstrates the strategy just discussed. The Locking Status indicator starts out red, indicating this instance of **LockFile** does not have exclusive control of the lock file (which is located in the /tmp directory, so any program will have access to it). When the user clicks the Lock button, the program attempts to obtain control of the lock file. If it succeeds, the indicator will turn green. If not, the indicator will turn yellow, and **LockFile** will continue its attempt to gain control.

By running two copies of **LockFile**, you can have a little fun. Acquire a lock with the first copy, and the indicator will be green. When you attempt a lock with the second copy, its indicator will turn yellow. As soon as you click the Release button on the first copy, its indicator will return to red, and the indicator on the second copy will turn green.

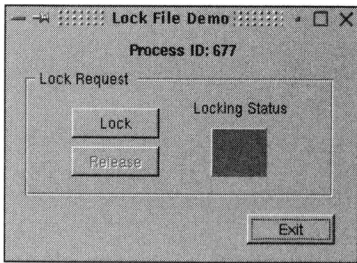

Figure 7.3
The **LockFile** program.

The code for **LockFile** is shown in Listing 7.3. The core routine in the program is the **FileLocked** function, which uses the low-level **open** function in an attempt to atomically create and gain exclusive access to the lock file. If the attempt succeeds, the program owns the file. When the Release button is clicked, the lock file is closed. Then it is deleted with the **unlink** library call. The remainder of the **LockFile** code simply operates the "mechanism," providing control for the buttons and a timer that reattempts to open the file every 250 ms while the program is in the "pending" mode, awaiting a lock.

Listing 7.3　The **LockFile** program.

```
unit LockFileMain;

interface

uses
  SysUtils, Types, Classes, Variants, QGraphics, QControls, QForms, QDialogs,
  QStdCtrls, QExtCtrls, QTypes, Libc, QButtons;

type
  TLockFileMainForm = class(TForm)
    ExitBtn: TButton;
    PIDLabel: TLabel;
    GroupBox1: TGroupBox;
    StatusPanel: TPanel;
    Label1: TLabel;
    LockBtn: TButton;
    ReleaseBtn: TButton;
    Monitor: TTimer;
    procedure UpdateControls;
    procedure ExitBtnClick(Sender: TObject);
    procedure FormCreate(Sender: TObject);
    procedure LockBtnClick(Sender: TObject);
    procedure ReleaseBtnClick(Sender: TObject);
    procedure MonitorTimer(Sender: TObject);
```

```
  private
    { Private declarations }
  public
    { Public declarations }
  end;

type
  TLockStatus = (tsdUnlocked, tsdPending, tsdLocked);

const
  LockFileName = '/tmp/LCK.LockFileDemo';

var
  LockFileMainForm: TLockFileMainForm;
  LockStatus : TLockStatus;
  FD : Integer;

implementation

{$R *.xfm}

function FileLocked : Integer;
begin
 Result := open(LockFileName, O_RDWR or O_CREAT or O_EXCL, 438);
end;

procedure TLockFileMainForm.UpdateControls;
begin
 case LockStatus of
  tsdUnlocked : begin
                  StatusPanel.Color := clRed;
                  LockBtn.Enabled := True;
                  ReleaseBtn.Enabled := False;
                end;
  tsdPending  : begin
                  StatusPanel.Color := clYellow;
                  LockBtn.Enabled := False;
                  ReleaseBtn.Enabled := False;
                end;
  tsdLocked   : begin
                  StatusPanel.Color := clGreen;
                  LockBtn.Enabled := False;
                  ReleaseBtn.Enabled := True;
                end;
 end; { case }
end;
```

```
procedure TLockFileMainForm.ExitBtnClick(Sender: TObject);
begin
 { We do this housekeeping just for this demo! }
 if FileExists(LockFileName) then unlink(LockFileName);
 Close;
end;


procedure TLockFileMainForm.FormCreate(Sender: TObject);
begin
 PIDLabel.Caption := 'Process ID: ' + IntToStr(getpid);
 LockStatus := tsdUnlocked;
 UpdateControls;
end;


procedure TLockFileMainForm.LockBtnClick(Sender: TObject);
begin
 FD := FileLocked;
 if FD <> -1
  then LockStatus := tsdLocked
  else begin
        LockStatus := tsdPending;
        Monitor.Enabled := True;
        end;
 UpdateControls;
end;


procedure TLockFileMainForm.ReleaseBtnClick(Sender: TObject);
begin
 __close(FD);
 unlink(LockFileName);
 LockStatus := tsdUnlocked;
 UpdateControls;
end;


procedure TLockFileMainForm.MonitorTimer(Sender: TObject);
begin
 FD := FileLocked;
 if FD <> -1
  then begin
        LockStatus := tsdLocked;
        UpdateControls;
        Monitor.Enabled := False;
        end;
end;


end.
```

Solution 7.4: Implementing Record-Level File Locking

Locking entire files, as described in Solution 7.3, may be fine for simple applications, but it is certainly inefficient when your program needs to access medium-to-large databases. In these situations, it's necessary to lock individual records. Fortunately, Linux provides a robust capability for managing advisory locks on specified portions of files.

Before we dig any deeper, you need to know that the common format for Linux database files is straight ASCII text, laid out in fixed-length records. Although this might not be the most sophisticated and exciting setup in the world, it is sane, straightforward for programming purposes, and most important of all—it *works*. What we're really looking for in terms of record locking, then, is the ability to place and honor locks on fixed-length groups of bytes—*regions*—throughout a file.

Linux provides this capability in spades. In fact, it enables you to lay claim to regions within a file on a byte-by-byte basis. These regions can be of varying lengths (down to a single byte), and they can even overlap. Unlike file locking, which uses the lock file as a traffic signal, here Linux, in effect, keeps a database with an entry for every byte in the file. Each entry contains the byte's current advisory read/write permissions and the pid of the process that currently holds those permissions.

> **Tip**
>
> *If you are programming for a situation where more than one program may need to read a data file simultaneously but you don't need to manage the data file at the record level, you can declare a single region consisting of the first byte in the file. This enables two or more programs to share the file while reading, and when a program needs to update any data, it can obtain an exclusive write lock. It's one way of creating a more flexible file-level lock that allows shared reading.*

The File-Locking Commands

There are actually two ways to implement region locking under Linux—one using the **lockf** library function and the other using the **fcntl** library function. For this discussion, I'll stick with using **fcntl**, which is the more common method.

The **fcntl** function is a low-level system call that can duplicate files, get and set file descriptor flags, and manage advisory file locking. The source code for the Kylix **Libc** unit specifies the following declaration for **fcntl**:

```
function fcntl(Handle: Integer; Command: Integer;
            var Lock: TFlock): Integer; cdecl; overload;
```

Like most library functions, **fcntl** returns a value of –1 if an error occurred during its execution. If so, the value of the error can be found in **errno**. The **Handle** argument is actually an ordinary file descriptor, returned by the **open** function. The **Command** argument is one of three commands of interest for our purpose: **F_GETLK**, **F_SETLK**, or **F_SETLKW**. (I'll go into more detail on each of these in just a moment.) The **TFlock** structure is a record containing the various pieces of information that will be provided to and returned by the call to **fcntl**. The fields in the **TFlock** structure are detailed in Table 7.2.

The *F_GETLK* Command

This command does not actually try to obtain a lock. Instead, it will let you know if you *could have* obtained the lock you specified, at the instant the command was issued. To use **F_GETLK**, you must specify values for all the fields except l_pid. The allowable values for l_type for **F_GETLK** are **F_RDLCK** and **F_WRLCK**.

The call to **fcntl** returns immediately and should always succeed (that is, return a value other than –1) for **F_GETLK**. If this is the case, you can check your results by examining the l_type field within the **TFlock** structure. If the value you specified for l_type has been replaced by **F_UNLCK**, you would have been able to obtain the lock. If not, you can check the l_pid field; it will contain the pid of the process currently holding the lock.

The *F_SETLK* Command

This command enables you to set a read or write lock on a region or to clear an existing lock on a region. All fields in the **TFlock** record except l_pid must be specified, and the allowed values for l_type are **F_RDLCK** and **F_WRLCK**. The call to **fcntl** returns immediately. If it fails, it will return with a value of –1 and **errno** will be set to one of the system constants (**EACCES** or **EAGAIN**). If **fcntl** returns any other value, the lock was obtained.

The *F_SETLKW* Command

The **F_SETLKW** command is identical to **F_SETLK**, except that instead of returning immediately, it attempts to wait until the lock is achieved. If a signal that is to be caught is

Table 7.2 Fields in the TFlock structure.

Identifier	Description
l_type	Specifies the type of lock sought. If this value is set to **F_RDLCK**, the lock will be a shared (read) lock. If the value is **F_WRLCK**, the lock will be an exclusive (write) lock. A value of **F_UNLCK** is used to unlock (clear) existing locks.
l_whence	Specifies the basis for the offset to the region within the file. The acceptable values are **SEEK_SET** (the first byte in the file), **SEEK_CUR** (the current position within the file), and **SEEK_END** (the end of the file).
l_start	The offset to the first byte in the desired region. The byte pointed to will actually be that specified by **l_whence**, offset by **l_start**.
l_len	The length of the region, in bytes.
l_pid	A value returned by the call, specifying the pid of the process holding a lock on the specified region. (This only applies when the **F_GETLK** command is issued.)

received while **fcntl** is waiting, the **fcntl** call is interrupted and (after the signal handler has returned) it returns immediately with the value –1 and **errno** set to **EINTR**.

A Hypothetical Case

For a solution that will demonstrate the use of all the region-locking commands just covered, let's assume we have a data file like the one shown in Figure 7.4. This file consists of five fixed-length records. Each of the records has a variable-length format with three fields, separated by colons. The three fields will contain the number of the record (1–5), the pid of the process that last updated the record, and a random number in the range 1–32,768. (Okay, in a normal situation, you would never include the record number as part of a record. I've done it here just to satisfy myself that records are being written to the correct place.)

We'll have one application that is able to update our data file. When it does, it will write a single record that contains the record number to be written, its own pid, and a random number, so updates can easily be recognized. A second application will monitor the contents of each of the records and give us a dynamic picture of the locks being placed on the data file.

Solution Example: The **LockWriter** Program

The first application is shown in Figure 7.5. **LockWriter** enables its user to select one of the five records and update it by clicking the Update button. If a lock is acquired, the record is updated and the indicator flashes momentarily.

Listing 7.4 contains the code for **LockWriter**. Its **onCreate** event handler takes care of creating an initial data file if one does not exist; then the file is closed and reopened for reading or writing. Note that although it is possible to create the file with Object Pascal file routines, the program must use the Linux low-level **open** function to be compatible with **fcntl**.

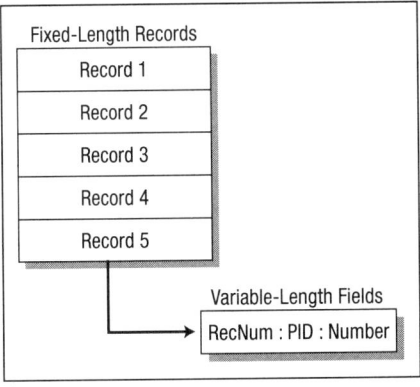

Figure 7.4
Model of the database to be used by the demo programs.

Figure 7.5
The **LockWriter** program.

A **TTimer** object is used to trigger the "real" event handler for the Update button, so the button won't be stuck in the down position during the rather lengthy time the update action is taking place. The actual updating is accomplished by the **UpdateRecord** procedure. First, the **TFlock** structure (**LockRec**) is stuffed with the information that requests an exclusive write lock and that specifies the offset and length of the record to be accessed. Then, depending on the **Checked** property of the checkbox, either **F_SETLK** or **F_SETLKW** is used in the **fnctl** call. If anything but –1 is returned, the lock was granted and the **__write** function is used to perform the record update.

Once the update has been accomplished, the lock is held for a period of time (it has been set to 500 ms by default). This is purely for demonstration purposes, so the monitoring application will have time to see and display an indication of the updating action. When the timeout has completed, **fcntl** is called once again—this time using the **F_UNLCK** value in **LockRec** to release the lock.

Listing 7.4   The **LockWriter** program.

```
unit LockWriterMain;

interface

uses
  SysUtils, Types, Classes, Variants, QGraphics, QControls, QForms, QDialogs,
  QStdCtrls, Libc, QExtCtrls, QTypes, QComCtrls;

type
  TLockWriterMainForm = class(TForm)
    ExitBtn: TButton;
    UpdateBtn: TButton;
    ProcLabel: TLabel;
    RecNumRBGroup: TRadioGroup;
    WaitForWriteCB: TCheckBox;
    GroupBox1: TGroupBox;
    UpdatePanel: TPanel;
    Trigger: TTimer;
```

```
    StatusBar: TStatusBar;
    Procedure UpdateRecord;
    procedure ExitBtnClick(Sender: TObject);
    procedure FormCreate(Sender: TObject);
    procedure UpdateBtnClick(Sender: TObject);
    procedure TriggerTimer(Sender: TObject);
  private
    { Private declarations }
  public
    { Public declarations }
  end;

const
  WriteDelay = 500; { milliseconds }
  DataFileName = '/tmp/LockRegion.data';
  NumRecs = 5;
  RecLen = 20;

var
  LockWriterMainForm: TLockWriterMainForm;
  PID : pid_t;
  PIDStr : String;
  DF : Integer;
  ErrResult : Integer;


implementation

{$R *.xfm}

procedure TLockWriterMainForm.UpdateRecord;
var
 RecNum : Integer;
 RandNum : Integer;
 LockRec : TFlock;
 Buf : array[0..RecLen] of char;
 DataStr : String;
begin
 StatusBar.SimpleText := '';
 RecNum := RecNumRBGroup.ItemIndex + 1;

 { Go for an exclusive lock }
 LockRec.l_type := F_WRLCK;
 LockRec.l_whence := SEEK_SET;
 LockRec.l_len := RecLen;
 LockRec.l_pid := -1;
 LockRec.l_start := RecLen * (RecNum - 1);
 if WaitForWriteCB.Checked
```

```
      then begin
          StatusBar.SimpleText := 'Waiting to write...';
          ErrResult := fcntl(DF, F_SETLKW, LockRec);
        end
    else ErrResult := fcntl(DF, F_SETLK, LockRec);
  if ErrResult <> -1
    then begin { We've got an exclusive lock }
          StatusBar.SimpleText := '';
          UpdatePanel.Color := clLime;
          Application.ProcessMessages;
          RandNum := Integer(Random(32768));
          DataStr := PIDStr + ' : ' + IntToStr(RecNum)
           + ' : ' + IntToStr(RandNum);
          if Length(DataStr) > RecLen
           then DataStr := copy(DataStr, 1, RecLen)
           else while Length(DataStr) < RecLen do
                 DataStr := DataStr + ' ';
          StrPCopy(Buf, DataStr);
          lseek(DF, RecLen * (RecNum - 1), SEEK_SET);
          __write(DF, Buf, RecLen);

          Sleep(WriteDelay);

          { Release the lock for this record }
          LockRec.l_type := F_UNLCK;
          LockRec.l_whence := SEEK_SET;
          LockRec.l_len := RecLen;
          LockRec.l_pid := -1;
          LockRec.l_start := RecLen * (RecNum - 1);
          fcntl(DF, F_SETLK, LockRec);
          StatusBar.SimpleText := 'Updated successfully';
        end
  else begin
       StatusBar.SimpleText := 'Not able to obtain lock';
       UpdatePanel.Color := clRed;
       Application.ProcessMessages;
       Sleep(WriteDelay);
      end;

 UpdatePanel.Color := clGreen;
end;

procedure TLockWriterMainForm.ExitBtnClick(Sender: TObject);
begin
 Close;
end;
```

```
procedure TLockWriterMainForm.FormCreate(Sender: TObject);
var
 F : TextFile;
 i : Integer;
 s : String;
begin
 Randomize;
 PID := getpid;
 PIDStr := IntToStr(PID);
 ProcLabel.Caption := 'Process ID: ' + PIDStr;
 if not FileExists(DataFileName)
  then begin { Create the data file }
        AssignFile(F, DataFileName);
        Rewrite(F);
        for i := 1 to NumRecs do
         begin
           s := PIDStr + ' : ' + IntToStr(i) + ' : 0';
           while Length(s) < RecLen do s := s + ' ';
           write(F, s);
         end; { for }
        CloseFile(F);
       end;
 DF := open(DataFileName,  O_RDWR);
 if DF = -1
  then begin
        UpdateBtn.Enabled := False;
        ShowMessage('Error opening data file!');
       end;
end;

procedure TLockWriterMainForm.UpdateBtnClick(Sender: TObject);
begin
 Trigger.Enabled := True;
end;

procedure TLockWriterMainForm.TriggerTimer(Sender: TObject);
begin
 Trigger.Enabled := False;
 UpdateBtn.Enabled := False;
 UpdateRecord;
 UpdateBtn.Enabled := True;
end;

end.
```

Solution Example: The **LockReader** Program

The second half of this record-locking demonstration is performed by **LockReader**, which is depicted in Figure 7.6. Once its Start/Stop button is clicked, **LockReader** repeatedly monitors and displays the status of the locks on each of the records, as well as displays the actual contents of those records. The type of lock currently granted on a record (exclusive, shared, or none) is displayed in color on an indicator next to the record.

Each time you click the Update button on **LockWriter**, the indicator for the selected record will flash and its contents will be updated on **LockReader**'s display. Clicking the Start/Stop button again stops the monitoring process.

Two controls are provided for modifying the behavior somewhat to account for the processing speed differences between machines. The **ReadDelay** control provides a selection of delay times that determine how long status indicators will stay lit, whereas the **Sampling Delay** control offers a selection of time delays that determine how often the records are examined.

Listing 7.5 contains the complete code for **LockReader**'s main unit. Like its partner, **LockWriter**, this program creates the data file if it doesn't exist, so there will for certain be a file to monitor. This time, however, the data file is opened in read-only mode.

Clicking the Start/Stop button enables **DisplayMonitor**, the **TTimer** object used to sample the status of data and locks. Each time **DisplayMonitor** fires, it calls **UpdateStatusDisplay**, and one time out of three it also calls **UpdateDataDisplay**.

Each time it is called, the **UpdateStatusDisplay** procedure checks the status of the locks on each record. The logic used for this process is not obvious from the code (it certainly had me scratching my head for a while!), so I'll summarize it here:

1. If we can obtain an exclusive lock on a record, that record must currently have no lock associated with it. No locks present. We're done.

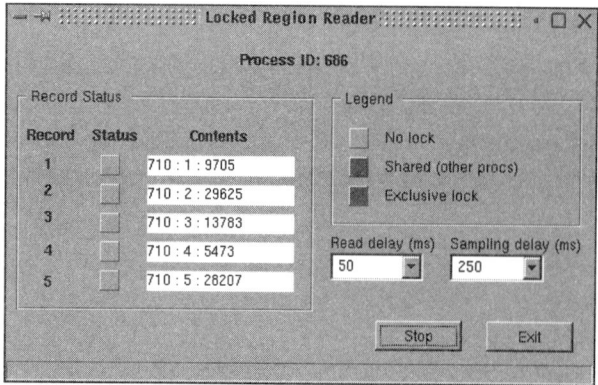

Figure 7.6
The **LockReader** program.

2. If we can't obtain an exclusive lock, there must already be one or more locks associated with the record. There could be one exclusive lock or any number of shared locks. We now see whether we can obtain a shared lock.

3. If there is no lock associated with the record, our **fcntl** call requesting the shared lock will return **F_UNLCK** in the **l_type** field of **LockRec**. The lock(s) must be of the shared type. We're done.

4. If the **fcntl** call doesn't return **F_UNLCK**, there must be an exclusive lock in place (and we can find out who owns it by examining the **l_pid** field of the record). Once again, we're through.

This logic is implemented in the **UpdateStatusDisplay** procedure. Once all the machinations are complete, the **Sleep** procedure is called using the value of **ReadDelay** (determined by the selection in **ReadDelayCombo**) to provide some "dwell" time to keep the indicator "lit."

Each time it is called, the **UpdateDataDisplay** procedure reads and displays the contents of each record by obtaining a shared read lock on the record and then pulling in its data with the **__read** library function. Once again, a delay is imposed for improved display; following the delay, the lock is cleared.

Tip

*Running **LockWriter** and **LockReader** is more instructive (and a whole lot more fun) if you run multiple copies of **LockReader**. Because the **UpdateStatusDisplay** and **UpdateDataDisplay** procedures are not interrupt-driven, they always run in sequential fashion. So even though **UpdateDataDisplay** requests a shared lock for each record, this operation is invisible to **UpdateStatusDisplay**.*

*If you launch multiple instances of **LockReader** (the more, the merrier), each instance will see the shared locks implemented by the other instances, and the "light show" gets more interesting. Even though the instances are not synchronized, on a lightly loaded machine they will seem to be, as the light flashes fall into a repeatable pattern. Stopping and then restarting the monitoring on one of the instances will change the pattern.*

Listing 7.5   The **LockReader** program.

```
unit LockReaderMain;

interface

uses
  SysUtils, Types, Classes, Variants, QGraphics, QControls, QForms, QDialogs,
  QStdCtrls, QExtCtrls, QComCtrls, Libc, QTypes;
```

```
type
  TLockReaderMainForm = class(TForm)
    StartBtn: TButton;
    ExitBtn: TButton;
    ProcLabel: TLabel;
    StatusBar: TStatusBar;
    GroupBox1: TGroupBox;
    Label4: TLabel;
    Label5: TLabel;
    Label6: TLabel;
    Label8: TLabel;
    Label9: TLabel;
    Label10: TLabel;
    Label11: TLabel;
    Label12: TLabel;
    Rec1Panel: TPanel;
    Rec2Panel: TPanel;
    Rec3Panel: TPanel;
    Rec4Panel: TPanel;
    Rec5Panel: TPanel;
    Rec1Label: TLabel;
    Rec2Label: TLabel;
    Rec3Label: TLabel;
    Rec4Label: TLabel;
    Rec5Label: TLabel;
    GroupBox2: TGroupBox;
    Panel6: TPanel;
    Label1: TLabel;
    Panel1: TPanel;
    Label2: TLabel;
    DisplayMonitor: TTimer;
    Panel2: TPanel;
    Label3: TLabel;
    ReadDelayCombo: TComboBox;
    Label7: TLabel;
    Label13: TLabel;
    SampleDelayCombo: TComboBox;
    procedure ClearStatusDisplay(Color : TColor; Visible : Boolean);
    procedure UpdateStatusDisplay;
    procedure UpdateDataDisplay;
    procedure ExitBtnClick(Sender: TObject);
    procedure FormCreate(Sender: TObject);
    procedure DisplayMonitorTimer(Sender: TObject);
    procedure StartBtnClick(Sender: TObject);
```

```
    procedure ReadDelayComboClick(Sender: TObject);
    procedure SampleDelayComboClick(Sender: TObject);
  private
    { Private declarations }
  public
    { Public declarations }
  end;

const
  DefaultSampleDelay = 250; { milliseconds }
  DefaultReadDelay = 50; { milliseconds }
  NumRecs = 5;
  RecLen = 20;
  DataFileName = '/tmp/LockRegion.data';
var
  LockReaderMainForm: TLockReaderMainForm;
  PID : pid_t;
  PIDStr : String;
  DF : Integer;
  ErrResult : Integer;
  Running : Boolean;
  SyncCntr : Integer;
  SampleDelay : Integer;
  ReadDelay : Integer;

implementation

{$R *.xfm}

procedure TLockReaderMainForm.ClearStatusDisplay(Color : TColor;
             Visible : Boolean);
begin
 Rec1Panel.Visible := Visible;
 Rec1Panel.Color := Color;
 Rec2Panel.Visible := Visible;
 Rec2Panel.Color := Color;
 Rec3Panel.Visible := Visible;
 Rec3Panel.Color := Color;
 Rec4Panel.Visible := Visible;
 Rec4Panel.Color := Color;
 Rec5Panel.Visible := Visible;
 Rec5Panel.Color := Color;
end;
```

```
procedure TLockReaderMainForm.UpdateStatusDisplay;
var
 i : Integer;
 Color : TColor;
 LockRec : TFlock;
begin
 for i := 1 to NumRecs do
  begin
   { Check for exclusive locks }
   LockRec.l_type := F_WRLCK;
   LockRec.l_whence := SEEK_SET;
   LockRec.l_len := RecLen;
   LockRec.l_pid := -1;
   LockRec.l_start := RecLen * (i - 1);
   ErrResult := fcntl(DF, F_GETLK, LockRec);
   if ErrResult = -1
    then begin
         ShowMessage('Error trying to read file status!'
          + ' Closing...');
         Close;
        end;


  if lockrec.l_type = F_UNLCK
  then begin { No locks present }
        Color := clSilver;
       end
  else begin { Can't have an exclusive lock - why? }
        { See if there's a shared read lock }
        LockRec.l_type := F_RDLCK;
        LockRec.l_whence := SEEK_SET;
        LockRec.l_len := RecLen;
        LockRec.l_pid := -1;
        LockRec.l_start := RecLen * (i - 1);
        ErrResult := fcntl(DF, F_GETLK, LockRec);
        if ErrResult = -1
         then begin
              ShowMessage('Error trying to read file status!'
                + ' Closing...');
              Close;
             end;
        if LockRec.l_type = F_UNLCK
         then Color := clTeal { Another shared lock exists }
         else Color := clRed { Exclusive lock exists }
       end;
```

```
  case i of
    1 : Rec1Panel.Color := Color;
    2 : Rec2Panel.Color := Color;
    3 : Rec3Panel.Color := Color;
    4 : Rec4Panel.Color := Color;
    5 : Rec5Panel.Color := Color;
    end; { case }
  end; { for }

 Sleep(ReadDelay);

 end;

procedure TLockReaderMainForm.UpdateDataDisplay;
var
 i : Integer;
 LockRec : TFlock;
 Buf : array [0..RecLen] of char;
begin
 for i := 1 to NumRecs do
  begin
   LockRec.l_type := F_RDLCK;
   LockRec.l_whence := SEEK_SET;
   LockRec.l_len := RecLen;
   LockRec.l_pid := -1;
   LockRec.l_start := RecLen * (i - 1);
   ErrResult := fcntl(DF, F_SETLK, LockRec);
   if ErrResult <> -1
    then begin { We've got a shared lock }
           lseek(DF, RecLen * (i - 1), SEEK_SET);
           __read(DF, Buf, RecLen);
           Buf[RecLen] := chr(0);
           case i of
             1 : Rec1Label.Caption := Buf;
             2 : Rec2Label.Caption := Buf;
             3 : Rec3Label.Caption := Buf;
             4 : Rec4Label.Caption := Buf;
             5 : Rec5Label.Caption := Buf;
           end; { case }

           Sleep(ReadDelay);

           { Let the lock go for this record }
           LockRec.l_type := F_UNLCK;
           LockRec.l_whence := SEEK_SET;
```

```
            LockRec.l_len := RecLen;
            LockRec.l_pid := -1;
            LockRec.l_start := RecLen * (i - 1);
            fcntl(DF, F_SETLK, LockRec);
          end;
  end; { for }
end;

procedure TLockReaderMainForm.ExitBtnClick(Sender: TObject);
begin
 Close;
end;

procedure TLockReaderMainForm.FormCreate(Sender: TObject);
var
 F : TextFile;
 i : Integer;
 s : String;
begin
 SampleDelay := DefaultSampleDelay;
 DisplayMonitor.Interval := SampleDelay;
 ReadDelay := DefaultReadDelay;

 ClearStatusDisplay(clSilver, False);
 Running := False;
 PID := getpid;
 PIDStr := IntToStr(PID);
 ProcLabel.Caption := 'Process ID: ' + PIDStr;
 if not FileExists(DataFileName)
  then begin { Create the data file }
        AssignFile(F, DataFileName);
        Rewrite(F);
        for i := 1 to NumRecs do
         begin
           s := PIDStr + ' : ' + IntToStr(i) + ' : 0';
           while Length(s) < RecLen do s := s + ' ';
           write(F, s);
         end; { for }
        CloseFile(F);
       end;
 DF := open(DataFileName,  O_RDONLY);
 if DF = -1
  then begin
        StartBtn.Enabled := False;
```

```
            ShowMessage('Error opening data file!');
            StatusBar.SimpleText := 'Error opening data file';
          end;
end;

procedure TLockReaderMainForm.DisplayMonitorTimer(Sender: TObject);
begin
  Inc(SyncCntr);
  if SyncCntr mod 3 = 0 then UpdateDataDisplay;
  UpdateStatusDisplay;
end;

procedure TLockReaderMainForm.StartBtnClick(Sender: TObject);
begin
  if Running
    then begin
          ClearStatusDisplay(clSilver, False);
          DisplayMonitor.Enabled := False;
          StartBtn.Caption := 'Start';
          Running := False;
        end
    else begin
          ClearStatusDisplay(clSilver, True);
          StartBtn.Caption := 'Stop';
          DisplayMonitor.Enabled := True;
          Running := True;
        end;
end;

procedure TLockReaderMainForm.ReadDelayComboClick(Sender: TObject);
begin
  ReadDelay :=
    StrToInt(ReadDelayCombo.Items[ReadDelayCombo.ItemIndex]);
end;

procedure TLockReaderMainForm.SampleDelayComboClick(Sender: TObject);
begin
  SampleDelay :=
    StrToInt(SampleDelayCombo.Items[SampleDelayCombo.ItemIndex]);
  DisplayMonitor.Interval := SampleDelay;
end;

end.
```

Solution 7.5: Obtaining File Attributes and Information

Occasionally applications need to know information about files on the system. For high-level applications, the information required might include the file size. For low-level utility applications, it might be the file's inode number (see the sidebar). This information and more can be obtained using the **stat** family of system calls (**stat**, **fstat**, and **lstat**).

In Solution 7.1, I used **stat** to obtain the permission mask for a file. There are several additional pieces of information returned in a **TStatBuf** record, however, including the file's size, type, group, owner, and time last modified as well as the serial number assigned by the system to ensure the file's uniqueness. The **TStatBuf** record filled by **stat** has the following format (some fields used for padding the record have been removed for clarity):

```
TStatBuf = {packed} record
  st_dev: __dev_t;                    { Device. }
  st_ino: __ino_t;                    { File serial number. }
  st_mode: __mode_t;                  { File mode. }
  st_nlink: __nlink_t;                { Link count. }
  st_uid: __uid_t;                    { User ID of the file's owner. }
  st_gid: __gid_t;                    { Group ID of the file's group. }
  st_rdev: __dev_t;                   { Device number, if device. }
  st_size: __off_t;                   { Size of file, in bytes. }
  st_blksize: __blksize_t;            { Optimal block size for I/O. }
  st_blocks: __blkcnt_t;              { Number 512-byte blocks allocated. }
  st_atime: __time_t;                 { Time of last access. }
  st_mtime: __time_t;                 { Time of last modification. }
  st_ctime: __time_t;                 { Time of last status change. }
end;
```

In Solution 7.1, I used the **st_mode** field to get file permissions. That field is also used to store the type of file. The information in Table 7.1 still applies here, and it goes along with the information in Table 7.3. This table shows the new file type constants as well as the

Table 7.3 File mode constants.

Constant	Test Function	Meaning
__S_IFDIR	S_ISDIR	Directory
__S_IFCHR	S_ISCHR	Character device
__S_IFBLK	S_ISBLK	Block device
__S_IFREG	S_ISREG	Regular file
__S_IFIFO	S_ISFIFO	FIFO
__S_IFLNK	S_ISLNK	Symbolic link
__S_IFSOCK	S_ISSOCK	Socket

An Inode by Any Other Name Is Still the Same File

As you saw in Chapter 2, it is possible to create any number of links to a single file. This is possible because files under Linux aren't identified by name but rather by unique integral values called *inode numbers*. It is perfectly legal to have multiple directory entries (names) that point to the same inode. In fact, when a hard link is created (soft links do not follow this rule), that is exactly what is done—a new directory entry is created and the reference count on the inode is incremented. When a file is deleted, the entry in the directory is removed, and the inode's reference count is decremented. If the reference count goes to zero, the inode—the actual file itself—will be deleted.

It is important to note that inode numbers are unique only within a single filesystem. If you have a drive partition mounted as /home, for example, it is likely that inode numbers will be duplicated between that partition and your root partition.

At times, it is desirable to refer to a specific inode rather than a filename. These times can include removing files with corrupted names or with control characters embedded in their names. The inode number can be obtained using the sample program shown here or by using the **ls** command-line utility with the **-i** option.

Finding all directory entries that refer to a specific inode is more difficult and is a job for the **find** command. Here's how to do it: First, use **ls -i** to find the inode number (999, for example) and then use the **find** command from the mount point of the filesystem to find all file names that refer to that inode number (**find /home -inum 999 -print**). Remember: if you conduct this search from your root directory, it is possible to obtain file names from other filesystems. Always limit these searches to the filesystem containing the inode of interest.

---

names of some functions provided in the **Libc** unit that are used to test the **st_mode** values. I'll be using these functions in my sample code for this section.

The **TStatBuf** field **st_ino** is used to hold the unique file serial number—called the inode number—allocated for this file. Two other useful fields from the **TStatBuf** record are the **st_uid** and **st_gid** fields, which contain the numeric values for the uid and gid of the file's owner. (These numeric values can be converted to textual names with the assistance of the **getpwuid** and **getgrgid** functions.) An in-depth description of each of the fields in a **TStatBuf** record is available on the stat man page (type "man stat").

Solution Example: The **FileInfo** Program

The **FileInfo** application shown in Figure 7.7 lists the files contained in a directory and allows the user of the application to view several of the more important attributes of those files.

Listing 7.6 contains two of the methods from the **FileInfo** application. The first is **populateFileList,** the method that populates the file list. This method uses our old friends **FindFirst** and **FindNext,** which have made a return appearance from Delphi. They are used in almost exactly the same manner in Kylix.

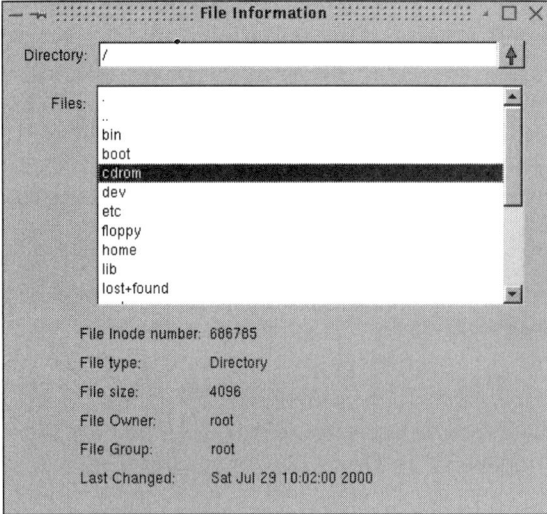

Figure 7.7
The **FileInfo** Program.

The second method contained in Listing 7.6, **lbFilesClick**, is used to populate the file information fields on the form when a user clicks one of the files in the list. This method shows the use of the **getpwuid** and **getgrgid** functions to retrieve the names of the file's group and owner.

Listing 7.6   Selected methods from the FileInfo application.

```
procedure TForm1.populateFileList;
var
    searchRec: TSearchRec;
    rv: Integer;
    savedCursor: TCursor;
begin
    savedCursor := Screen.Cursor;
    Screen.Cursor := crHourGlass;

    lbFiles.Clear;

    rv := FindFirst( String( tbDirectory.Text ) + '/*',
                    faAnyFile, searchRec );

    while ( rv = 0 ) do
        begin
        lbFiles.items.Add( searchRec.Name );
        rv := FindNext( searchRec );
        end;
```

```
    FindClose( searchrec );
    lbFiles.ClearSelection;
    Screen.Cursor := savedCursor;
end;


procedure TForm1.lbFilesClick(Sender: TObject);
var
    rv: Integer;
    filename: String;
    statbuf: TStatBuf;
    passrec: PPasswordRecord;
    grprec: PGroup;
begin
        // get the details for the selected file and fill in the form
    filename := constructFilename;
    rv := lstat( PChar( filename ), statBuf );
    if ( rv = -1 ) then
        begin
        ShowMessage( 'Unable to stat file.' );
        exit;
        end;

        // display the file's inode number
    lblInode.Caption := IntToStr(statBuf.st_ino );

        // display the mode (type) of the file
    if ( S_ISDIR( statBuf.st_mode) = true ) then
        lblType.Caption := 'Directory'
    else if ( S_ISCHR( statBuf.st_mode) = true ) then
        lblType.Caption := 'Character device'
    else if ( S_ISBLK( statBuf.st_mode) = true ) then
        lblType.Caption := 'Block device'
    else if ( S_ISREG( statBuf.st_mode) = true ) then
        lblType.Caption := 'Regular file'
    else if ( S_ISFIFO( statBuf.st_mode) = true ) then
        lblType.Caption := 'FIFO'
    else if ( S_ISLNK( statBuf.st_mode) = true ) then
        lblType.Caption := 'Symbolic link'
    else if ( S_ISSOCK( statBuf.st_mode ) = true ) then
        lblType.Caption := 'Socket'
    else
        lblType.Caption := 'Unknown...';
```

```
        // display the file size
    lblSize.Caption := IntToStr(tatBuf.st_size);

        // display the owner of the file
    passrec := getpwuid( statBuf.st_uid );
    lblOwner.Caption := passrec.pw_name;

        // display the group of the file
    grprec := getgrgid( statBuf.st_gid );
    lblGroup.caption := grprec.gr_name;

        // display the last modification time of the file
    lblModified.Caption := ctime( Addr( statBuf.st_mtime ) );
end;
```

Solution 7.6: Mounting Other Filesystems

Let's be honest. Most applications will be perfectly content with the filesystem mounted on the machine when they start up. Sometimes, though, they'll need to mount a CD drive, Zip drive, or some other device that isn't already mounted. Whether for CD authentication or data backup, some applications will need to access other filesystems. And if Murphy plays as big a role on your system as he does on mine, it's almost a certainty that the user will forget to mount the needed drive before starting the program.

When that happens, it'll impress your users to no end that your program is able to do this automatically, without requiring them to raise a finger. The drawback is that only the superuser can **mount** filesystems. There's always a catch, but at least we've discussed this one—see Solution 5.12 in Chapter 5 for information on running your program with superuser privileges.

Tip

*The fact that only the superuser can mount filesystems is true, but only by default. The file **/etc/fstab** contains the information used by the system to mount known filesystems. Within this file is a column containing mount options. If the "user" option is specified for a filesystem in this list, ordinary users will be able to mount and unmount that filesystem, using the **mount** command-line utility, without the need for superuser status. Unfortunately, though, this will only help you from the command-line side because the **fstab** file is used only by the **mount** command-line utility (which runs as setuid root anyway) and has no bearing on the **mount** system call. What this means for you as an applications programmer is that if you want to mount filesystems programmatically, your program will need root privileges. If you want to prompt the normal user who is running your program to mount the CD-ROM, then having the admin set the user flag in the **fstab** file will allow the user to do that.*

Mounting and unmounting other filesystems is accomplished with the **mount** and **umount** system calls. These calls are made available to your program when you use the **Libc** unit and are fully documented in the system man pages, so I'll only summarize them here.

*Because of the name collision between the **mount** and **umount** system calls and the **mount** and **umount** command-line utilities, you'll need to specify the section number when you attempt to read these man pages. The command line required to do this is*

```
man 2 mount
```

or

```
man 2 umount
```

Section 2 of the man pages is for system calls, whereas the command line utilities are all in section 1.

The **mount** Function

The **mount** system call takes five arguments and has the following format:

```
function mount(__special_file: PChar;
               __dir: PChar;
               __fstype: PChar;
               __rwflag: Cardinal;
               __data: Pointer): Integer; cdecl;
```

The first argument to mount, **__special file**, contains a pointer to the name of the special device that will be mounted. This is usually the name of a device file from the /dev directory (/dev/cdrom, for example). The second argument, **__dir**, contains a pointer to the name of a directory on the system that will be used as the device's mount point. For example, an empty directory called /cdrom could be used as the mount point for the CD-ROM drive. This directory can be anywhere on the system.

The third argument, **__fstype**, is the filesystem type. A list of supported filesystem types can be found on your system in the file **/proc/filesystems**. The fourth argument, **__rwflag**, specifies the options that will be used when mounting the device. The argument is a combination of a magic number—available as the named constant **MS_MGC_VAL**—bitwise or'ed with one or more of the constants in Table 7.4. The final argument is **__data**, a pointer whose meaning and usage will depend on the type of filesystem you are mounting. If the call to mount succeeds, it returns 0; if it fails, it returns –1 and enters an appropriate value in **errno**.

Table 7.4 Options for the **mount** system call.

Option Constant	Description
MS_RDONLY	Mount read-only
MS_NOSUID	Ignore **suid** and **sgid** bits
MS_NODEV	Disallow access to device special files
MS_NOEXEC	Disallow program execution
MS_SYNCHRONOUS	Writes are synced at once
MS_REMOUNT	Alter flags of a mounted filesystem
MS_MANDLOCK	Allow mandatory locks on an filesystem
S_WRITE	Write on file/directory/symlink
S_APPEND	Append-only file
S_IMMUTABLE	Immutable file
MS_NOATIME	Do not update access times
MS_NODIRATIME	Do not update directory access times
MS_BIND	Bind directory at different place

The *umount* Function

The **umount** system call is substantially easier to use than **mount**. The **umount** system call takes the following form:

```
function umount(__special_file: PChar): Integer; cdecl;
```

As you can see, the **umount** function has only one argument—the name of the special device you're unmounting. Like **mount**, **umount** can be executed only by the superuser. If it succeeds, it returns 0; if it fails, it returns –1 and places a meaningful error code in errno.

The *setmntent, getmntent* and *endmntent* Functions

Linux keeps information on filesystems known to the system (in **/etc/fstab**) and on filesystems that are already mounted (in **/proc/mounts**). (Linux also keeps information on mounted filesystems in the **/etc/mtab** file, for the convenience of the **mount** command-line utility, but this data is not necessarily current.) The function library thoughtfully provides a set of three functions that make it easy to pull information from any of these files: **setmntent**, **getmntent**, and **endmntent**.

The **setmntent** function returns an open file stream to the selected filesystem data file. As its arguments, **setmntent** takes a variable of type **PChar** pointing to the name of the file and another variable of type **PChar** that indicates whether the stream will be opened for reading (**r**) or writing (**w**). The **setmntent** function takes the following form:

```
function setmntent(__file: PChar; _mode: PChar): PIOFile; cdecl;
```

The **getmntent** function is used to read from the file stream. Each time it is called, it reads a line from the stream and parses it into fields, filling in a **TMountEntry** record. Here's the form of **getmntent**:

```
function getmntent(__stream: PIOFile): PMountEntry; cdecl;
```

The **PMountEntry** record returned by **getmntent** contains fields that represent each of the possible fields within a mounting specification. Here is the declaration of the **TMountEntry** record:

```
PMountEntry = ^TMountEntry;
TMountEntry = {packed} record
    mnt_fsname: PChar;                      { Device or server for filesystem. }
    mnt_dir: PChar;                         { Directory mounted on. }
    mnt_type: PChar;                        { Type of filesystem: ufs, nfs, etc. }
    mnt_opts: PChar;                        { Comma-separated options for fs. }
    mnt_freq: Integer;                      { Dump frequency (in days). }
    mnt_passno: Integer;                    { Pass number for 'fsck'. }
  end;
```

When all the records in the filesystem data file have been read, you need to close the stream. That's done with **endmntent**:

```
function endmntent(__stream: PIOFile): Integer; cdecl;
```

These functions make child's play of extracting information from the mounted device tables.

Solution Example: The **MountTool** Program

The **MountTool** program, shown in Figure 7.8, demonstrates the use of both the **mount** and **umount** system calls to mount and unmount external filesystems, such as CD-ROM and floppy drives.

MountTool builds a list of known mountable devices by parsing the information stored in **/etc/fstab**. After selecting any of the devices in the list box, the user will be allowed to mount or unmount the selected device, depending on whether it is already mounted on the system. (Remember that the user will need to be root in order to execute these operations.)

Warning

As with many of the solutions presented here, misuse of this sample program could be hazardous to the health of your system. Very little sanity checking is performed by the application itself. Use it with caution. It is generally quite safe to mount and unmount CD-ROM drives and floppy disks, but use caution when playing with the devices that are already in use on your system. In a further attempt to provide a little more safety with this application, filesystems will only be mounted for read-only access.

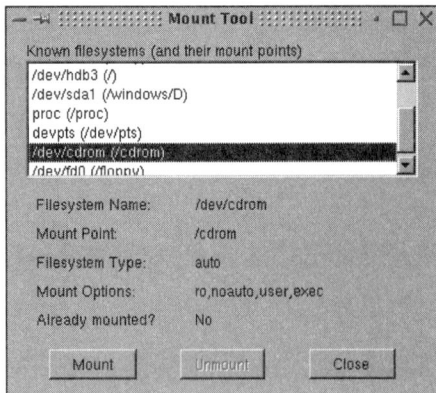

Figure 7.8
The **MountTool** program.

Relevant code from the **MountTool** application is presented in Listing 7.7. The **FillForm** procedure first examines the **/proc/mounts** file and builds a string list containing the mount points of all mounted drives (that is, the directory where the device is attached). The **fstab** file is then processed, and the list of all known filesystems is placed in the list box.

When the **onClick** event handler is called for the Mount button, it uses the **ItemIndex** property of the list box (which indicates the selected item) as an index into the list of mount points. The information in **mntEntList** is then used as arguments for a call to **mount**. The **onClick** event handler for the Unmount button works in a similar fashion, taking information from **mntEntList** to make its call to **umount**. The **RefreshForm** procedure is used by several routines to update the fields on the form to reflect the current status.

Listing 7.8 details the **onFormLoad** event handler for the dialog box called by the **MountTool** application. This dialog box offers a choice of specific filesystem types when an "auto" parameter is detected in a mount specification (for a CD-ROM drive, for example). As you can see, the routine easily picks up a list of all possible device types by reading the **/proc/filesystems** file.

Listing 7.7   Excerpts from **MountForm.pas**.

```
procedure TForm1.FillForm;
var
 f: PIOFile;
 mntEnt: PMountEntry;
 mntIdx: Integer;
begin
 mntIdx := 0;

 if ( getuid <> 0 ) then
  ShowMessage( 'You are not running as root. You will only be able ' +
               'to examine the mount information, not change it.' );
```

```
// first, get the mount points of all mounted drives
f := setmntent( '/proc/mounts', 'r' );
if not Assigned( f ) then
 begin
  ShowMessage( 'Fatal: Unable to open /proc/mounts' );
  exit;
 end;

mntEnt := getmntent( f );
while ( mntEnt <> nil ) do
 begin
  mounts.Add( mntEnt.mnt_dir );
  mntEnt := getmntent( f );
 end;
endmntent( f );

// now, populate the list of known filesystems in the list box
// and keep track of 'em for later use.
f := setmntent( _PATH_FSTAB, 'r' );
if ( not Assigned( f ) ) then
 begin
  ShowMessage( 'Fatal: Unable to open ' + _PATH_FSTAB );
  exit;
 end;

mntEnt := getmntent( f );
while ( mntEnt <> nil ) do
 begin
  lbFilesystems.Items.Add( mntEnt.mnt_fsname
      + ' (' + mntEnt.mnt_dir + ')' );
  persistMntEntry( mntIdx, mntEnt );

  mntEnt := getmntent( f );

  Inc( mntIdx );
 end;

 endmntent( f );
end;

procedure TForm1.persistMntEntry( idx: Integer; mntEnt: PMountEntry );
begin
 mntEntList[idx].fsName := mntEnt.mnt_fsname;
 mntEntList[idx].mountPoint := mntEnt.mnt_dir;
 mntEntList[idx].fsType := mntEnt.mnt_type;
 mntEntList[idx].fsOpts := mntEnt.mnt_opts;
 if ( mounts.IndexOf( mntEnt.mnt_dir ) <> -1 ) then
  mntEntList[idx].mounted := true
 else
```

```
    mntEntList[idx].mounted := false;
  end;

procedure TForm1.btnMountClick(Sender: TObject);
var
 idx: Integer;
 rv: Integer;
 str: String;
begin
 idx := lbFilesystems.ItemIndex;
 if ( mntEntList[idx].fstype = 'auto' )
  then begin
        TTypeSelect.ShowModal;
        str := TTypeSelect.selectedType;
       end
  else
    str := mntEntList[idx].fstype;

 // mount read only for safety in this example
 rv := mount( PChar( mntEntList[idx].fsName ),
              PChar( mntEntList[idx].mountPoint ),
              PChar( str ),
              MS_MGC_VAL Or MS_RDONLY,
              nil );
 if ( rv <> 0 )
  then ShowMessage( strerror( errno ) )
  else begin
        mntEntList[idx].mounted := true;
        RefreshForm;
        btnMount.Enabled := false;
        btnUnmount.Enabled := true;
       end;
end;

procedure TForm1.btnUnmountClick(Sender: TObject);
var
 idx: Integer;
 rv: Integer;
begin
 idx := lbFilesystems.ItemIndex;
 rv := umount( PChar( mntEntList[idx].fsName ) );
 if ( rv <> 0 )
  then ShowMessage( strerror( errno ) )
  else begin
        mntEntList[idx].mounted := false;
        RefreshForm;
        btnMount.Enabled := true;
        btnUnmount.Enabled := false;
```

```
        end;
end;

procedure TForm1.RefreshForm;
var
 idx: Integer;
begin
 idx := lbFilesystems.ItemIndex;
 lblFsName.Caption := mntEntList[idx].fsName;
 lblMountPoint.Caption := mntEntList[idx].mountPoint;
 lblFsType.Caption := mntEntList[idx].fsType;
 lblMntOptions.Caption := mntEntList[idx].fsOpts;
 if ( mntEntList[idx].mounted )
  then begin
        lblMounted.Caption := 'Yes';
        btnMount.Enabled := false;
        btnUnmount.Enabled := true;
       end
  else begin
        lblMounted.Caption := 'No';
        btnMount.Enabled := true;
        btnUnmount.Enabled := false;
       end;
end;
```

Listing 7.8   Excerpt from SelectForm.pas.

```
procedure TTTypeSelect.FormLoaded(Sender: TObject);
var
 F: TextFile;
 str: String;
begin
 AssignFile( F, '/proc/filesystems' );
 FileMode := fmOpenRead;
 Reset( F );
 Readln( F, str );
 {$I-}
 while ( Length( str ) > 0 ) do
  begin
   str := Trim( str );
   if ( Pos( 'nodev', str ) = 0 )
    then lbFsTypes.Items.Add( str );
   Readln( f, str );
  end;
 CloseFile( F );
 {$I+}
end;
```

Chapter 8
Online Help

A GUI application should have online help. It's as simple as that. Even if they receive a printed manual, users are loath to actually read it, and with electronic distribution of applications becoming increasingly more prevalent, users more often than not don't even have a printed manual. Some developers try to get away with creating README files in the distribution directories, but there's really no substitute for a good context-sensitive online help system that the user can access by pressing F1.

Other than man pages, which are inadequate for GUI programs' online help, there is no recognized standard for online documentation in the Linux world. There are some competing technologies available either from vendors or as free software, but none has emerged as an overwhelming favorite among developers. One proprietary product, HyperHelp from Bristol Technologies (**www.bristol.com**), provides a cross-platform emulation of the Windows WinHelp engine and is the help system that Borland used for Kylix's online help. Kylix does not, however, include a help compiler for HyperHelp, and developers are not allowed to redistribute the HyperHelp viewer from the Kylix package.

This lack of an online help standard poses some interesting challenges for application developers in terms of actually creating online help content. Fortunately though, Borland endowed Kylix with a flexible help system architecture that makes it very easy to create an interface to any help system without changing the way that help is handled within the application.

Help System Architecture

Within a Kylix application, online help is provided by the global **HelpSystem** object. The **HelpSystem**, which is created at application startup, is a system-independent interface between the program code (**TApplication** object, **TForm** object, and other **TControl** descendents) and the system-dependent Help Viewer modules that interact with individual online help systems. Applications make online help requests to the **HelpSystem** object, which forwards those requests to the individual Help Viewer modules. Developers create or otherwise obtain (perhaps from third parties) Help Viewers for particular help systems.

All the machinery for responding to users' help requests is already built into Kylix controls. The **TControl** class, from which all controls descend, has help-related properties that allow you to define the help file that contains the control's online help, as well as the topic identifier or keyword string that identifies the help text within that file. All you need to do is set those properties for each control at design time. If you do not define a help file for a particular control, Kylix will use the parent form's help file. And if the Form has no help file defined, the Application's help file is used. When the user presses F1 at runtime, a help request is forwarded through the **HelpSystem** object to the **HelpManager** and on to the Help Viewer.

The Help Viewer module forwards help requests to the underlying online help system—be it HyperHelp, man pages, a Web browser, or something else. Note that, although the Help Viewer is included in the application, no application code calls it directly. Rather, the Help Viewer's initialization code registers the viewer with the **HelpManager**.

This architecture makes it very easy to move an application from one help system to another, or even to provide information from multiple help systems in the same program. The hardest part is creating the Help Viewer module, and as you'll see, even that isn't terribly difficult.

Unlike the other chapters in this part of the book, where each solution can stand by itself, the solution examples in this chapter will build on each other. The example in Solution 8.2, for example, makes use of the example from Solution 8.1. Wherever possible, we have tried to minimize the dependencies between the individual examples.

Solution 8.1: Creating a Simple Help Viewer

A Help Viewer is a **TInterfacedObject** descendent that implements the **ICustomHelpViewer** interface or one of its descendent interfaces (**IExtendedHelpViewer** or **ISpecialWinHelpViewer**). These interfaces are defined in the **HelpIntfs.pas** unit, which is located in your **kylix/source/clx** directory.

The **ICustomHelpViewer** interface defines the base interface that all Help Viewers must implement. Table 8.1 lists all the methods and provides a brief description of each.

Table 8.1   The methods of the ICustomHelpViewer interface.

Method	Description
GetViewerName	function **GetViewerName: String;** The **HelpManager** calls this function to obtain the viewer's name. The viewer's name is a string that identifies the viewer to the user (for example, 'Simple Help Viewer').
UnderstandsKeyword	function **UnderstandsKeyword (const HelpString: String): Integer;** The **HelpManager** calls this function to ask whether the viewer can provide help for the keyword identified by the **HelpString** parameter. The return value is the number of topics associated with that keyword. A return value of 0 indicates that the viewer has no topics that match the keyword.
GetHelpStrings	function **GetHelpStrings (const HelpString: String): TStringList;** The **HelpManager** calls this function to obtain the names of the topics that match the keyword identified by **HelpString**. The **HelpManager** interface guarantees that this function will only be called after **UnderstandsKeywords** returns a value greater than 0. The **HelpManager** will not ask for a list of topics for a keyword that the viewer does not understand.
CanShowTableOfContents	function **CanShowTableOfContents: Boolean;** The **HelpManager** calls this function to see whether the viewer is capable of showing a table of contents. The viewer should return True if it can display the contents and False if no table of contents is available.
ShowTableOfContents	procedure **ShowTableOfContents;** The **HelpManager** calls this function to have the viewer display the table of contents. The **HelpManager** will not call this procedure if the **CanShowTableOfContents** method returns False.
ShowHelp	procedure **ShowHelp (const HelpString: String);** The **HelpManager** calls this procedure to instruct the Viewer to display help for a particular keyword. The **HelpString** parameter contains the keyword of the topic to be displayed. The **HelpManager** guarantees that it will never call this procedure unless it has called **UnderstandsKeywords** first.
NotifyID	procedure **NotifyID (const ViewerID: Integer);** The **HelpManager** calls this function after the viewer has been registered to provide the viewer with a unique identifier that identifies it with the **HelpManager**. The viewer uses this identifier to communicate with the **HelpManager**.
SoftShutDown	procedure **SoftShutDown;** The **HelpManager** calls **SoftShutDown** to shut down all external subsystems without actually shutting down the viewer. The viewer should close any windows it has created and shut down any external subsystems (the **HyperHel**p viewer, for example).
ShutDown	procedure **ShutDown;** The **HelpManager** calls **ShutDown** to completely shut down the viewer. The viewer should shut down all external subsystems and release its reference to the **HelpManager**.

A Help Viewer is typically implemented in a separate unit and included in the **uses** clause of the application's main module. No application code calls functions in the **Viewer** unit. Rather, the unit's **initialization** code creates the viewer and registers it with the **HelpManager** at system startup, and the **finalization** code destroys the viewer when the program exits.

Solution Example: The **TSimpleHelpViewer** Class

When you're learning a new technology, it's usually helpful to implement the smallest possible working example so that you can see how to interface with the underlying system without having to worry about details specific to your particular application. That way, you can verify that your subsystem is communicating correctly with the rest of the system. You can always add specific functionality later.

The smallest possible Help Viewer in Kylix is one that implements the **ICustomHelpViewer** interface and always displays the same text regardless of what keyword is requested. The viewer's **UnderstandsKeyword** function always returns 1, and the **ShowHelp** method simply displays a message box that contains the name of the topic for which help was requested. The result isn't much of a help system, but it does show how to write the interface code. Adding support for individual topics and a table of contents becomes almost trivial after you get the interface hooked up. Figure 8.1 shows the application and the help message displayed by the viewer.

Before starting on the Help Viewer, you need to create an application that makes help requests. To do that, just create a new application with a blank form. Save the form as **frmHelpSample.pas** and save the project as **HelpSample.dpr**. In the Object Inspector, change the form's **HelpKeyword** property to "Main". This tells Kylix to request help on the "Main" keyword when the user presses F1. We'll discuss **HelpKeyword** and the other help-related properties in more detail in Solution 8.2, "Adding Help to an Application."

Now, select New from Kylix's File menu and click the "unit" icon to create a new unit. This unit will contain your simple Help Viewer module. Save this file as **SimpleHelpViewer.pas**. You're now ready to start building the Help Viewer.

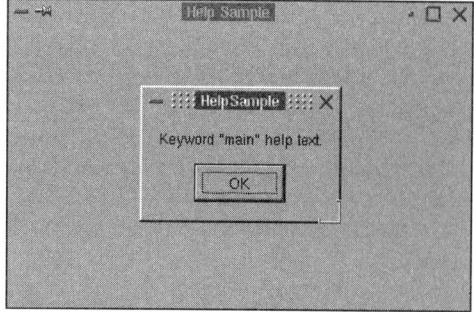

Figure 8.1
Getting help from a simple Help Viewer.

Because the Help Viewer module doesn't expose an interface (it *implements* an interface), there is nothing in the **interface** section of the unit. Remember, no application code calls the Help Viewer directly. Rather, the Help Viewer registers itself during program startup by passing its address to the **HelpManager**. The **HelpManager** uses this pointer to access the **ICustomHelpViewer** methods implemented by the viewer. The **uses** clause and everything else to do with the module is declared in the **implementation** section. Listing 8.1 contains the first part of the unit, which declares the **TSimpleHelpViewer** class.

Listing 8.1   The TSimpleHelpViewer class declaration.

```
{
  SimpleHelpViewer.pas - Implements the simplest possible Help Viewer.
}
unit SimpleHelpViewer;

interface

{ This unit has no interface! }

implementation

uses
  SysUtils, classes, HelpIntfs,
  QDialogs;

const
  STR_VIEWER_NAME = 'Simple Help Viewer';

type
  TSimpleHelpViewer = class (TInterfacedObject, ICustomHelpViewer)
  private
    FHelpManager: IHelpManager;
    FViewerID: Integer;
    FHelpStrings: TStringList;
    procedure InternalShutdown;
  public
    constructor Create;
    destructor Destroy; override;
    { ICustomHelpViewer methods }
    function  GetViewerName : String;
    function  UnderstandsKeyword(const HelpString: String): Integer;
    function  GetHelpStrings(const HelpString: String): TStringList;
    function  CanShowTableOfContents : Boolean;
    procedure ShowTableOfContents;
    procedure ShowHelp(const HelpString: String);
    procedure NotifyID(const ViewerID: Integer);
```

```
    procedure SoftShutDown;
    procedure ShutDown;
  end;


var
  { HelpViewer is a module global that is initialized at program startup }
  HelpViewer: TSimpleHelpViewer;
```

The **FHelpManager** member variable is used to hold a reference to the **HelpManager**. The viewer uses this pointer to call **IHelpManager** methods that the **HelpManager** implements. **FViewerID** is the unique identifier assigned to the viewer by the **HelpManager** during registration. **FHelpStrings** is used internally by the viewer to cache the help strings found by the **UnderstandsKeyword** function so that it can return the list when **GetHelpStrings** is called. This particular feature—caching the help strings—isn't strictly necessary for this demonstration, but it will become very useful later when we extend the Viewer. Implementation of this simple viewer is straightforward, as shown by the code in Listing 8.2.

Listing 8.2   Implementation of the **TSimpleHelpViewer** class.

```
{ TSimpleHelpViewer }
constructor TSimpleHelpViewer.Create;
begin
  inherited Create;
  FHelpStrings := TStringList.Create;
end;

destructor TSimpleHelpViewer.Destroy;
begin
  FHelpStrings.Free;
  inherited Destroy;
end;

{
  The unit finalization code calls InternalShutdown to shutdown the Viewer
  and notify the HelpManager that the Viewer is gone.
}
procedure TSimpleHelpViewer.InternalShutdown;
begin
  if Assigned (FHelpManager) then
    FHelpManager.Release (FViewerID);
  Shutdown;
end;

{
  The HelpManager calls GetViewerName to provide a unique string identifier
  that users can use to select among multiple help systems.
}
```

```
function  TSimpleHelpViewer.GetViewerName : String;
begin
  Result := STR_VIEWER_NAME;
end;


{
  The HelpManager calls UnderstandsKeywords to ask if the Viewer supports
  a particular keyword. The Viewer responds with the number of topics
  that match the keyword. A return value of 0 indicates that the
  viewer doesn't support that keyword.
}
function  TSimpleHelpViewer.UnderstandsKeyword
  (const HelpString: String): Integer;
begin
  // SimpleHelpViewer always understands keywords
  FHelpStrings.Clear;
  FHelpStrings.Add ('Main');
  Result := FHelpStrings.Count;
end;


{
  When more than one Viewer supports help for a particular keyword, and
  the HelpManager needs to display a UI element to allow the user to select
  a keyword, it will call GetHelpStrings to get the string list that the
  Viewer built during UnderstandsKeywords.

  The HelpManager guarantees that it will only call this function
  after calling UnderstandsKeywords, so it's OK to build the list during
  that function and return it here.
}
function  TSimpleHelpViewer.GetHelpStrings
  (const HelpString: String): TStringList;
begin
  Result := FHelpStrings;
end;


{
  The HelpManager calls this function to ask if the Viewer can display
  a table of contents. If the viewer can display the TOC, it should
  return True.
}
function  TSimpleHelpViewer.CanShowTableOfContents : Boolean;
begin
  { No TOC in this Viewer }
  Result := false;
end;
```

```
{
  The HelpManager calls this procedure when it wants the Viewer to
  display the table of contents. The HelpManager should only call
  this function if CanShowTableOfContents returns True.
}
procedure TSimpleHelpViewer.ShowTableOfContents;
begin
  { Should never get here, but raise just in case... }
  raise EHelpSystemException.Create ('Unable to show table of contents');
end;


{
  The HelpManager calls this procedure when it wants the Viewer to
  display help for a particular topic.
}
procedure TSimpleHelpViewer.ShowHelp(const HelpString: String);
begin
  ShowMessage (Format ('Keyword "%s" help text.', [HelpString]));
end;


{
  The HelpManager calls NotifyID after successful registration to provide
  the viewer with a unique value that identifies the viewer in communications
  with the HelpManager.
}
procedure TSimpleHelpViewer.NotifyID(const ViewerID: Integer);
begin
  FViewerID := ViewerID;
end;


{
  The HelpManager calls SoftShutDown to shut down all visible portions
  of the Viewer without actually shutting down the Viewer.
}
procedure TSimpleHelpViewer.SoftShutDown;
begin
  // nothing to do
end;


{
  The HelpManager calls ShutDown to shut down the Viewer.
  Since the HelpManager ordered the Viewer to shut down, we don't need
  to notify it.
}
procedure TSimpleHelpViewer.ShutDown;
```

```
begin
  if Assigned(FHelpManager) then FHelpManager := nil;
end;

initialization
  {
    Create and initialize the Viewer,
    and register it with the HelpManager.
  }
  if not Assigned(HelpViewer) then
  begin
    HelpViewer := TSimpleHelpViewer.Create;
    HelpIntfs.RegisterViewer(HelpViewer, HelpViewer.FHelpManager);
  end;

finalization
  { Shutdown and free the Viewer. }
  if Assigned(HelpViewer) then
  begin
    HelpViewer.InternalShutDown;
    HelpViewer.Free;
  end;

end.
```

In addition to the **ICustomHelpViewer** methods described in Table 8.1, **TSimpleHelpViewer** has a constructor, a destructor, and a private method called **InternalShutDown**. The constructor and destructor simply handle creating and destroying the **FHelpStrings** list. **InternalShutDown** is a helper function that is called by the unit finalization code to shut down the viewer and notify the **HelpManager** that the viewer is no longer present. Note that the **ShutDown** method does not notify the **HelpManager** of the viewer's impending demise. Because the **HelpManager** calls **ShutDown** directly, there's no need for the notification—the **HelpManager** already knows that the viewer is being destroyed.

Add the code from Listings 8.1 and 8.2 to your **SimpleHelpViewer** unit, save the file, and then run the program. When the main form is displayed, press the F1 key. You should see the help text appear in a message box, just like in Figure 8.1. Granted, **TSimpleHelpViewer** is not much of a help system, but it does supply a very simple implementation of the **ICustomHelpViewer** interface—an implementation onto which we can add other features.

Solution 8.2: Adding Help to an Application

Within normal application code (that is, excluding the Help Viewer), there are two objects that provide hooks into the help system. The global **Application** object has two public methods (**ContextHelp** and **KeywordHelp**) that you can call to invoke help on a context identifier or on a particular keyword. Calls to these functions are forwarded on to the **HelpManager** (through the **HelpSystem**), which processes them by calling the registered Help Viewers. Table 8.2 describes these two methods. In addition, applications can access the **HelpSystem** directly through the **Application** object's **HelpSystem** property.

In addition to the **Application** object's help functions, the **TControl** object from which all controls descend exposes four help-related properties and a method called **InvokeHelp**, which the application can call to pass a request to the **HelpSystem**. **TControl**'s help-related properties are described in Table 8.3.

The **Application** object also has a property called **HelpFile** that defines the application's default help file name. Individual controls' **HelpFile** property settings override the application's **HelpFile** property. That is, if the **HelpFile** property for an individual control is blank, then the parent control's **HelpFile** is used. If the parent's (and its parent's, etc.) **HelpFile** is blank, then the **Application's HelpFile** property is used.

Context help is based on an integer topic identifier similar to the Windows Help engine's context identifiers. **HyperHelp** supports context help, but most other Linux help systems do not, and Borland recommends that you use keyword-based help unless absolutely necessary. Another advantage of using only keyword-based help is that you don't have to implement the **IExtendedHelpViewer** interface, which is required in addition to **ICustomHelpViewer** for context help.

Table 8.2   The Application object's help methods.

Method	Description
ContextHelp	function **ContextHelp(const HelpContext:THelpContext): Boolean;** Displays the help topic identified by the **HelpContext** parameter
KeywordHelp	function **KeywordHelp(const HelpKeyword: String): Boolean;** Displays the help topic identified by the **HelpKeyword** parameter

Table 8.3   The TControl object's help-related properties.

Property	Description
HelpContext	The control's help context identifier. This value is only used if **HelpType** is set to **htContext**.
HelpFile	The name of the file that contains the control's help information. If the help system does not use file names (the man page system, for example), this property should be blank.
HelpKeyword	The keyword that identifies the control's help topic within the help system. This value is only used if **HelpType** is set to **htKeyword**.
HelpType	Specifies which of the values (**HelpContext** or **HelpKeyword**) is to be used when help for the control is accessed.

If you've used **WinHelp** in the past, you may be confused by the use of the term *keyword* in the Kylix help system. Keywords in **WinHelp** are index entries, and it's very common for a single keyword to reference multiple topics. In the Kylix help system, *keyword* is a more general concept: it is a string that identifies one or more topics. It's possible to use keywords in Kylix to mimic the **WinHelp** keyword system, but it's not required. In a simple help system, a keyword may simply be a unique string that identifies a single help topic.

The **InvokeHelp** method of **TControl** is the mechanism that actually forwards help requests from the control to the **HelpSystem**. **InvokeHelp** calls the appropriate **Application** help method (**ContextHelp** or **KeywordHelp**) based on the value of the control's **HelpType** property. Application code can call the control's **InvokeHelp** method directly, but that's not often necessary.

When the user presses the F1 key, the control's **KeyDown** method calls **InvokeHelp**. In the case of keyword help, **InvokeHelp** examines the control's **HelpKeyword** property. If **HelpKeyword** is not blank, **InvokeHelp** calls **Application.KeywordHelp**, passing it the keyword value. If **HelpKeyword** is blank, **InvokeHelp** calls the parent control's **InvokeHelp** method. This setup allows you to define a single help keyword for a form and individual keywords for selected controls. If a control has its own keyword, that control's help topic is displayed. Otherwise, the form's help topic is displayed when the user presses F1. The mechanism for context help is similar: If the control's **HelpContext** value is nonzero, **Application.ContextHelp** is called with that value. Otherwise, the parent control's **InvokeHelp** method is called.

Tip

*Handling of the **HelpFile** property in the first release of Kylix is broken, and the intention is somewhat ambiguous. Unlike the Delphi 5 VCL, where **HelpFile** is a property of the **TCustomForm** class, in Kylix's CLX, **HelpFile** is a property of **TControl**. It appears that the intention is for **HelpFile** to work in much the same way as the **InvokeHelp** method: If a control's **HelpFile** property is blank, the underlying help machinery should use the **HelpFile** property of the control's parent or **Application.HelpFile** if the control's parent is **nil**. The CLX code that obtains the current help file (**Application.GetCurrentHelpFile**), though, is written to work the same as in the Delphi 5 VCL. It completely ignores the control's **HelpFile** property and inspects only the form's and application's **HelpFile** properties. This problem will probably be fixed by the time this book is available, and there will likely be a fix posted to Borland's Web site (**www.borland.com/kylix**).*

Applications that want to display the help system's table of contents must call the **HelpSystem** object's **ShowTableOfContents** method directly. This code fragment shows how to do that:

```
Application.HelpSystem.ShowTableOfContents;
```

Solution Example: Adding Help to the Sample Application

To illustrate how the help system works, we have added some controls to the **HelpSample** application's main form from the previous example. Figure 8.2 shows the resulting form.

Add the controls shown in Figure 8.2 to your sample program's main form. Be sure to add the main menu control as well as create the menu items shown in Table 8.4.

After you have created the menu and the new controls, set their help-related properties as shown in Table 8.5. If a control is not shown in Table 8.5, leave its help properties at the defaults.

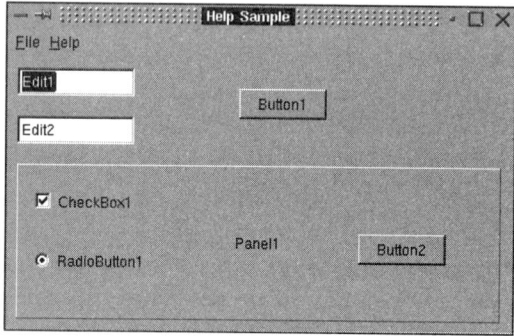

Figure 8.2
The enhanced **HelpSample** main form.

Table 8.4   New menu items.

Menu	Item	Name
File		File1
File	Exit	Exit1
Help		Help1
Help	Contents	Contents1

Table 8.5   Help property settings for the new controls.

Control Name	HelpKeyword	HelpType
Form1	Main	htKeyword
Edit1	Edit1	htKeyword
Panel1	Panel1	htKeyword
CheckBox1	CheckBox1	htKeyword
File1	File1	htKeyword
Exit1	Exit1	htKeyword
Help1	Help1	htKeyword

Finally, add these two **OnClick** event handlers for the buttons:

```
procedure TForm1.Button1Click(Sender: TObject);
begin
  // could be Form1.InvokeHelp
  Button1.InvokeHelp;
end;

procedure TForm1.Button2Click(Sender: TObject);
begin
  // could be Panel1.InvokeHelp
  Button2.InvokeHelp;
end;
```

After making those additions, compile and run the program. If you tab among the different controls on the form and press the F1 key, you'll see how the controls' **InvokeHelp** methods work. For example, if Edit1 is the selected control on the form, pressing F1 will display help for the "Edit1" topic. However, if you move focus to the Edit2 control and press F1, the form's help topic ("Main") is displayed because Edit2 does not have a defined help keyword. Similarly, if you move the focus to RadioButton1 and press F1, the help text for Panel1 is displayed because RadioButton1 has no help keyword, and Panel1 is the parent control of RadioButton1.

Solution 8.3: Interfacing to an External Help System

Because there is no standard online help system for Linux GUI applications, you will have to create or otherwise obtain a Help Viewer module to link with your Kylix applications. If you're fortunate enough to be using **HyperHelp**, you can use the sample viewer (**WinHelpViewer.pas**) supplied in your **kylix/demos/helpviewers** directory. If you will be using any other help system, you'll have to write your own viewer to interface with that help system. It's still instructive to examine the sample viewers supplied with Kylix because they illustrate some very important techniques for interfacing with external help systems.

In this section, we develop a very simple help system that is implemented in forms invoked directly by the Help Viewer. Although this doesn't illustrate the specific interprocess communications techniques you might use to communicate with a true external help system, it does serve to show the bookkeeping requirements of the viewer.

The **SimpleHelp** Forms

Our help system consists of two forms: the topic display form, shown in Figure 8.3, and the table of contents form. The topic display form contains a single **TMemo** control in which topic help text is displayed.

Figure 8.3
The **SimpleHelp** topic display form.

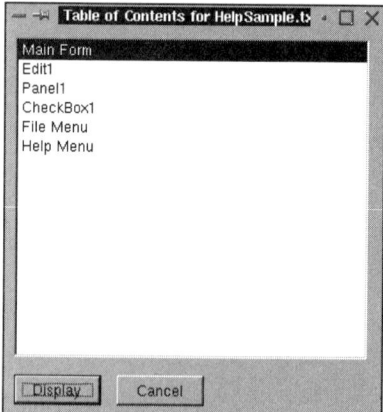

Figure 8.4
The **SimpleHelp** table of contents form.

Note that our help system does not support topic links or other advanced help system features. The table of contents form, shown in Figure 8.4, is equally simple. It contains a single list box that lists all the help system topics and allows the user to choose and display a topic. Before you see the implementation of these two forms, the format of the files used to supply online help information needs to be defined.

The Help File Format

The **SimpleHelp** system's help file is a text file that contains one line for each help topic. Each topic line contains three comma-separated values: the topic name, the keyword associated with the topic, and the help text for that topic. Listing 8.3 shows the **HelpSample.txt** file, which supplies help topics for the sample program developed in Solution 8.2.

Listing 8.3   The HelpSample.txt help file.
```
Main,"Main Form","This application illustrates how to use online help."
Edit1,"Edit1","Enter some text here."
Panel1,"Panel1","A panel can have its own help topic, too."
CheckBox1,"CheckBox1","Check this box to turn this option on."
File1,"File Menu","This topic describes items on the File menu."
Help1,"Help Menu","This topic describes items on the Help menu."
```

Strings that contain embedded spaces, tabs, or commas must be quoted. This makes it possible to read and parse the help file using the **TStringList** functions.

Solution Example: Implementing the **SimpleHelp** Help System

Implementing the **SimpleHelp** system consists of building the topic display form and the table of contents form, and modifying the Help Viewer from Section 8.1 so that it displays topics and the table of contents.

Implementing the Topic Display Form

The topic display form is implemented in a module called **frmHelpTopic.pas**. The form itself contains no custom code. However, two global procedures are called by the **SimpleHelpViewer** module. The **ShowTopic** procedure sets the form's caption and populates the memo box with the topic text, and the **ShutDown** procedure destroys the form. **ShutDown** is called by the **SimpleHelpViewer** module's **SoftShutDown** procedure. The implementation of the topic display form is shown in Listing 8.4.

Listing 8.4   The topic display form (frmHelpTopic.pas).
```
unit frmHelpTopic;

interface

uses
  SysUtils, Types, Classes, Variants, QGraphics, QControls, QForms, QDialogs,
  QStdCtrls;

type
  TfrmshTopic = class(TForm)
    Memo1: TMemo;
  end;

var
  frmshTopic: TfrmshTopic;

procedure ShowTopic (const sTopicName: String; const sTopicText: String);
procedure ShutDown;

implementation
```

```
{$R *.xfm}
procedure ShowTopic (const sTopicName: String; const sTopicText: String);
begin
  if not Assigned (frmshTopic) then
    frmshTopic := TfrmshTopic.Create (nil);

  frmshTopic.Caption := Format ('Simple Help - %s', [sTopicName]);
  frmshTopic.Memo1.Lines.Text := sTopicText;

  frmshTopic.Show;
end;

procedure ShutDown;
begin
  if Assigned (frmshTopic) then
    FreeAndNil (frmshTopic);
end;

end.
```

Implementing the Table of Contents Form

The table of contents form, implemented in **frmTOC.pas**, is slightly more involved than the topic display form. It, too, contains two global procedures. **ShowTOC** is called by **SimpleHelpViewer.ShowTableOfContents** to actually display the help file contents. Like the topic display form, **frmTOC** also contains a **ShutDown** procedure. In addition, the Display button's event handler contains code to show the help text for a selected topic. The code for **frmTOC** is shown in Listing 8.5.

Listing 8.5   The table of contents form (frmTOC.pas).

```
unit frmTOC;

interface

uses
  SysUtils, Types, Classes, Variants, QGraphics, QControls, QForms, QDialogs,
  QStdCtrls,
  frmHelpTopic;

type
  TfrmshTOC = class(TForm)
    btnDisplay: TButton;
    btnCancel: TButton;
    lbTopics: TListBox;
    procedure btnDisplayClick(Sender: TObject);
    procedure FormCreate(Sender: TObject);
    procedure FormDestroy(Sender: TObject);
```

```
  private
    FlstHelp: TStringList;
  end;

var
  frmshTOC: TfrmshTOC;

procedure ShowTOC (const sFilename: String; lstHelp: TStringList);
procedure ShutDown;

implementation

{$R *.xfm}
procedure ShowTOC (const sFilename: String; lstHelp: TStringList);
var
  i: Integer;
  lstLine: TStringList;
begin
  if not Assigned (frmshTOC) then
    frmshTOC := TfrmshTOC.Create (nil);

  frmshTOC.FlstHelp.Assign (lstHelp);
  frmshTOC.Caption := Format ('Table of Contents for %s', [sFileName]);

  frmshTOC.lbTopics.Clear;
  lstLine := TStringList.Create;
  try
    for i := 0 to lstHelp.Count-1 do
    begin
      lstLine.CommaText := lstHelp[i];
      if lstLine.Count >= 3 then
        frmshTOC.lbTopics.Items.Add (lstLine[1]);
    end;
    frmshTOC.lbTopics.ItemIndex := 0;
  finally
    lstLine.Free;
  end;

  frmshTOC.Show;
end;

procedure ShutDown;
begin
  if Assigned(frmshTOC) then
    FreeAndNil (frmshTOC);
end;
```

```
procedure TfrmshTOC.btnDisplayClick(Sender: TObject);
var
  lstLine: TStringList;
begin
  if lbTopics.ItemIndex <> -1 then
  begin
    lstLine := TStringList.Create;
    try
      lstLine.CommaText := FlstHelp[lbTopics.ItemIndex];
      frmHelpTopic.ShowTopic (lstLine[1], lstLine[2]);
      Hide;
    finally
      lstLine.Free;
    end;
  end;
end;

procedure TfrmshTOC.FormCreate(Sender: TObject);
begin
  FlstHelp := TStringList.Create;
end;

procedure TfrmshTOC.FormDestroy(Sender: TObject);
begin
  FlstHelp.Free;
end;

end.
```

Modifying the Simple Help Viewer to Display the Forms

We had to make a number of modifications to **SimpleHelpViewer.pas** so that it will load the help file from disk, display topics and the table of contents, and manage the destruction of the forms in response to **SoftShutDown** and **ShutDown** procedure calls from the **HelpManager**.

In order to keep track of the current help file, we have added the following two data members to the private section of the **TSimpleHelpViewer** class:

```
FlstHelpFile: TStringList;  // string list containing the help file text
FLastHelpFileName: String;  // name of the currently-loaded help file
```

FLastHelpFileName is maintained to prevent having to reload the help file for every request.

In addition to these two data members, we have added a private procedure called **LoadHelpFile**, which is declared like this:

```
procedure LoadHelpFile;
```

One other new procedure, **GetHelpFileName**, is defined at global scope. This procedure is a replacement for the **Application.GetCurrentHelpFile** procedure, which in the first release of Kylix contains a bug. The **LoadHelpFile** procedure calls **GetHelpFileName** to obtain the name of the help file to load. Normally, **LoadHelpFile** would call the **HelpManager**'s **GetHelpFile** procedure. However, **THelpManager.GetHelpFile** relies on **Application. GetCurrentHelpFile**. The implementations of **GetHelpFileName** and **LoadHelpFile** are shown in Listing 8.6.

Listing 8.6 The GetHelpFileName and LoadHelpFile procedures.

```
{
  GetHelpFileName is a replacement for THelpManager.GetHelpFile, because
  Application.GetCurrentHelpFile is broken.
}
function GetHelpFileName: String;
var
  ActiveForm: TCustomForm;
begin
  ActiveForm := Screen.ActiveCustomForm;
  if Assigned(ActiveForm) and (ActiveForm.HelpFile <> '') then
    Result := ActiveForm.HelpFile
  else
    Result := Application.HelpFile;
end;
{ LoadHelpFile loads the current help file into a TStringList }
procedure TSimpleHelpViewer.LoadHelpFile;
var
  HelpFile: String;
begin
  if FlstHelpFile = nil then
    FlstHelpFile := TStringList.Create;
  { Would use FHelpManager.GetHelpFile, but that function is broken. }
  HelpFile := GetHelpFileName;
  { Check prevents reloading the same help file }
  if HelpFile <> FLastHelpFileName then
  begin
    FlstHelpFile.LoadFromFile (HelpFile);
    FLastHelpFileName := HelpFile;
  end;
end;
```

Because we now can display the table of contents, we've modified **CanShowTableOfContents** to return True, and the **ShowTableOfContents** procedure now loads the help file and calls the **ShowTOC** procedure that's located in **frmTOC.pas**. **UnderstandsKeywords** has been modified so that it searches for the specified keyword in the help file, and we have modified the **ShowHelp** procedure so that it locates the help topic text for the specified keyword and calls the **ShowTopic** procedure (located in **frmHelpTopic.pas**) to display the topic form. These modifications are shown in Listing 8.7.

Listing 8.7   Changed table of contents and topic display functions.

```
{
  The HelpManager calls UnderstandsKeywords to ask if the Viewer supports
  a particular keyword. The Viewer responds with the number of topics
  that match the keyword. A return value of 0 indicates that the
  viewer doesn't support that keyword.
}
function  TSimpleHelpViewer.UnderstandsKeyword
  (const HelpString: String): Integer;
var
  lstLine: TStringList;
  i : Integer;
begin
  LoadHelpFile;
  lstLine := TStringList.Create;
  try
    FHelpStrings.Clear;
    for i := 0 to FlstHelpFile.Count-1 do
    begin
      lstLine.CommaText := FlstHelpFile[i];
      if lstLine.Count >= 3 then
        if SameText (lstLine[0], HelpString) then
          FHelpStrings.Add (lstLine[1]);
    end;
  finally
    lstLine.Free;
  end;
  Result := FHelpStrings.Count;
end;
{
  The HelpManager calls this function to ask if the Viewer can display
  a table of contents. If the viewer can display the TOC, it should
  return True.
}
function  TSimpleHelpViewer.CanShowTableOfContents : Boolean;
begin
  Result := True;
end;
```

```
{
  The HelpManager calls this procedure when it wants the Viewer to
  display the table of contents. The HelpManager should only call
  this function if CanShowTableOfContents returns True.
}
procedure TSimpleHelpViewer.ShowTableOfContents;
begin
  LoadHelpFile;
  ShowTOC (GetHelpFileName, FlstHelpFile);
end;


{
  The HelpManager calls this procedure when it wants the Viewer to
  display help for a particular topic.
}
procedure TSimpleHelpViewer.ShowHelp(const HelpString: String);
var
  lstLine: TStringList;
  i: Integer;
begin
  LoadHelpFile;
  lstLine := TStringList.Create;
  try
    { Locate the first occurrence of HelpString in the file }
    for i := 0 to FlstHelpFile.Count-1 do
    begin
      lstLine.CommaText := FlstHelpFile[i];
      if SameText (lstLine[0], HelpString) then
      begin
        frmHelpTopic.ShowTopic (lstLine[1], lstLine[2]);
        exit;
      end;
    end;
  finally
    lstLine.Free;
  end;
end;
```

Finally, we have changed the **SoftShutDown** procedure so that it calls the **ShutDown** procedures in the individual forms' units in order to destroy the table of contents and topic display forms. In addition, **ShutDown** has been modified so that it calls **SoftShutDown**. The modified procedures are shown in Listing 8.8.

Listing 8.8   Modified **ShutDown** and **SoftShutDown** procedures.

```
{
  The HelpManager calls SoftShutDown to shut down all visible portions
  of the Viewer without actually shutting down the Viewer.
```

```
}
procedure TSimpleHelpViewer.SoftShutDown;
begin
  frmTOC.ShutDown;
  frmHelpTopic.ShutDown;
end;

{
  The HelpManager calls ShutDown to shut down the Viewer.
  Since the HelpManager ordered the Viewer to shut down, we don't need
  to notify it.
}
procedure TSimpleHelpViewer.ShutDown;
begin
  SoftShutDown;
  if Assigned(FHelpManager) then
    FHelpManager := nil;
end;
```

Putting It All Together

After you create the new forms and make the preceding changes to the **SimpleHelpViewer**
module, change the **SimpleHelpViewer**'s **uses** statement to include **QForms**, **frmTOC**, and
frmHelpTopic. **QForms** is required for the **GetHelpFileName** function, and the other two
are required in order to access the new forms. The new **uses** statement should look like this:

```
uses
  SysUtils, classes, HelpIntfs,
  { Required for GetHelpFileName fix }
  QForms,
  frmHelpTopic, frmTOC;
```

Then, in the **HelpSample** program's main program (**HelpSample.dpr**), add a line that sets
the **Application** object's **HelpFile** property to **'HelpSample.txt'**. This code fragment shows
how this is done:

```
begin
  Application.Initialize;
  { Specify the help file that the application will use }
  Application.HelpFile := 'HelpSample.txt';
  Application.CreateForm(TForm1, Form1);
  Application.Run;
end.
```

After making these changes, you should be able to compile and run the application.

The Future of Help with Kylix

Because Kylix is new, there aren't many viewer modules available to interface with existing Linux help systems. In fact, the only ones that we know of are the man page viewer and WinHelp viewer that are shipped with Kylix. As more developers start using Kylix, we expect viewers for KDE Help, GNOME Help, and other Linux help systems to appear. If you're not willing to wait, though, you can use the information in this chapter in combination with the documentation for your external help system to develop your own viewer.

If you do develop a Kylix Help Viewer for an existing Linux help system, consider submitting it to the JEDI project (**www.delphi-jedi.org**) so that Kylix programmers can benefit from it as well.

Chapter 9
The Drawer

It seems that in every household there is a designated drawer with a very special purpose: to store your *really important stuff*. At our house The Drawer is located in the kitchen. Just before writing this introduction, I took an inventory of its contents. The short list of what I found includes:

♦ seven pens, four of them dried up,

♦ four distinctly different types of batteries (several of each),

♦ six pencils in dire need of sharpening,

♦ thirteen rubber bands of various sizes,

♦ one partial packet of pipe cleaners,

♦ one small can of "3-in-1" oil,

♦ one large box of push pins,

♦ one green automobile aerial ball from Central Market,

♦ two books of safety matches,

♦ one night light, and

♦ two locked padlocks with unknown combinations (I'm just *sure* I'll remember those combinations someday).

A pretty strange assortment, to be certain—but *invaluable* when you're suddenly faced with an unplanned situation that calls for prying, poking, fastening (or locking) some wayward device. Whenever such a dilemma arises, the perfect tool will be found in The Drawer.

This chapter is to the book what The Drawer is to my kitchen. It contains a variety of solutions that just wouldn't comfortably fit elsewhere in the book. Just as certainly as I'll need that green aerial ball, a situation will undoubtedly arise for you that will call for one of the solutions included in this chapter.

Solution 9.1: Getting a List of Logged-in Users

At times, it can be valuable to know who the other users are who are currently logged in. These situations might include admin programs monitoring the state of the system, accounting programs designed to bill users for time spent online, and the ever-important need to tell when the boss has logged in so you know when to quit playing Civ.

Linux keeps track of information on its online users in two data files—one for those currently logged in, and one that contains historical data on previous logins. Both files consist of **TUserTmp** records, and are generally referred to as "utmp" data files. Table 9.1 describes the various fields in a **TUserTmp** record.

The primary field of interest for this solution is **ut_user**, but knowing when the user logged in (**ut_tv**) could also give us some valuable information. Table 9.2 illustrates the structure of a **TTimeval** record.

Table 9.1   Description of fields in a TUserTmp record.

Field Name	Description
ut_type	A **Smallint** that represents the type of login executed. The **utmp** files maintain records on changes in boot times, changes in runlevels, logins, user process startups, among other things.
ut_pid	The process ID of the login process.
ut_line	A packed array of characters that contains the name of the device the login came from.
ut_id	A packed array of characters containing the ID from the initialization table. This is most frequently used as a lookup value.
ut_user	A packed array of characters containing the name of the logged-in user.
ut_host	A packed array containing the hostname, if this login was executed from a remote location.
ut_exit	A structure containing the exit status of a login process, if it was marked as a "dead" process.
ut_session	A **Longint** containing a representation of the session ID. This is used for windowing purposes.
ut_tv	A **TTimeval** structure containing the time this entry was made in the file.
ut_addr	The Internet (IP) address of the host, if this login was executed from a remote location.
__unused	A 20-character area reserved for future use.

Table 9.2   Description of fields in a TTimeval record.

Field Name	Description
tv_sec	Elapsed time since the epoch, in whole seconds.
tv_usec	Remaining fractional elapsed time, in microseconds.

About Epoch Time

Every calendar must have a starting point from which to measure the current date and time. That point is usually called the *start of the epoch*. For MS-DOS systems, the epoch start was at midnight Universal Coordinated Time on January 1, 1980. For Unix and Linux systems, it was January 1, 1970. Other operating systems use other epoch start times.

The **Libc** unit contains several routines that can read and (if you're the superuser) even *manipulate* utmp-type files. Let's take a look at the four routines that will be critical to creating a list of current users, starting with **utmpname**:

```
function utmpname(__file: PChar): Integer; cdecl;
```

The **utmpname** function opens the file to be examined, using its fully qualified path name. The system constants **_PATH_UTMP** and **_PATH_WTMP** are provided for this purpose, making the job a little easier by providing the fully qualified paths to the current and historical user files. If the call to **utmpname** fails, it returns a nonzero value.

The next routine that will help in the reading of **utmp**-type files is **setutent:procedure setutent(); cdecl;**:

The **setutent** procedure simply "rewinds" the file pointer to the beginning of the **utmp** file. It is recommended that you call this routine before calling any other access routines.

The third of the four routines needed to read the files is **getutent**:

```
function getutent(): PUserTmp; cdecl;
```

The **getutent** function returns a pointer to the current **TUserTmp** record, and then it increments the file pointer to the next record. If a call to **getutent** fails, it returns nil.

Finally, we have the **endutent** procedure, which simply closes the file:

```
procedure endutent(); cdecl;
```

Solution Example: The **LogUser** Program

The **LogUser** program is shown in Figure 9.1. The program gives the user the choice of viewing the current or historical log, displaying the list of users and login times.

Listing 9.1 contains the source code for the **LogUser** program. The main functionality of the program is contained in the **onClick** event handler for the Start button.

The setting of the radio button is used to determine which utmp file to access, and then the selected file is opened and rewound to its beginning with the **utmpname** and **setutent** routines. A **repeat..until** loop is then executed to repetitively call **getutent**. Each time through

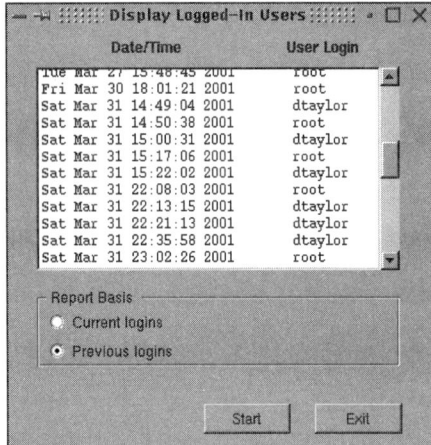

Figure 9.1
The **LogUser** program.

the loop, the username and the time values are extracted. When **getutent** returns **nil**, all the matching records have been processed.

Time representation and conversion always seems to be a challenge in operating systems, and Linux is no exception—it has at least as many time and date–related data types as MS-DOS (and maybe more). All of them finally boil down to the representation of elapsed time since the epoch, expressed in seconds (or microseconds). Getting data from one of those representations to another can be a challenge, however. The **ctime** library function returns a formatted string containing the date and time, expressed in seconds.

Listing 9.1 Program listing for LogUser.

```
unit LogUserMain;

interface

uses
  SysUtils, Types, Classes, Variants, QGraphics, QControls, QForms, QDialogs,
  QStdCtrls, QExtCtrls, Libc;

type
  TForm1 = class(TForm)
    ExitBtn: TButton;
    Memo: TMemo;
    StartBtn: TButton;
    BasisRBGroup: TRadioGroup;
    Label1: TLabel;
    Label2: TLabel;
    procedure ExitBtnClick(Sender: TObject);
    procedure StartBtnClick(Sender: TObject);
```

```
  private
    { Private declarations }
  public
    { Public declarations }
  end;

var
  Form1: TForm1;

implementation

{$R *.xfm}

procedure TForm1.ExitBtnClick(Sender: TObject);
begin
 Close;
end;

procedure TForm1.StartBtnClick(Sender: TObject);
var
 PLoginRec : PUserTmp;
 LoginTime : TTime_T;
 s : String;
begin
 if BasisRBGroup.ItemIndex = 0
  then utmpname(_PATH_UTMP) { Current logins }
  else utmpname(_PATH_WTMP); { Previous logins }

 LoginTime := 0;
 setutent;
 repeat
  PLoginRec := getutent;
  if Assigned(PLoginRec)
   then begin
     if PLoginRec^.ut_type = USER_PROCESS
      then begin
           LoginTime := PLoginRec^.ut_tv.tv_sec;
           s := ctime(@LoginTime);
           s := copy(s, 1, Length(s) - 1); { Chop the nl }
           Memo.Lines.Add(s + '        ' + PLoginRec^.ut_user);
         end;
       end;
 until not Assigned(PLoginRec);
 endutent;
end;

end.
```

Solution 9.2: Checking for Unread Email

A spiffy feature to add to applications is a notification to users when they receive an email message. Fortunately, this is not a difficult process, mainly because the format of email messages has been standardized (by RFC 822 and others).

The file containing all a user's mail is normally located in **/var/mail**, and it bears the name of its user. The format of the file is standard across all Linux systems, making it easy pickings to read and interpret. It is important to remember that this file is used by the system to store mail it receives from the outside world addressed to you; however, mail you retrieve using POP3 or IMAP (or any other mail retrieval protocol) can be stored in locations determined by the package you use to retrieve the mail, and as such can't be addressed by this general solution. The Indy components contain a nice POP3 client that you can use to extend this solution into that domain as well.

The basis for this solution is simple. The filesystem tracks two timestamps for each file: the time last modified and the time last accessed (read). New mail (whether it has been read or not) is present by definition when the mail file's modification timestamp is later than its access timestamp. In addition, the headers of individual messages within the mail file are, as a matter of course, modified by email clients that manage those messages. Headers can be read and subjects displayed by an application without that application actually "reading" a message, which can result in some interesting definitions of the term "new mail." For purposes of discussion here, "old" mail will refer to messages that either have been read or have been accessed (their subjects displayed by an email client, for example) but not actually read.

Because a file's modification and access times can, themselves, be manipulated independent of file contents, we have a way we can read the mail file and then cover our tracks. This allows other dedicated email clients to determine the existence of new mail as well, using the same technique we use. We simply buffer the timestamps before we read the file, and then we restore them when we're done. This "dirty work" is done with two library functions: **stat** (which reads the timestamps) and **utime** (which writes them). You met **stat** back in Solution 7.1 in Chapter 7. Let's now examine **utime**:

```
function utime(FileName: PChar; FileTimes: PUTimeBuffer): Integer; cdecl;
```

As you can see, **utime** takes as its arguments the name of the file to modify and the pointer to a **TUTimeBuffer** record. Here is its declaration:

```
TUTimeBuffer = {packed} record
    actime: __time_t;              { Access time. }
    modtime: __time_t;             { Modification time. }
  end;
```

It's all very straightforward, and it's kind of fun, too. If you would like to explore the subject of email further, check out RFC 822 and the other standards documents at **www.faqs.org/ rfcs/**. Right now, let's see this strategy put into action.

Solution Example: The **CheckMail** Program

Figure 9.2 shows **CheckMail**, a simple demo application that gives the user two choices for checking for new mail. If he chooses the Just See If There's Any New Mail option and clicks the Check button, a dialog box will pop up to tell him whether *any* new mail is waiting.

Choosing the Tell Me The Number Of New Items option and clicking the Check button pops up a dialog box displaying the number of new messages. Listing 9.2 shows the code for the underlying **CheckMailStuff** unit. This unit exports one function, **CheckNewMail**, which takes as arguments the name of the user and a mode type that specifies whether you want **CheckNewMail** to report that the user has new mail or report the actual number of new messages. (Be aware that unless you are the superuser, you won't be allowed to read anyone else's mail file—and if you *are* the superuser, you'd better have a good reason for snooping in other people's email.)

If the **CheckNewMail** function is called with the mode type **MSG_NOCOUNT**, it only examines the mail file's modification time and size. If messages are waiting, in this mode, **CheckNewMail** returns 1; if there are no messages, it returns 0. If an error occurred, –1 is returned.

If **CheckNewMail** is instead called with **MSG_COUNT**, a much more thorough checking takes place: Each line of the file is examined, headers are parsed, and an actual count of new messages is computed. If an error occurs, **CheckNewMail** returns –1; otherwise, it returns the number of new messages.

Listing 9.3 contains the source code for the **CheckMail** program, demonstrating the use of the **CheckNewMail** function exported by the **CheckMailStuff** unit.

> **Tip**
>
> *You might want to run **CheckMail** outside the Kylix IDE. The function **ForceIntConversion**, local to the **isFrom** function, forces Kylix's **StrToInt** function to evaluate strings that frequently are not numerical string representations, which results in thrown exceptions. Although you won't see those exceptions during normal execution, you will definitely see them while running inside the IDE—which is somewhat of a distraction.*

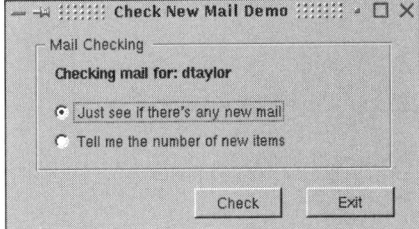

Figure 9.2
The **CheckMail** program.

Listing 9.2   Code for the CheckMailStuff unit.

```pascal
unit CheckMailStuff;

interface

uses
  SysUtils, Libc;

type
 CountType = (MSG_COUNT, MSG_NOCOUNT);

 // The CheckNewMail function returns values that indicate
 // whether or not user logName has new mail waiting. When called
 // with opType set to MSG_COUNT, CheckNewMail will return
 // the number of new email messages waiting. When called
 // with opType set to MSG_NOCOUNT, it will return 0 if there
 // are no new mail messages waiting, or 1 if new messages are
 // present. Either mode will  return -1 in case of an error.
 function CheckNewMail(logName: String; opType: CountType): Integer;

implementation
var
 mailFile: String;
 mailCount: Integer;
 new_mailCount: Integer;
 old_mailCount: Integer;
 newMsgs: Integer;
 oldMsgs: Integer;
 lastMTime: Time_T;
 lastSize: Off_T;
 isInternal: boolean;

function isOld( buf: String ): boolean;
begin
 Result := False;
 if ( Pos( 'S', buf ) <> 1 ) and ( Pos( 'X', buf ) <> 1 )
  then Exit;

 // Now check for new status from normal mail clients...
 if Pos( 'Status:', buf ) = 1
  then begin
   if ( Pos( 'R', buf ) <> 0 ) or ( Pos( 'O', buf ) <> 0 )
    then begin
     Result := True;
     Exit;
    end;
  end;
```

```
// ...and check for new status from Netscape clients
if ( Pos( 'X-Mozilla-Status:', buf ) = 1 )
 and ( Pos( '0000', buf ) = 19 )
  then begin
   Result := True;
   Exit;
  end;

end;

function isFrom( buf: String): boolean;
var
 sender: String;
 dayNum: Integer;

  function GetWord(s : String; idx : Integer) : String;
  var
   i : Integer;
   s1 : String;
   w : String;
  begin
   s1 := s;
   w := '';
   for i := 1 to idx do
    begin
     while (Length(s1) > 0) and (s1[1] in [' ', ^I]) do
      Delete(s1, 1, 1);
     while (Length(s1) > 0) and not (s1[1] in [' ', ^I]) do
      begin
       if i = idx then w := w + s1[1];
       Delete(s1, 1, 1);
      end; { while }
    end; { for }
   Result := w;
  end;

  function ForceIntConversion(s : String) : Integer;
  var
   i : Integer;
  begin
   if Length(s) > 0
    then begin
          try
           i := StrToInt(s);
          except
           i := 0;
```

```
            end; { try }
          end
      else i := 0;
    Result := i;
  end;


begin
 sender := '';
 Result := False;

 // If the first 5 chars of the string are
 // not "From ", return false.
  if Pos( 'From ', buf ) <> 1 then Exit;

 // See if the sending address is missing, by looking
 // for the day of the month in field 4 or 5.
 dayNum := ForceIntConversion(GetWord(buf, 4));
 if dayNum = 0
  then begin
        sender := GetWord(buf, 2);
        dayNum := ForceIntConversion(GetWord(buf, 5));
        if (Length(sender) = 0) or (dayNum = 0)
         then Exit;
       end;

 if dayNum > 31 then Exit;

 // Needed for an "is_Internal" check outside this function.
 // THIS IS A SIDE EFFECT.
 if strcmp( PChar( sender), 'MAILER-DAEMON' ) = 0
  then isInternal := True;

 Result := True;

end;

function isMultipartMsg( buf: String;
                         var sepLine: String ): boolean;
var
 idxField: Integer;
 idxSep: Integer;
 lenSep: Integer;
begin
 Result := false;

 // If the string doesn't start with 'Content-Type: ' return False
 if Pos( 'Content-Type: ', buf ) <> 1 then Exit;
```

```
if Pos( 'multipart/', Copy( buf, 15, 10 ) ) <> 1 then Exit;

// Starting at the 15th character...
idxField := 15;

// ...loop to the end of the string.
while idxField <= Length( buf ) do
 begin
  // find the next ';' character
  while ( idxField <= Length( buf ) )
   and (Copy( buf, idxField, 1 ) <> ';' ) do Inc( idxField );

  if Copy( buf, idxField, 1 ) = ';' then Inc( idxField );

  // Now find the next non-space character
  while ( idxField <= Length( buf ))
   and (Copy( buf, idxField, 1 ) = ' ' ) do Inc( idxField );

  // If where we are right now says 'boundary='
  if Copy( buf, idxField, 9 ) = 'boundary=' then
   begin
    idxSep := idxField + 9;
    if Copy( buf, idxSep, 1 ) = '"' then
     begin
      Inc( idxSep );
      lenSep := 0;

      // Count the number of chars between '"' chars
      while ( Copy( buf, idxSep + lenSep, 1 ) <> '"' )
       and ( Copy( buf, idxSep + lenSep, 1 ) >= ' ' )
         do Inc( lenSep );
     end
    else
     begin
      lenSep := 0;

      // Count the number of chars until a ';' char
      while ( Copy( buf, idxSep + lenSep, 1 ) <> ';' )
       and ( Copy( buf, idxSep + lenSep, 1 ) >= ' ' )
         do Inc( lenSep );
     end;

    // copy the separator string into the supplied buffer
    sepLine := '--';
    sepLine := sepLine + Copy( buf, idxSep, lenSep );
    sepLine := sepLine + '--';
```

```
      Result := True;
    end;
  end;
end;

function CheckNewMail(logName: String;opType: CountType): Integer;
var
 F: TextFile;
 statBuf: TStatBuf;
 timeBuf: TUTimeBuffer;
 line: String;
 sepStr: String;
 inHeader: boolean;
 markedRead: boolean;
 isMultipart: boolean;
begin
 inHeader := False;
 markedRead := False;
 isMultipart := False;
 timeBuf.actime := 0;
 timeBuf.modtime := 0;

 // First, what is the name of our mail file?
 mailFile := _PATH_MAILDIR + '/' + logName;

 // stat the file into the statbuf. If we fail, the file isn't
 // accessible and we automatically return a -1 (error)
 if stat( PChar(mailFile), statbuf ) <> 0
  then begin
        mailCount := 0;
        newMsgs := 0;
        oldMsgs := 0;
        Result := -1;
        Exit;
      end;

 // If we're running in "no-count" mode then we'll report new mail
 // based on the mailbox file's modification time and size.
 if opType = MSG_NOCOUNT
  then begin
        if   ( statbuf.st_size > 0 )
          and ( statbuf.st_size >= lastSize )
          and ( statbuf.st_mtime >= statbuf.st_atime )
          then new_mailCount := 1
          else new_mailCount := 0;
```

```
        // We're not counting, so simply use the fields as a
        // boolean value (that is, either there's mail there,
        // or there isn't).
        if statbuf.st_size > 0
         then mailCount := 1
         else mailCount := 0;


        old_mailCount := 0;


        // Keep track of the size and modification time of the file.
        lastSize := statBuf.st_size;
        lastMTime := statBuf.st_mtime;


        // If there's new mail, return 1. Otherwise, return 0.
        if new_mailCount <> 0
         then begin
              Result := 1;
              Exit;
              end
          else begin
              Result := 0;
              Exit;
              end;
     end;


// We're running in "count" mode.
// If the mailboxes have been modified since last check,
// count the new/total messages.
if  ( statBuf.st_mtime <> lastMTime )
 or ( statBuf.st_size <> lastSize )
 then begin
       // Open the mail file for reading. If we can't,
       // return -1 (error).
       {$I-}
       AssignFile( F, mailFile );
       Reset( F );
       if IOResult <> 0
        then begin
              {$I+}
              Result := -1;
              Exit;
              end;


       mailCount := 0;
       old_mailCount := 0;
       // Read a line from the file, and loop on whether or not
```

```
// it is available. When we run out of lines we're done.
while not EOF( F ) do
 begin
  Readln( F, line );
  // If is_multipart is true, AND in_header is false
  if isMultipart and not inHeader
   then begin
        // Skip to last line of multipart mail
        if Pos( sepStr, line ) = 1
          then isMultipart := False;
       end
   // Else if the line is empty (first char is a newline)
   else begin
   if Length( line ) = 0
    then begin
         inHeader := False;
         isInternal := False;
        end
   // Else if we're on a From: line (see function above)
   else begin
        if isFrom( line )
          then begin
               Inc( mailCount );
               inHeader := True;
               markedRead := False;
              end
   // Else if inHeader is true AND status_is_old (see above)
   // returns true AND markedRead is false
   else begin
        if ( inHeader and isOld( line ) and not markedRead)
          then begin
               Inc( old_mailCount );
               markedRead := True;
              end
   // Else if in_header is true AND mailstats.is_internal
   // is true
   else begin
        if inHeader and isInternal
          then begin
               if Pos( 'From: Mail System Internal Data',
                  line ) = 1
                 then begin
                      inHeader := False;
                      Dec( mailCount );
                      isInternal := False;
```

```
                                    end;
                            end
                     // Else if in_header is true AND this is a
                     // multipart mail message
                     else if inHeader
                             and isMultipartMsg( line, sepStr )
                               then isMultipart := True;
             end;
             end;
             end;
             end; { If line is empty }
             end; { while }

        // Close the file - we're done with it.
        CloseFile( F );
        {$I+}

        // Restore the mailfile stat time so that other mail
        // checking programs will function correctly.
        timeBuf.actime := statBuf.st_atime;
        timeBuf.modtime := statBuf.st_mtime;
        utime( PChar(mailFile), @timeBuf );

        // Keep track of things for next time
        lastMtime := statBuf.st_mtime;
        lastSize := statBuf.st_size;

        // Compute the number of new messages
        new_mailCount := mailCount - old_mailCount;

       end; { if statBuf.st_mtime <> stats.lastMTime }

  Result := new_mailCount;
end;

end.
```

Listing 9.3 Program listing for the CheckMail program.
```
unit CheckMailMain;

interface

uses
  SysUtils, Types, Classes, Variants, QGraphics, QControls,
  QForms, QDialogs, CheckMailStuff, QStdCtrls, Libc, QExtCtrls;
```

```
type
  TCheckMailForm = class(TForm)
    ExitBtn: TButton;
    CheckBtn: TButton;
    GroupBox1: TGroupBox;
    UserNameLabel: TLabel;
    NoCountRB: TRadioButton;
    CountRB: TRadioButton;
    procedure ExitBtnClick(Sender: TObject);
    procedure FormCreate(Sender: TObject);
    procedure CheckBtnClick(Sender: TObject);
  private
    { Private declarations }
  public
    { Public declarations }
  end;

var
  CheckMailForm: TCheckMailForm;
  UserName: String;

implementation

{$R *.xfm}

procedure TCheckMailForm.ExitBtnClick(Sender: TObject);
begin
 Close;
end;

procedure TCheckMailForm.FormCreate(Sender: TObject);
var
 PPWRec  : PPasswordRecord;
 uid     : Integer;
begin
 uid := getuid;
 PPWRec := getpwuid(uid);
 UserName := PPWRec^.pw_name;
 UserNameLabel.Caption := 'Checking mail for: ' +    UserName;
end;

procedure TCheckMailForm.CheckBtnClick(Sender: TObject);
var
 QtyNewMail: Integer;
 Result : Integer;
```

```
begin
 if NoCountRB.Checked
  then begin
        Result := CheckNewMail(UserName, MSG_NOCOUNT);
        case Result of
          0 : ShowMessage('No new mail for you.');
          1 : ShowMessage('You have new mail.');
         -1 : ShowMessage('An error occurred during the check!');
        end; { case }
       end
  else begin
        QtyNewMail := CheckNewMail(UserName, MSG_COUNT);
        if QtyNewMail <> -1
          then ShowMessage('User ' + UserName + ' has '
                + IntToStr(QtyNewMail) + ' new mail item(s).')
          else ShowMessage('An error occurred during the check!');
       end;
 end;

 end.
```

Solution 9.3: Sending Email to Local Destinations

There are times you may want to notify an end user of a condition occurring within a program being run by another user—or there may be no actual user at all. Let's take a hypothetical situation in which you have produced a set of groupware applications. You would like to monitor the activities of the members of the group to see whether they have updated their own files on a project. Wouldn't it be nice to have a little application that would be scheduled with **cron** to wake up, inspect the file dates and times, and send you a report via email?

A client of mine who is running a network on Windows told me he was having trouble getting some of his team members (those with notebook computers) to perform their regular backup operations to the data server. My solution was twofold. First, I created a small application (with Delphi) to remind the users to back up. (Okay, after they ignore it long enough, it *hounds* them to back up.) A second application, run once each day on the server by the Task Scheduler, examines the timestamps for the individual files reserved exclusively for the notebook users. Part of this second application's job is to prepare a report of who backed up their files and then email that report to the administrator. (By the way, the other function of the program is to remove backup files aged more than a specified number of days).

Linux provides several ways to send mail, and perhaps the simplest is by using the **mail** program, which is a *mail user agent* (MUA). This is a program invoked by the user to send and receive mail but does not, itself, perform the actual transport. The **mail** program is usually located in the **/bin directory**, but on some systems it is found in the **/usr/bin directory**.

The **mail** program is a command-line utility that, although lacking the visual elegance of even the mail client in KDE 1.0, gets the job done nicely. When executed from the command line, **mail** can specify a subject, carbon and blind carbon copies, and the user to whom email will be sent. Here's an example:

```
mail [-s subject] [-c cc-addr] [-b bcc-addr] to-addr
```

Once invoked, **mail** will send the lines typed in by its user. As you'll see, **mail** can be called to send a message from a GUI application by using a pipe. Note also that **mail** actually interfaces with the Linux **sendmail** utility—an industrial-strength mail transport agent (MTA) that handles the transmission of just about every email message that leaves a Linux-based machine. The **sendmail** program (and **mail**, which uses it) is quite capable of sending email to any valid address in the world—not just to a user on the local system.

Solution Example: The **PipeMail** Program

Figure 9.3 depicts the **PipeMail** program, which has been created to demonstrate the use of **mail** to send email to a local user. The user enters a subject line and a message and then clicks the Send button. The message will be sent to the currently logged in user.

The code for **PipeMail** is shown in Listing 9.4. On startup, **PipeMail** determines the user's login name so it can use this name as the sole recipient for messages it creates.

When the Send button is clicked, its event handler creates a string to be passed to **mail** on its command line. In this case, the string consists of the path to the mail program, the **-s** option flag, the subject string entered by the user, and the recipient's login. The string is used to open a pipe, using the **w** (write) option. Each line in the memo is then appended with a linefeed character and sent down the pipe.

It's quick, simple, and dirty, and it works.

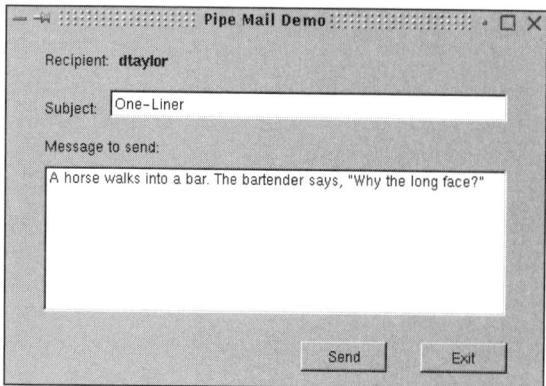

Figure 9.3
The **PipeMail** program.

Warning

*You must always take special care when writing applications that use the **system** function and the **popen** function (which calls the **system** function internally)— especially when you pass to either of these routines as an argument a string that has been entered by the user. Because the command will be executed by the Bourne Shell (/**bin/sh**) a potential security hole is opened every time the **popen** function is used. It is entirely possible for a malicious user to compose a "subject" line containing characters that have special meaning to that shell, and that will cause the subject line to be executed as a process. If this happens the process will be executed just as if the user had typed it at the command line, and it will be executed with all the user's current permissions and privileges.*

*A complete description of all security pitfalls and how to avoid them is way, way beyond the scope of this book. There are many good books and articles written on this topic; you might start with one at **www.linuxfocus.org/English/January2001/ article182.shtml**.*

Listing 9.4 Program listing for **PipeMail**.

```
unit PipeMailMain;

interface

uses
  SysUtils, Types, Classes, Variants, QGraphics, QControls, QForms, QDialogs,
  QStdCtrls, Libc;

type
  TPipeMailMainForm = class(TForm)
    Memo: TMemo;
    Label1: TLabel;
    Label2: TLabel;
    RecipientLabel: TLabel;
    SendBtn: TButton;
    ExitBtn: TButton;
    Label3: TLabel;
    Edit: TEdit;
    procedure RefreshDisplay;
    procedure ExitBtnClick(Sender: TObject);
    procedure MemoChange(Sender: TObject);
    procedure FormCreate(Sender: TObject);
    procedure SendBtnClick(Sender: TObject);
    procedure EditChange(Sender: TObject);
  private
    { Private declarations }
  public
    { Public declarations }
  end;
```

```
const
  LF = #10; { ASCII linefeed/newline }
  MAILPROG = '/bin/mail'; { location of mail file }

var
  PipeMailMainForm: TPipeMailMainForm;
  Recipient : String;

implementation

{$R *.xfm}

procedure TPipeMailMainForm.RefreshDisplay;
begin
 SendBtn.Enabled := (Memo.Lines.Count > 0)
   and (Length(Edit.Text) > 0);
end;

procedure TPipeMailMainForm.ExitBtnClick(Sender: TObject);
begin
 Close;
end;

procedure TPipeMailMainForm.MemoChange(Sender: TObject);
begin
 RefreshDisplay;
end;

procedure TPipeMailMainForm.FormCreate(Sender: TObject);
var
 PPWRec  : PPasswordRecord;
 uid     : Integer;
begin
 uid := getuid;
 PPWRec := getpwuid(uid);
 Recipient := PPWRec^.pw_name;
 RecipientLabel.Caption := Recipient;
end;

procedure TPipeMailMainForm.SendBtnClick(Sender: TObject);
var
 MailFile : PIOFile;
 s : String;
 i : Integer;
begin
 s := MAILPROG + ' -s ''' + Edit.Text + ''' ' + Recipient;
```

```
 MailFile := popen(PChar(s), 'w');
 for i := 0 to Memo.Lines.Count - 1 do
   fprintf(MailFile, PChar(Memo.Lines[i] + LF));
 pclose(MailFile);
 ShowMessage('Message sent to ' + Recipient + '.');
end;

procedure TPipeMailMainForm.EditChange(Sender: TObject);
begin
 RefreshDisplay;
end;

end.
```

Solution 9.4: Using **sendmail** from an Application

Solution 9.3 sent email by connecting a pipe to the mail MUA and then sending a message to the MUA through the pipe. Now I'd like to present an alternative to Solution 9.3, both in terms of how the message is formed and how it is sent. This time we'll use the **sendmail** MTA directly, and we'll do that by sending it a complete file through redirection. Sending a file in this manner is the way MIME-encoded mail is handled; it is first encoded and then sent as a file. (If you really want the sophistication of MIME-encoding, you should use an Indy component instead.)

Sending with **sendmail**

If you have ever suffered through the experience of installing a Perl script on a Web site, you've probably already heard of **sendmail**, and you know it can be located in one of several places, but most commonly in **/usr/lib**. There is no pretty front end to **sendmail**; it's strictly a workhorse that offers a laundry list of option flags. For this example, we'll use only two: the **–oi** and the **–t** options. To fully understand what these options do, you must first know what an *envelope* is, at least in email terms. Figure 9.4 depicts a complete email message stored as a file.

Have you ever received a blue, lightweight air mail letter from overseas—the kind that consists of a single sheet of paper that you write on and then fold up so it becomes its own envelope? That's a pretty good real-world model for the email envelope depicted in Figure 9.4. There are three sections to an email envelope. The first section consists of the headers, which correspond to the front of the air mail message envelope, where you'll find the addresses. The headers in the email file contain the return address and the address to which the message will be sent. In addition, the headers contain any "carbon copy" and "blind carbon copy" addresses, and even the subject. (In fact, you can put just about anything you want in the headers; those field names defined in RFC 822 and the MIME RFCs will be handled by most email clients.)

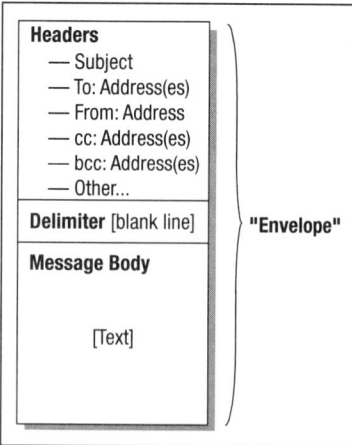

Figure 9.4
Representation of an email envelope.

The blank delimiter line signals the end of the headers and the beginning of the message text. It corresponds to the fold lines on the paper envelope example. Finally, there is the message itself. The **sendmail** MTA looks for its input on stdin, so we will send it a file—a file that contains a completely formed email message, as shown in Figure 9.4. Using the **–t** option flag tells **sendmail** to examine the headers and automatically construct a list of envelope recipients. The other option combination, **-oi**, is a standard specification when using input files.

As you will see, the distinct advantage to this method is that we will not be allowing a user to enter anything that will eventually be passed to the system in a way it can be executed. This offers increased security over the piping method used in Solution 9.3.

Solution Example: The **FileMail** Program

A demo program that implements the strategy just discussed is shown in Figure 9.5. To send a message with **FileMail**, the user simply types in a list of recipients, a subject line, and the message. Clicking the Send button speeds the message on its way.

The complete source code for **FileMail** is contained in Listing 9.5. On startup, **FileMail** searches for **sendmail** in the usual locations, and if it is not found, the controls are disabled. This is perhaps an unusual way of handling this situation, but I included it here as *yet another way to think about problem solving* (YAWTTAPS). The **Libc** unit provides us with the constant **_PATH_SENDMAIL**, which should work in *most* situations. Also, some Linux distributions establish file links for the traditional **sendmail** locations, pointing to the actual location on the system. These links makes using the **_PATH_SENDMAIL** constant

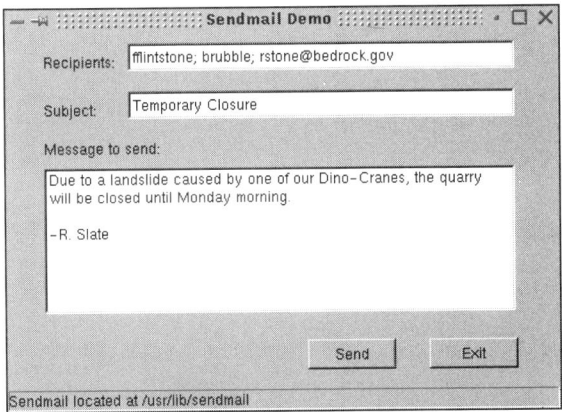

Figure 9.5
The **FileMail** program.

an even safer bet. The startup code in the **onCreate** event handler also uses the **tmpnam** library function to select a unique name for the temporary file that **FileMail** will use to store the email envelope it creates.

The primary function of this program is accomplished in the **SendMail** procedure. It first opens a stream with a unique file name. Once open, **SendMail** writes out the minimal header information collected in the recipient and subject controls. The blank delimiter line is then written, followed by all the lines in **MsgMemo**. The stream is then closed.

The **SendMail** procedure now creates a string that will be sent to the **sendmail** program. The string consists of the fully qualified path name to **sendmail**, the **sendmail** option flags, the input redirection symbol (**<**), and the name of our temporary file. This string is then fed to the **Libc** unit's **system** command, which executes it as if it had all been keyed in at a console. Mission accomplished.

Listing 9.5   Program listing for FileMail.

```
unit FileMailMain;

interface

uses
  SysUtils, Types, Classes, Variants, QGraphics, QControls, QForms, QDialogs,
  QStdCtrls, Libc, QExtCtrls, QComCtrls;

type
  TFileMailMainForm = class(TForm)
    MsgMemo: TMemo;
    Label1: TLabel;
    Label2: TLabel;
```

```
      SendBtn: TButton;
      ExitBtn: TButton;
      Label3: TLabel;
      SubjectEdit: TEdit;
      RecipientsEdit: TEdit;
      StatusBar: TStatusBar;
      procedure SendMail;
      procedure RefreshDisplay;
      procedure ExitBtnClick(Sender: TObject);
      procedure MsgMemoChange(Sender: TObject);
      procedure FormCreate(Sender: TObject);
      procedure SendBtnClick(Sender: TObject);
      procedure SubjectEditChange(Sender: TObject);
      procedure FormDestroy(Sender: TObject);
      procedure RecipientsEditChange(Sender: TObject);
    private
      { Private declarations }
    public
      { Public declarations }
    end;

const
  LF = #10; { ASCII linefeed/newline }
  SMNumPaths = 3;
  SMSearchPaths : array[1..SMNumPaths] of string
    = ('/usr/lib/sendmail',
       '/usr/sbin/sendmail',
       '/usr/libexec/sendmail');

var
  FileMailMainForm: TFileMailMainForm;
  SMPath : String;
  MailFileName : array[0..128] of Char;
  Recipients : String;
  Subject : String;

implementation

{$R *.xfm}

procedure TFileMailMainForm.SendMail;
var
  i : Integer;
  MailFile : PIOFile;
  Cmd : array[0..512] of Char;
```

```
begin
 MailFile := fopen(MailFileName, 'w');
 if not Assigned(MailFile)
  then begin
        ShowMessage('Cannot open temporary mail file!');
        Exit;
       end;

 { write out the header information }
 fprintf(MailFile, 'To: %s', Recipients);
 fputc(ord(LF), MailFile);
 fprintf(MailFile, 'Subject: %s', Subject);
 fputc(ord(LF), MailFile);

 { write out the end of header }
 fputc(ord(LF), MailFile);

 { write out the message }
 for i := 0 to MsgMemo.Lines.Count - 1 do
  begin
   if Length(MsgMemo.Lines[i]) > 0
    then fprintf(MailFile, '%s', MsgMemo.Lines[i]);
   fputc(ord(LF), MailFile);
  end; { for }

 fclose(MailFile);

 { Hand the file to sendmail }
 sprintf(Cmd, '%s -oi -t < %s', SMPath, MailFileName);
 if Libc.system(Cmd) <> 0
  then ShowMessage('Error occurred while sending mail!')
  else ShowMessage('Message sent to recipient(s).');

end;

procedure TFileMailMainForm.RefreshDisplay;
begin
 SendBtn.Enabled := (MsgMemo.Lines.Count > 0)
  and (Length(SubjectEdit.Text) > 0)
  and (Length(RecipientsEdit.Text) > 0);
end;

procedure TFileMailMainForm.ExitBtnClick(Sender: TObject);
begin
 Close;
end;
```

```pascal
procedure TFileMailMainForm.MsgMemoChange(Sender: TObject);
begin
 RefreshDisplay;
end;

procedure TFileMailMainForm.FormCreate(Sender: TObject);
var
 i : Integer;
 SMFound : Boolean;
begin
 { Find the sendmail application }
 for i := 1 to SMNumPaths do
  begin
   SMFound := FileExists(SMSearchPaths[i]);
   if SMFound then Break;
  end; { for }

 if SMFound
  then begin
        SMPath := SMSearchPaths[i];
        StatusBar.SimpleText := 'Sendmail located at ' + SMPath;
       end
  else begin
        RecipientsEdit.Enabled := False;
        SubjectEdit.Enabled := False;
        MsgMemo.Enabled := False;
        StatusBar.SimpleText := 'Sendmail program not located!';
        ShowMessage('Sendmail program not located!');
       end;

 { Get a unique file name }
 tmpnam(MailFileName);

end;

procedure TFileMailMainForm.SendBtnClick(Sender: TObject);
begin
 SendMail;
end;

procedure TFileMailMainForm.SubjectEditChange(Sender: TObject);
begin
 Subject := SubjectEdit.Text;
 RefreshDisplay;
end;
```

```
procedure TFileMailMainForm.FormDestroy(Sender: TObject);
begin
 if FileExists(MailFileName) then unlink(MailFileName);
end;

procedure TFileMailMainForm.RecipientsEditChange(Sender: TObject);
begin
 Recipients := RecipientsEdit.Text;
 RefreshDisplay;
end;

end.
```

Solution 9.5: Dealing with Octal Permissions Masks

Unless you're used to thinking in octal, permissions masks can be thoroughly frustrating. Once you've learned to do it, using groups of three bits to represent the permissions for owner, group, and everyone (plus the additional set for **setuid**, **setgrp**, and sticky bits) makes perfect sense. However, here's the rub: You're creating a file with the **Libc** routines, and you must specify an octal constant for the permissions—but the library function forces you to do it as a decimal number. What's a programmer to do?

Solution Example: The **OctalConv** Program

Figure 9.6 depicts **OctalConv**, a simple octal-decimal converter. As you type a decimal number in the left edit control, it is instantly converted to octal in the right edit control. Entering an octal number on the right converts it to decimal on the left. You can copy and paste the result right into the Kylix editor.

As an added bonus, if the number entered in either edit control looks like a valid permissions mask, a representation of the mask (à la the results from the **ls** utility) is displayed in an area below the edit controls. Listing 9.6 contains the code for **OctalConv**. There's nothing particularly noteworthy here—just some pretty straightforward coding. I've found this to be a handy little utility. Who knows—you might even decide to add this to the programs on the Tools menu in the Kylix IDE.

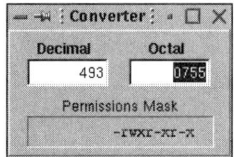

Figure 9.6
The **OctalConv** program.

Listing 9.6   Program listing for **OctalConv**.

```
unit OctalConvMain;

interface

uses
  SysUtils, Types, Classes, Variants, QGraphics, QControls, QForms, QDialogs,
  QStdCtrls, QMask, Math, QExtCtrls, Libc;

type
  TOctalConvMainForm = class(TForm)
    Panel1: TPanel;
    Label1: TLabel;
    Label2: TLabel;
    DecEdit: TEdit;
    OctEdit: TEdit;
    Bevel1: TBevel;
    Label3: TLabel;
    MaskLabel: TLabel;
    procedure DecEditKeyPress(Sender: TObject; var Key: Char);
    procedure OctEditKeyPress(Sender: TObject; var Key: Char);
    procedure OctEditChange(Sender: TObject);
    procedure DecEditChange(Sender: TObject);
  private
    { Private declarations }
  public
    { Public declarations }
  end;

var
  OctalConvMainForm: TOctalConvMainForm;

implementation

{$R *.xfm}

function CreatePermissionMask(OctStr : String) : String;
var
 i : Integer;
 OctBits : array[1..3] of Boolean;
 SetUID : Boolean;
 SetGID : Boolean;
 SetSticky : Boolean;
 s : String;
```

```
begin
 s := '-';
 SetUID := False;
 SetGID := False;
 SetSticky := False;
 if Length(OctStr) <= 4
  then for i := 1 to Length(OctStr) do
        begin
          OctBits[1] := StrToInt(OctStr[i]) and 4 <> 0;
          OctBits[2] := StrToInt(OctStr[i]) and 2 <> 0;
          OctBits[3] := StrToInt(OctStr[i]) and 1 <> 0;
          if i = 1 { Special bits }
           then begin
                  SetUID := OctBits[1];
                  SetGID := OctBits[2];
                  SetSticky := OctBits[3];
                end
           else begin
                  if OctBits[1]
                   then s := s + 'r'
                   else s := s + '-';
                  if OctBits[2]
                   then s := s + 'w'
                   else s := s + '-';

                  case i of
                   2 : if SetUID
                         then if OctBits[3]
                                then s := s + 's'
                                else s := s + 'S'
                         else if OctBits[3]
                                then s := s + 'x'
                                else s := s + '-';

                   3 : if SetGID
                         then if OctBits[3]
                                then s := s + 's'
                                else s := s + 'S'
                         else if OctBits[3]
                                then s := s + 'x'
                                else s := s + '-';

                   4 : if SetSticky
                         then if OctBits[3]
                                then s := s + 't'
                                else s := s + 'T'
```

```
                        else if OctBits[3]
                                then s := s + 'x'
                                else s := s + '-';



                end; { case }
              end;
        end; { for }


 Result := s;
end;

function ConvertDecToOct(DStr : String) : String;
var
 s : array[0..32] of Char;
 v : Longint;
begin
 if StrToInt(DStr) = 0
  then Result := '0'
   else begin
        v := StrToInt(DStr);
        sprintf(s, '%o', v);
        Result := s;
        if Length(Result) < 4
         then Result := '0' + Result;
        end;
end;

function ConvertOctToDec(OStr : String) : String;
var
 i : Integer;
 Value : Longint;
 Exp : Extended;
begin
 Value := 0;
 for i := Length(OStr) downto 1 do
  begin
   Exp := Length(OStr) - i;
   Value := Value + (StrToInt(OStr[i]) * Trunc(Power(8,Exp)));
  end; { for }
 Result := IntToStr(Value);
end;

procedure TOctalConvMainForm.DecEditKeyPress(
 Sender: TObject; var Key: Char);
```

```
begin
 if Key in ['0'..'9', Chr(8)]
  then inherited
  else Key := Chr(0);
end;

procedure TOctalConvMainForm.OctEditKeyPress(
 Sender: TObject; var Key: Char);
begin
 if Key in ['0'..'7', Chr(8)]
  then inherited
  else Key := Chr(0);
end;

procedure TOctalConvMainForm.OctEditChange(Sender: TObject);
begin
 if OctEdit.Focused
  then if Length(OctEdit.Text) > 0
        then begin
              DecEdit.Text := ConvertOctToDec(OctEdit.Text);
              if Length(OctEdit.Text) = 4
               then MaskLabel.Caption := CreatePermissionMask(OctEdit.Text)
               else MaskLabel.Caption := '';
             end
        else begin
              DecEdit.Text := '';
              MaskLabel.Caption := '';
             end;
end;

procedure TOctalConvMainForm.DecEditChange(Sender: TObject);
begin
 if DecEdit.Focused
  then if Length(DecEdit.Text) > 0
        then begin
              OctEdit.Text := ConvertDecToOct(DecEdit.Text);
              if Length(OctEdit.Text) = 4
               then MaskLabel.Caption := CreatePermissionMask(OctEdit.Text)
               else MaskLabel.Caption := '';
             end
        else begin
              OctEdit.Text := '';
              MaskLabel.Caption := '';
             end;
end;

end.
```

Solution 9.6: Running as the Superuser (Revisited)

Solution 5.12 in Chapter 5 provided some overall guidance regarding running programs that need superuser privileges. That discussion described some of the machinations necessary to protect system integrity when you're not the system administrator. If all that seemed like a hassle, you're not alone. The truth is, if you're developing applications that require superuser privileges, it's just easier to develop them on a system on which you have those privileges—which may mean setting up your own Linux box for development. Even though you will then have total control, it's strongly recommended that you do not run as root unless you are performing administrative system functions—again, this is just "good practice."

When you installed Kylix, you had two options: install Kylix for a single user, so only he has access to it, and install it as root, so anyone can run it. If you install Kylix for a single user and then try to execute a program as root (either by logging on as root or by running the **su** utility), you'll get error messages. If you install Kylix as root and attempt to execute a program as an ordinary user, you'll also get error messages (or if you created a desktop icon, clicking it will only cause the disk to thrash briefly).

What, then, are your options? To answer that, we must first lay some groundwork, and we're going to dig down deep into the ground—you may want to grab a pair of gardening gloves and something with caffeine in it. We'll need a basis to talk from, so I'll assume you've installed for a single user (I save discussing the ramifications of installing as root until a little later). Also, there are several shells to choose from, but I'll limit the discussion to the one I use (**bash**); the operation of the other shells is very similar.

Heredity and the Environment

Solution 5.1 in Chapter 5 highlighted the **exec** family of library calls. If you remember, some of those functions will launch a new process by using the environment of the current (parent) process. Other functions in the **exec** family require that you pass them a pointer to an array of strings that contain environment variables. When a new process is launched by the system (such as from a shell running in a terminal window), the new process always inherits the environment of its parent. (Well, *almost* always. You'll hear more about that in just a moment.)

We'll now refine our target discussion a bit, limiting it for the moment to executing a program from a terminal window. The example I'll present in Solution 9.7 (**SysLog**) requires root privileges for part of its functionality, so I'll use its name here.

Take a look at Figure 9.7. This is a representation of what we might see if we run **SysLog** in one terminal window and, while it is still running, we run the **ps** utility with the –**el** options in another terminal window. (Note that the representation of **ps**'s output in this figure—and in all the figures for this solution—has been highly simplified for the sake of clarity.)

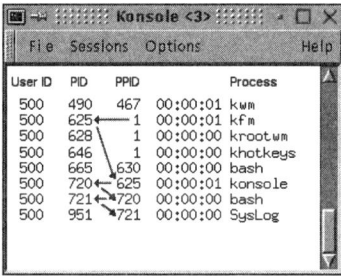

Figure 9.7
Representation of **ps** output when **SysLog** is run from the console.

In Figure 9.7, you can see that the **SysLog** program bears a pid of 951 and that its parent process's pid is 721—which is an invocation of **bash**, the system shell. If we keep backtracking the family lineage (marked with arrows in the figure), we eventually end up with **init**, the equivalent of Adam. The **init** process is Linux, inheriting and dutifully dispatching zombies whenever they're found—plus a whole lot of other responsibilities.

It would be natural to assume that **SysLog** would inherit the environment of its ancestors, right back to **init**. There is an exception to the rule of inheritance, however, and that's why I said *almost* always a little earlier. Whenever a system shell is run interactively (which will be the case any time a user is interacting with the shell, as opposed to the shell being run by **cron**, for example), it loads the environment that has been specified for its user. This configuration specification is located in a configuration file (or files) in that user's home directory. In the case of **bash**, these files are called **.profile** and **.bashrc**.

The shell configuration is very important because part of its contents is any special path information—including the path to the **Kylix** shared object library, which is required to run your compiled Kylix application. (You probably know where I'm heading with this.) Assuming we know the root password, let's say we now run the **su** utility (with the "-" option) in one terminal window and run **ps** in the other terminal window. An example with abbreviated output is shown in Figure 9.8.

Take a look at the first two invocations of **bash** (pids 653 and 681). Everything is perfectly normal here, and as you can see, it knew its user was me (User ID 500), and loaded the Kylix library path information as part of the environment. But see what happens when **su** is run: Suddenly, the user ID becomes 0, which is the superuser, by definition. From that point on, it is loading the configuration for the superuser, not me—and if his shell hasn't been configured for Kylix paths, we're toast as far as running any compiled Kylix applications is concerned. Whether you have logged in as root or have run the **su** utility, the result is the same—the all-powerful superuser wouldn't know how to run one of your applications if it crawled up and sat in his lap.

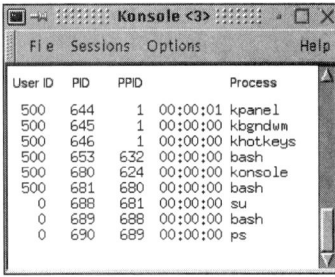

Figure 9.8
Representation of **ps** output after the **su** utility is run.

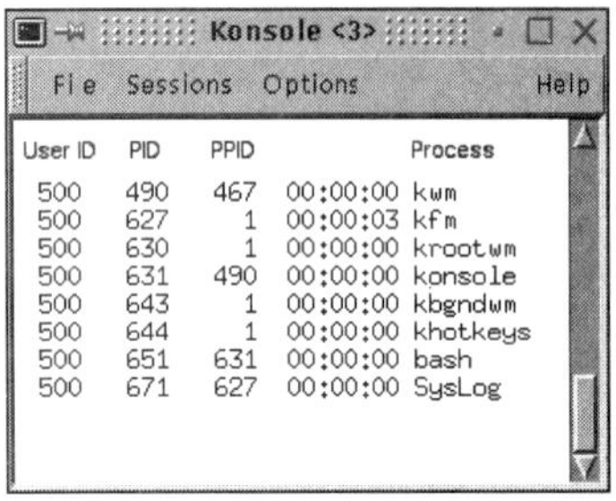

Figure 9.9
Representation of **ps** output after **SysLog** is launched from an icon.

Just one more point of interest before we jump to the solutions. Have you ever wondered what happens in terms of processing when you click an icon on the desktop? Figure 9.9 reveals the answer. This time, **SysLog** (pid 671) inherits everything directly from its parent, **kfm** (the KDE file manager, pid 627). And where does **kfm** get its environment information? From the user's shell configuration, of course. That's why the disk just thrashes momentarily when you install an icon on the superuser's desktop and click it: It finds the application, but it can't find the Kylix shared object library files.

Solution Example: Change Your Configurations

The first solution that comes to mind is simply to change the configuration settings for your shell. If you have installed Kylix as root, that is exactly what you'll need to do for each user you want to be able to run Kylix (or any applications compiled with it) so that **LD_LIBRARY_PATH** points to the correct place. If you are the superuser, you can establish a default configuration for each new account created so that any shell the new user creates will automatically include the path proper library path. (Directions for setting these defaults can be found in the man pages for the shell you use.)

If you have installed Kylix for a single user, I don't recommend modifying the superuser's shell configuration to include the path. Yes, it will work, but it's poor practice to configure the system administrator's settings so that they're reliant on those of an ordinary user. It's the first step on a relatively short road to chaos. Trust me on this. Instead, consider using the shell scripts presented in the two solution examples that follow.

Solution Example: The **runsu1** Script

If running a program (or script) as the superuser always loads the environment specified for the superuser, how can we get the path known only to the user's environment—and do this only when we need it? The answer lies in the fact that environment variables can be added at any time. That means we can save the user's path environment variable to disk and then load it later as the superuser.

Listing 9.7 shows **runsu1**, a very simple shell script that accomplishes this task. The first line calls the X Window system and tells it to open up the permissions on the X Server. Normally, to provide better security, only programs invoked by the user running the X Server are allowed to display applications on the X Server. The **xhost** application modifies the permission settings of the X Server, making it possible for *any* application to be displayed there, regardless of who invoked it. The second line performs the function of writing the library path variable to a file named **libpath.tmp**, located in the user's home directory. The **chmod** utility is called in the next line, ensuring unrestricted access will be given to the file.

Finally, the **su** utility is called. If you can supply the superuser's password, you will be placed inside another shell where you will have all of his privileges, power, and responsibilities (and all of his environment variables). You should find yourself in the same directory you were in, but your command-line prompt will likely change.

Warning
While operating in this terminal window, you are the superuser. Be very careful.

You'll need to run this script each time you wish to have superuser privileges. (Remember to **chmod** this script so that its execute bits are set. A recommended value is 0755.) To exit the superuser "mode," just type "exit" at the prompt; you will drop back to life as an ordinary user.

After running this script, you're halfway there. You now need to skip to the next example and execute **runsu2**.

Listing 9.7   The **runsu1** script.
```
# runsu1: Shell script to log on as superuser
# Usage: runsu1
# Note: Shares display with all processes, writes the
#       library path command to the user's home directory,
#       then starts the logon as superuser.
```

```
xhost + > /dev/null
echo "LD_LIBRARY_PATH="$LD_LIBRARY_PATH > ~/libpath.tmp
chmod 777 ~/libpath.tmp
su
```

Solution Example: The **runsu2** Script

Once you have executed **runsu1**, you're ready to execute your program as root. To accomplish this, run your program from inside a shell, first pulling in the library path information.

Listing 9.8 shows **runsu2**, a simple shell script that performs this operation. It *must* be executed in the user's home directory where the **libpath.tmp** file was written. The script uses the **source** and **export** commands to pull in the contents of **libpath.tmp** and export them into the environment variables for this new shell created with superuser privileges. The command specified on the command line that launched **runsu2** is launched (with up to seven program arguments) by the last line of the script.

While the script is executing, you'll notice that the cursor does not return in your terminal window. When you exit the program, the cursor will return, and the temporary shell will be no more—and the same goes for the path information loaded into that shell.

Tip

*Here's a handy way to use **runsu2** as you're developing and testing an application: While you're running Kylix on one desktop, go to a clean, uncluttered desktop and open a terminal window. In that terminal window, execute **runsu1** and then execute your application with **runsu2** to gain the superuser privileges. Use your Page Up key (in **bash**; other command-line history mechanisms exist in other shells) to recall the last command line (**runsu2**) in your terminal window. Now you can flip between the two desktops to write and compile in one and test in the other.*

Tip

*If you want to execute your program by logging in as the superuser instead of merely running the **su** utility, you can do that, too. Once you've logged in as root, change to the user's home directory where you previously ran **runsu1**. Executing **runsu2** will now temporarily pick up the path environment variable, just as it did when you ran **runsu2** as user-turned-superuser.*

Warning

There's an obvious security problem with these scripts, of course: Files are being left around that are owned and writable by normal users, yet the superuser must run them to set up his environment. This leads to a situation in which the user who owns the files can basically take over the system by modifying the contents of the files before root runs the script. Obviously, this mechanism should be used for development only—and not on a production system. If for some reason this mechanism must be deployed, the script files must be owned and be writable only by root.

Listing 9.8   The runsu2 script.

```
# runsu2: Shell script to run a program as superuser - Part 2
# Usage: runsu2 <executable_file_name> [arg1] [arg2] .. [arg7]
# Notes: 1. It's assumed you've already logged on as the superuser
#           by running the runsu1 script.
#        2. The file libpath.tmp is located in the *user's* home directory,
#           *not* in root's home directory!

# Get the path to the Kylix shared objects library
source libpath.tmp
export LD_LIBRARY_PATH

# Now run the program
"$1" "$2" "$3" "$4" "$5" "$6" "$7" "$8"
```

Solution 9.7: Using System Logging for Debugging

Integrated software debugging is a real blessing. But what happens when you put your software in the hands of users, and you want to collect any further bug reports or usage information? My experience has been that users are much more interested in getting their work done than reporting bugs, and when it comes to usage data—well, just forget it.

However, that information can be critical for an application developer. The value of bug reports is obvious, but usage data can tell you *how* a user is making use of your program, which can help you polish the user interface or even add new capabilities. Also, if the end user of your application is a system administrator, you can add value to that application by logging critical events, such as a user unsuccessfully attempting to log in as the superuser.

Linux provides a system logging function that it makes available to all programs. On a typical Linux system, the log files are kept in **/var/log** and may include **maillog** (for logging all messages from the mail system) and **debug** (a general bug-reporting capability). One log file common to all systems is messages, which contains all system messages.

System Logging Routines

The **Libc** unit provides three functions that manage logging operations. Used with a wide array of available options, these calls offer powerful logging capabilities. Let's take a brief look at the three routines and the various option constants. We'll start with **openlog**:

```
procedure openlog(__ident: PChar;
                  __option: Integer;
                  __facility: Integer); cdecl;
```

True to its name, the **openlog** procedure opens a connection to the system logger. The **__ident** argument is a pointer to a string that you would like to have included in each message logged. Typically, this will point to the name of a program, but if you're collecting usage information it might be handy to provide the argument with the name of the user instead. The __option argument is one of the values listed in Table 9.3.

The __facility argument specifies the *facility* (the type of program) making the logging request. Depending on the facility, the system logger may handle the request a bit differently. Valid constants for this argument are listed in Table 9.4.

The second logging routine is **syslog**:

```
procedure syslog(__pri: Integer;
                 __fmt: PChar); cdecl; varargs;
```

The **syslog** procedure is the one that makes the request to the system logger. The __fmt argument is a pointer to a *formatted* string (that is, one created with the **sprintf** function). The __pri argument (short for *priority level*) is an integer value, one of the constants listed in Table 9.5. (The values are listed in order of decreasing importance.)

Table 9.3 Constants for the __option argument of an openlog call.

Constant	Option Description
LOG_CONS	If an error occurs while writing to the system logger, this constant writes a description of the error to the system console.
LOG_NDELAY	Normally, the connection to the system logger is not actually made until the first attempt to write to it. Selecting this option makes the connection immediately.
LOG_PERROR	This constant sends the log message to stderr as well as sending it to the system logger.
LOG_PID	This constant includes in the log entry the pid of the process submitting the entry.

Table 9.4 Constants for the __facility argument of an openlog call.

Constant	Facility Description
LOG_AUTHPRIV	A program that handles security authorization, requesting private message handling.
LOG_CRON	Either the **cron** or **at** scheduling utilities.
LOG_DAEMON	A daemon.
LOG_KERN	The Linux kernel.
LOG_LOCAL0 LOG_LOCAL7	Reserved for local use.
LOG_LPR	The line printer subsystem.
LOG_MAIL	The mail subsystem.
LOG_NEWS	The Usenet news subsystem.
LOG_SYSLOG	The system logger itself.
LOG_USER	Any user program. This is the default value.
LOG_UUCP	The UUCP system, used to copy files from one 'Nix system to another.

Table 9.5   Constants for the __pri argument of a syslog call.

Constant	Option Description
LOG_EMERG	The system has turned to jelly and is totally unusable.
LOG_CRIT	A critical condition exists in the system.
LOG_ERR	An error condition exists.
LOG_WARNING	A situation exists that requires a warning.
LOG_NOTICE	A normal (but significant) condition has been detected.
LOG_INFO	An informational message is to be logged.
LOG_DEBUG	A debug-level message is to be logged.

The third and final routine for managing logging requests is the **closelog** procedure:

```
procedure closelog; cdecl;
```

As you might expect, this closes the connection to the system logger.

The Man (Daemon) behind the Curtain

I've mentioned the system logger several times. Now it's time to name names. The logging operation is actually performed by **syslogd**, a daemon that accepts and carries out the logging requests.

The way that **syslogd** handles those requests depends on the values you give to your **openlog** and **syslog** calls—but it also depends on the configuration of the logging system, which is specified in **/etc/syslog.conf**. Depending on that configuration, a request marked **LOG_DEBUG** might be routed to debug, messages, or both—or it might be totally ignored.

The debug logging capability on my machine was disabled by default, and I had to study the configuration information (in man **syslog.conf**) a while before I finally got what I wanted—to send debug log messages to debug alone. Listing 9.9 contains my **syslog.conf** file, edited somewhat for brevity.

Listing 9.9   Example of a syslog.conf file.

```
# /etc/syslog.conf - Configuration file for syslogd(8)
#
# For info about the format of this file, see "man syslog.conf".
#

# print most on tty10 and on the xconsole pipe
#
kern.warn;*.err;authpriv.none /dev/tty10
kern.warn;*.err;authpriv.none|/dev/xconsole
*.emerg *
```

```
# enable this, if you want that root is informed
# immediately, e.g. of logins
#*.alert root

# all email-messages in one file
#
mail.*   -/var/log/mail

# all news-messages
#
# these files are rotated and examined by "news.daily"
news.crit  -/var/log/news/news.crit
news.err   -/var/log/news/news.err
news.notice   -/var/log/news/news.notice
# enable this, if you want to keep all news messages
# in one file
#news.*     -/var/log/news.all

# Warnings in one file
#
*.=warn;*.=err   -/var/log/warn
*.crit          /var/log/warn
#

# Debug info
#
*.=debug   /var/log/debug

# save the rest in one file
#
*.*;mail.none;news.none;*.!=debug    -/var/log/messages

# enable this, if you want to keep all messages
# in one file
#*.*    -/var/log/allmessages

kern.*   /var/log/firewall
```

Solution Example: The **SysLog** Program

Figure 9.10 shows **SysLog**, a program that demonstrates the use of system logging. The upper portion of the dialog box displays a maximum specified number of characters from either the messages log or the debug log. The user can enter a message in either one of these logs by keying in his message in the edit control, selecting the desired log with the radio buttons, and then clicking the Send button to initiate the logging process.

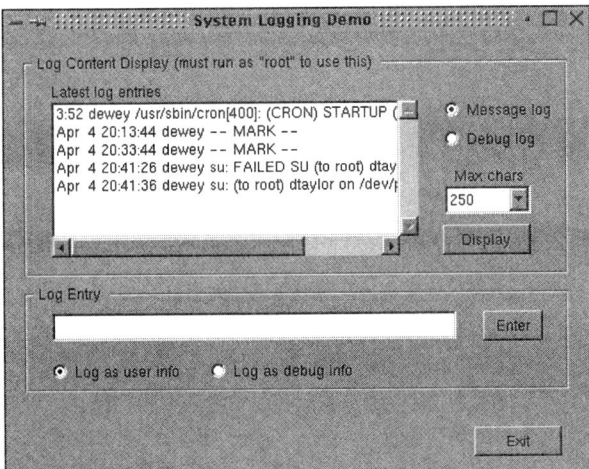

Figure 9.10
The **SysLog** program.

*Although any program can request that a message be logged, it is standard practice that only the superuser can read system logs. For the **SysLog** demo program to be fully functional, you will likely need to run it with superuser privileges. To explore your options for attaining this privilege level, refer to Solution 9.6.*

The code for **SysLog** is shown in Listing 9.10. For the purposes of displaying the logs, an assumption has been made as to their names and locations, which have been assigned to the constants **SYS_MSGS_FNAME** and **SYS_DEBUG_FNAME**. The user's authority to read the system log files is determined by the function **CanReadSysMsgsFile**, which simply attempts to open the messages file for reading.

Display of the log file contents is accomplished in a straightforward manner: by opening the selected file, reading up to the maximum number of characters, and displaying the characters in the memo. The core of **SysLog** is contained in the **onClick** event handler for the Enter button. This routine uses the three log file–related routines to create a log entry in the selected file, using constants that specify a user-level message that includes the pid of the requesting process and the name of the application.

Listing 9.10   Program listing for SysLog.

```
unit SysLogMain;

interface

uses
  SysUtils, Types, Classes, Variants, QGraphics, QControls, QForms, QDialogs,
  QStdCtrls, Libc;
```

```
type
  TSysLogMainForm = class(TForm)
    ExitBtn: TButton;
    MonitorGroup: TGroupBox;
    Memo: TMemo;
    NumCharsCombo: TComboBox;
    DisplayBtn: TButton;
    Label1: TLabel;
    Label2: TLabel;
    EditGroup: TGroupBox;
    EnterBtn: TButton;
    LogEdit: TEdit;
    LogInfoRB: TRadioButton;
    DebugInfoRB: TRadioButton;
    MsgLogRB: TRadioButton;
    DbgLogRB: TRadioButton;
    procedure ExitBtnClick(Sender: TObject);
    procedure DisplayBtnClick(Sender: TObject);
    procedure FormCreate(Sender: TObject);
    procedure NumCharsComboClick(Sender: TObject);
    procedure EnterBtnClick(Sender: TObject);
    procedure MsgLogRBClick(Sender: TObject);
    procedure DbgLogRBClick(Sender: TObject);
  private
    { Private declarations }
  public
    { Public declarations }
  end;

const
  SYS_MSGS_FNAME = '/var/log/messages';
  SYS_DEBUG_FNAME = '/var/log/debug';
var
  SysLogMainForm: TSysLogMainForm;
  SysMsgFileOK : Boolean;
  CharsToRead : Integer;
  AppName : String;

implementation

{$R *.xfm}

function CanReadSysMsgsFile : Boolean;
var
 FD : Integer;
```

```
begin
 FD := open(SYS_MSGS_FNAME, O_RDONLY);
 Result := FD <> -1;
 __close(FD);
end;

procedure TSysLogMainForm.ExitBtnClick(Sender: TObject);
begin
 Close;
end;

procedure TSysLogMainForm.DisplayBtnClick(Sender: TObject);
var
 FD : Integer;
 Buf : array[0..32768] of Char;
 SR : TSearchRec;
 FSize : Longint;
 s : String;
 MaxChars : Integer;
begin
 Memo.Lines.Clear;

 if MsgLogRB.Checked
  then begin
        FD := open(SYS_MSGS_FNAME, O_RDONLY);
        if FD = -1
         then begin
                ShowMessage('Can''t open system message log.');
                Exit;
              end;

        FindFirst(SYS_MSGS_FNAME, 0, SR);
       end
  else begin
        FD := open(SYS_DEBUG_FNAME, O_RDONLY);
        if FD = -1
         then begin
                ShowMessage('Can''t open system debug log.');
                Exit;
              end;

        FindFirst(SYS_DEBUG_FNAME, 0, SR);
       end;

 FSize := SR.Size;
 FindClose(SR);
```

```
  MaxChars := CharsToRead;
  if MaxChars > FSize then MaxChars := FSize - 1;
  if MaxChars > SizeOf(BUF) then MaxChars := SizeOf(BUF) - 1;
  lseek(FD,FSize - MaxChars, SEEK_SET);
  __read(FD, Buf, MaxChars);
  __close(FD);

  Buf[MaxChars] := chr(0);
  s := StrPas(Buf);
  Memo.Lines.Add(s);
end;

procedure TSysLogMainForm.FormCreate(Sender: TObject);
begin
 AppName := ExtractFileName(Application.ExeName);
 CharsToRead :=
   StrToInt(NumCharsCombo.Items[NumCharsCombo.ItemIndex]);
 SysMsgFileOK := CanReadSysMsgsFile;
 if not SysMsgFileOK
  then begin
        Memo.Enabled := False;
        DisplayBtn.Enabled := False;
        NumCharsCombo.Enabled := False;
        MsgLogRB.Enabled := False;
        DbgLogRb.Enabled := False;
        end;
end;

procedure TSysLogMainForm.NumCharsComboClick(Sender: TObject);
begin
 CharsToRead :=
   StrToInt(NumCharsCombo.Items[NumCharsCombo.ItemIndex]);
end;

procedure TSysLogMainForm.EnterBtnClick(Sender: TObject);
var
 s : String;
begin
 s := LogEdit.Text;
 openlog(PChar(AppName), LOG_PID, LOG_USER);
 if LogInfoRB.Checked
  then syslog(LOG_INFO, PChar(s))
  else syslog(LOG_DEBUG, PChar(s));
 closelog;
 ShowMessage('Message written to system log.');
 LogEdit.Text := '';
end;
```

```
procedure TSysLogMainForm.MsgLogRBClick(Sender: TObject);
begin
 Memo.Lines.Clear;
end;

procedure TSysLogMainForm.DbgLogRBClick(Sender: TObject);
begin
 Memo.Lines.Clear;
end;

end.
```

Index

G

Printed in Poland
by Amazon Fulfillment
Poland Sp. z o.o., Wrocław